This text was written to help preserve and in-ser... determine how technology can support the education of exceptional individuals. Several special features highlight the practical, classroom-oriented approach of this text.

TECHNIQUES FOR YOUR CLASSROOM

highlights specific methods that teachers can use to incorporate technology most effectively in the classroom.

T ECHNIQUES FOR YOUR CLASSROOM

Tips for Using Instructional Software for Remediation

When you use instructional software for remediation purposes, research suggests that you follow these guidelines (Fitzgerald & Koury, 1996):

1 Control the size of the instructional set. For example, break down concepts into smaller pieces. Instead of asking students to understand all of the aspects of estimation in one lesson, focus on vocabulary in the first lesson, then on procedures in another. Don't try to push too much information at one time.

[...] time delay and controlled response times to [...]d fluency (speed of reading). This means that [...]ons should give students "wait time" to think [...]ut what they've read and opportunities to break [...]ling texts down into smaller sections.

3 Maintain learning and build successful rates of responding by interspersing mastered items with new items.
4 Provide immediate and meaningful feedback.
5 Limit the use of extraneous graphics and arcade-game formats in skill-and-drill materials.
6 Provide opportunities for the learner to use hypermedia enhancements and speech synthesizers to support understanding.

These recommendations are particularly important to the child with a communication disorder. When you have children with communication difficulties in your classroom, carefully evaluate the software applications you are using to be sure they meet these standards.

T ECHNIQUES FOR YOUR CLASSROOM

Are They Safe Out There?

Whenever we talk about using the Internet, the issue of security emerges. Can students see pornographic or violent images or text by clicking on a button? These issues must be addressed before students start surfing around. Inappropriate content is easy to encounter.

Here are three methods for making the Internet "safe" for students:

1 Start students off on the Internet with a website that has links to sites you've already previewed. Avoid letting students use search engines when you don't know what they will find. You can do a quick Web search to find appropriate resource websites, and then bookmark these for use by students.
2 Use a filtering device. Programs such as Net Nanny (Net Nanny Software), Cyber Patrol (SurfControl), and CYBERsitter (Solidoak) scan web pages for words and pictures that have been identified as inappropriate. They include different levels of security (such as a filter for children under 5). In addition, the

network manager for your school or district may have installed a **proxy server**, which acts as a filter for all computers on the network.
3 Find out if your school system's connection to the Internet has a *proxy server*. A proxy server is a piece of software that runs at the school's (or school district's) main Internet connection server and blocks out web addresses known to be inappropriate for children. A *firewall* is a piece of equipment or software that blocks people (hackers) from getting unauthorized access to the schoolwide network.

All of these methods are useful, but none is more effective than the most basic method of keeping students safe on the Internet: supervise them! If you think of the Internet as the ultimate library and resource center, you know that you would never send a student off on this field trip without supervision. For more specific recommendations, refer to the Handbook of Resources at the back of this book.

PRINCIPLES AND PRACTICE

appears throughout the text to emphasize different elements of special education, such as regulations, controversial issues, and suggestions for good teaching strategies.

P RINCIPLES AND PRACTICE

The Ritalin Controversy: State Legislatures Respond

The use of behavior-modifying medications for students with any condition has always been a central issue in the minds of parents and teachers. In addition to concerns about side effects, many feel a natural desire to help children learn ways to manage their own behaviors.

Lately, Ritalin, a drug prescribed to many children with ADHD, has been a source of particular concern. In response to complaints of overprescription of Ritalin and similar medications used in the treatment of ADHD, some states have either passed or initiated legislation to limit or eliminate recommendations to parents that they seek drug treatment for their children. For example:

- In July 2001, Minnesota prohibited schools and child protection agencies from insisting that parents use drug treatments for disorders such as ADHD.
- In October 2001, a Connecticut law went into effect requiring that school personnel not discuss drug treatment with parents and that such discussions take place with physicians.
- Legislative action like that of Minnesota and Connecticut has been initiated in Arizona, New Jersey, New York, Utah, and Wisconsin.

Reporting these legislative actions, the *New York Times* noted an increase in the amount of

direct advertising to consumers by pharmaceutical companies that make drugs similar to Ritalin. According to a Drug Enforcement Administration official interviewed by the *Times*, such advertising, while not illegal, breaches agreements made in a 1971 international treaty not to market controlled substances directly to consumers (Zernike & Petersen, 2001).

On September 30, 2001, the American Academy of Pediatrics published for the first time its guidelines for the treatment of ADHD. The guidelines state that greater evidence indicates the effectiveness of medication—that is, stimulants like Ritalin—in ADHD treatment than for behavioral therapy. However, the guidelines recommend using behavioral techniques in combination with medication, as well as monitoring medication for side effects and appropriate dosage (American Academy of Pediatrics, 2001).

As we consider ways to make the most of advances in technology, particularly in the area of medicine, we must consider the total impact on each child and make our decisions accordingly. As a teacher who may work with medical doctors, keep in mind that our greatest promise should be to "do no harm."

P RINCIPLES AND PRACTICE   Hearing Tests

Hearing tests take many forms, but they often begin with the familiar hearing examination you might remember from your school days. In this test, called the *tone test*, you raise your hand when you hear a sound in one ear or the other. This classic test gives a rough estimate of hearing, but more specialized tests can identify minor hearing problems and isolate specific types of noises that the student finds challenging. These tests include the following:

- *Pure-tone audiometry.* The student puts on a pair of headphones and listens to tones at different pitch and decibel levels. Whenever the student hears a

tone in his left ear, he raises his left hand; for a tone in the right ear, he raises his right hand.
- *Speech audiometry.* Sounds are played through one earphone at a time. The sounds can range from whispers through normal speech and can include specific sounds such as a ticking clock. This test measures not only the decibel level, but also the ability to understand different elements of speech.
- *Specialized tests.* Specialized tests evaluate infants or people with more severe hearing loss to determine the degree of residual hearing. For example, with infants, the child usually sits on a parent's lap and sounds are played from behind the child. If the child turns to look for the sound, the tester determines that he or she heard it.

P ROFILE

Zachary Winters

A screen from Zack's HyperStudio project on space

The accompanying picture is a screen shot from a HyperStudio stack created by Zachary Winters, a student with learning disabilities. During a space study unit, Zachary worked with a team of his peers to create a project showing an imaginary adventure in which the children take the school bus into space and visit each of the planets. Along the way, the students present facts they have learned about space and planetary science.

For this particular screen, Zack took a digital picture of himself, cut out his face, and pasted it digitally onto the image of a spacesuit he found on the Internet. He then added the background, drew in the satellite and the moons, and added a button to move on to the next screen. In addition, if you click on Zack's face, you will hear him say, "Many moons and satellites rotate around the planet Jupiter."

According to Zack's mother, he had a normal early childhood, and when his teacher recommended that he stay an extra year in pre-kindergarten because of his "poor processing ability," she was stunned. After much turmoil in kindergarten, Zack's first grade teacher recommended that he be tested for learning disabilities, and the school psychologist found that he had major difficulties with perceptive and receptive language. The psychologist found Zack's verbal intelligence to be normal, but his performance IQ was in the eighth percentile, meaning that his score was well below average. During testing, Zack couldn't recall a word list, but he was able to answer questions about a story read to him. He was found to have difficulties with fine motor skills, as well as language problems that included an inability to recognize some sounds.

Halfway through the first grade, Zack started seeing a speech therapist at the school, and he began visiting the special education teacher three times a week for help with reading. Although his speech and language seemed to improve, his reading did not, and he continued to fall behind. In second

TECHNOLOGY FOR EXCEPTIONAL LEARNERS

TECHNOLOGY FOR EXCEPTIONAL LEARNERS

CHOOSING
INSTRUCTIONAL
TOOLS TO
MEET STUDENTS'
NEEDS

Sarah Irvine Belson
American University

WADSWORTH
CENGAGE Learning

Australia • Brazil • Japan • Korea • Mexico • Singapore • Spain • United Kingdom • United States

WADSWORTH
CENGAGE Learning

Technology for Exceptional Learners: Choosing Instructional Tools to Meet Students' Needs
Sarah Irvine Belson

Senior Sponsoring Editor: Sue Pulvermacher-Alt

Senior Development Editor: Lisa Mafrici

Project Editor: Ylang Nguyen

Editorial Assistant: Wendy Thayer

Production/Design Coordinator: Lisa Jelly Smith

Marketing Manager: Nicola Poser

Senior Manufacturing Coordinator: Marie Barnes

Photo Credits

P. 88, by Sarah Irvine Belson; p. 120, © Michael Zide; p. 140, by W. Randall Irvine; p. 162, by W. Randall Irvine; p. 209, by Rosemary Belson; p. 235, by Conrad Lotze; p. 253, by W. Randall Irvine; p. 285, by Jeff Hammill; p. 292, by Alexander Tomlinson.

Text Credits

P. 59, "Sample scope and sequence chart" retrieved from http://www.pde.psu.edu/connections/currdevl/res2-d.htm. Developed by Cisek, Lurant & Wilt/Berks County Intermediate Unit. Reprinted by permission of the Pennsylvania Department of Education; p. 132, from *Diagnosis in Speech-Language Pathology, 2nd edition*, by J.B. Tomblin, H.L. Morris, and D.C. Spriesterbach. Copyright (c) 2000. Reprinted with permission of Delmar, Cengage Learning. Fax 800-730-2215; p. 227, copyrighted material from the National Association for Gifted Children (NAGC). This material may not be reprinted without permission from NAGC, 1707 L Street, NW, Suite 550, Washington, DC 20036, 202-785-4628, www.nagc.org; p. 245, Shackelford, J. (2000). State and jurisdictional eligibility definitions for infants and toddlers with disabilities under IDEA. *NECTAS Notes*, No. 5 (April), revised, Table 1. Chapel Hill, NC: National Early Childhood Technical Assistance System.

For product information and technology assistance, contact us at
Cengage Learning Customer & Sales Support, 1-800-354-9706

For permission to use material from this text or product, submit all requests online at **www.cengage.com/permissions**
Further permissions questions can be emailed to
permissionrequest@cengage.com

Library of Congress Control Number: 2001133275

ISBN-13: 978-0-618-07359-7

ISBN-10: 0-618-07359-0

Wadsworth
10 Davis Drive
Belmont, CA 94002
USA

Cengage Learning is a leading provider of customized learning solutions with office locations around the globe, including Singapore, the United Kingdom, Australia, Mexico, Brazil, and Japan. Locate your local office at **www.cengage.com/global**

Cengage Learning products are represented in Canada by Nelson Education, Ltd.

To learn more about Wadsworth, visit **www.cengage.com/wadsworth**

Purchase any of our products at your local college store or at our preferred online store **www.ichapters.com**

Printed in the United States of America
3 4 5 6 7   16 15 14 13 12

FD044

BRIEF CONTENTS

CONTENTS

PREFACE

The majority of teachers in today's classrooms confront two fundamental issues related to the subject of this book. First, inclusion, or mainstreaming, is the most popular special education practice in school systems. Under this arrangement, children with a wide range of exceptionalities are being included in the general education classroom, and teachers require practical and up-to-date information about addressing these students' needs. Second, the influx of technology into classrooms has been enormous over the past decade. The majority of technology funding has supported hardware, software, and networking, and little focus has been placed on the professional development of teachers. Given these two factors, the time seems ripe for a book about integrating technology into the teaching of exceptional students, especially a text that takes a practical, classroom-oriented approach to the subject.

The idea behind this book is to put technology in its place—as one of many tools a teacher can use to meet particular curricular and learning needs and the goals of an individualized education program (IEP). Materials for teacher professional development in this area are currently inadequate, and it is my hope that this book can assist all those who teach students with exceptionalities—in mainstream classrooms, in "resource" settings, and in self-contained programs. The book is suited not only for courses in special education technology, but also for surveys of exceptionalities and for in-service professional development courses and training sessions.

FOCUS ON A VARIETY OF TECHNOLOGIES TO MEET STUDENTS' NEEDS

Most technology books related to special education focus almost exclusively on adaptive or assistive technologies. That is not the case here. This book does, of course, discuss such technologies, but it also includes mainstream software applications that have been shown to be effective for students with exceptionalities. For example, students with many types of expressive difficulties can benefit from using multimedia software applications. Although these applications are not specifically designed for children with learning differences, they can provide students with the opportunity to express ideas, be creative, and further their learning.

One of the book's core principles is that technological applications can and should be used in different ways with different students. Thus, all types of technology are included when they make sense in meeting a particular type of need. The book offers real-life examples of how technology has influenced the lives of children with exceptionalities as well as techniques for adapting state-of-the-art tools to better the education of all students.

However, this book cannot hope to discuss every technological tool that is available and effective. Advances in the development and distribution of technology tools appear much too quickly for all to be included here. The point of this book is not to prescribe certain tools that work in all cases, but to offer a perspective that helps teachers determine how technology can support the education of exceptional individuals.

How This Book Is Organized

Part I of this book, "Background Knowledge," sets out the structure and principles that inform the later chapters. Chapter 1 presents an overview of technology's role in teaching children with exceptionalities and develops the four core principles that underlie the entire text. Chapter 2 offers guidelines for teachers to use in selecting technological applications for their own students.

Part II, "The Students," describes technologies in the context of specific disabilities. Each of the ten chapters in this part discusses a category of disability and the related implications for learning and teaching. The chapters offer jargon-free descriptions of technologies that have been successful, along with frequent examples and illustrations. In addition, each chapter in this section contains a profile of a person with special needs who is using some of the technologies described in the chapter. (The profiles of individuals are typically based on an amalgamation of several people.) The profiles emphasize the practical nature of the book and help make the concepts more approachable.

Between Parts II and III is a special section called "Choosing Technology by Content Area." This section presents descriptions of useful technological applications organized according to curricular areas such as reading, mathematics, social studies, and social and life skills. Because children with different exceptionalities may have similar educational needs, this section can be a handy resource for teachers who are trying to meet IEP goals in particular academic areas.

Part III, "Tools for Educators," examines professional tools for teachers to use. Chapter 13 offers recommendations for using technology to develop IEPs, assessing students' progress, and communicating with parents and students. Chapter 14 then reviews the core principles introduced in the first chapter and discusses ways for teachers to keep up with ongoing changes in the field.

After the final text chapter, readers will find a Handbook of Resources with a wealth of useful reference material, including sources for locating online curriculum materials, discussion groups, and the software and hardware tools discussed in the text.

LEARNING FEATURES OF THIS BOOK

The book contains a variety of pedagogical features designed to help both novice and experienced teachers learn and reflect on the content.

Profiles, as mentioned earlier, offer portrayals of individuals (and in one case a school) who use the technologies described in the text.

Techniques for Your Classroom features, which appear in the majority of the book's chapters, highlight specific methods that teachers can use in the classroom to incorporate technology most effectively.

Principles and Practice features, also appearing throughout the text, highlight different elements of special education, including regulations, controversial issues, and ideas about good teaching.

Focus Questions at the beginning of each chapter help organize the reader and challenge him or her to think about the chapter's content.

Marginal Notes—short phrases in the page margins—reinforce important points and provide convenient markers for review.

Summary sections offer helpful recaps of each chapter's main ideas.

Key Terms appear at the end of each chapter, with page numbers indicating where each term is introduced or discussed.

Resources for Further Investigation, another section at the end of each chapter, offers a variety of helpful information, including valuable websites, sources for particular software and hardware products, and contact information for relevant organizations.

The *Handbook of Resources* at the back of the book, as mentioned, is another handy reference source for teachers as they apply the principles of this book to their own classroom practices.

The *Glossary* includes definitions for all the key terms.

In line with the practical nature of this book, the ***textbook website*** contains useful activities for learning about technology and special education, links to downloadable demonstrations of software applications, a discussion board where teachers and students can exchange ideas, and much more. The students' section of the site can be accessed from **www.cengage.com/education** and the instructors' section from **www.cengage.com/education**.

ACKNOWLEDGMENTS

Although the title page may suggest that I wrote this book on my own, this is certainly not the case. A number of people deserve recognition for the contributions they made to this project, either to the material within or to my sanity and stability as this book was put together—and in most cases to both. I first want to thank my editor, Doug Gordon, for his insights, kindness, and encouragement throughout this process. Without Doug's perspective on the usefulness of my ideas, this book would not have been completed. I also want to express my gratitude to my graduate/research/editorial assistant, Martha Cohen-Tomlinson, for her unique perspective and numerous contributions in terms of content and direction. My gratitude also goes to Erika Vaughn for her research and hard work in the beginning stages of this process. I want to thank Lisa Mafrici at Houghton Mifflin for her support and help with all the details of this project, and Sue Pulvermacher-Alt at Houghton Mifflin for her encouragement and support of my ideas. Ylang Nguyen was a wonderful project editor and had such great insights into the book's organization and presentation. Thanks for all your hard work! I also want to express special appreciation to Loretta Wolozin for approaching me with the idea for this book in the first place, and for her creative ideas that shaped much of what is evident in the final product.

The members of the faculty of the School of Education at American University have believed in me and encouraged me along the way. I especially want to convey my gratitude to my friend and colleague Sally L. Smith for sharing her ideas and creativity and for her inspiration. Thanks, Sally! A number of reviewers at other universities offered helpful comments; these include Karen Anderson, University of Memphis; Christina Curran, Central Washington University; Chris Givner, California State University, Los Angeles; Caron Mellblom, California State University, Dominguez Hills; Creighton Miller, Murray State College; June Szabo-Kifer, California State University, Los Angeles; Teresa A. Taber, Purdue University; and Cheryl Wissick, University of South Carolina. I also want to thank the students I've had over the years who showed genuine interest and strengthened my conviction that a book like this one is needed. I am particularly grateful to my former students and friends who served as inspiration for the profiles.

Finally, there are my family and friends. To my husband, Stephen—thanks for always encouraging me to sit down and write instead of lamenting about it! To my children, Deirdre and Griffin, for being such wonderful distractions and my daily inspirations. Thanks to my dad for his technical help with this book and to my mom for her research help and perspective on the ideas. My deepest appreciation also goes to the rest of my family, for their encouragement throughout the process, and to all my good friends for showing interest and for assuring me that I could do this.

TECHNOLOGY FOR EXCEPTIONAL LEARNERS

BACKGROUND KNOWLEDGE

When technology is carefully selected and matched to learning objectives, all students can benefit from its use as an educational tool.
(© Susie Fitzhugh)

PRINCIPLES FOR USING TECHNOLOGY WITH EXCEPTIONAL LEARNERS

FOCUS QUESTIONS

As you read this chapter, think about the following:

- What does the term *disability* mean to you? What does *exceptionality* mean?

- Do you know any "exceptional" individuals? Are we all in some way exceptional?

- What do you think of when you envision "classroom technology"?

- What particular idea or image do you form when you think of "technology for disabled people"?

This chapter provides an overview of this book's main principles and the types of technology used in teaching students with exceptionalities. The book is built on the concept of choosing technologies to meet the needs of individual students in both general and special education classrooms. It discusses technologies that go beyond assistive and adaptive tools for children with disabilities and in fact aims to integrate state-of-the-art, mainstream applications into the education of children with exceptionalities.

Students identified as having a disability or difference may have a wide variety of learning needs. Likewise, a group of children with a particular exceptionality do not necessarily share common academic needs or require the same instructional methods. In addition, many students may have special classroom needs even though they are not identified as having a disability. Certain technologies can bridge these gaps. Teachers may find, for example, that technologies that work with students with visual disabilities are also useful for children with learning disabilities. The technologies presented in this book increase the set of techniques at a teacher's disposal and help teachers meet the needs of all children.

TECHNOLOGY IN TODAY'S CLASSROOM

Today, if you ask an elementary school student about computer technology, you will likely hear about e-pals, researching on the Web, multimedia educational software, and computerized game stations. Book reports often become multimedia presentations. Today's school children are technologically savvy and they use technology to meet their own needs. Today's schools have taken technology beyond the role of reinforcer, drill-and-practice device, or reward. Technology is now an *instructional tool.*

Thinking about technology as a tool, like a pencil or a paintbrush, helps students and teachers alike use computers and other devices actively, whether their goal is to tell a story, produce a picture, or practice basic skills. Appropriate technologies can help your students become active, empowered learners and help you find innovative and exciting ways to meet the social and learning needs of a variety of students in a multitude of settings.

Nevertheless, using technology with special needs students can prove challenging. Finding age appropriate resources specifically focused on academics and matched to individual learning needs and educational goals can be difficult. This book can help you navigate the world of today's technologies and choose among today's technological tools to meet the diverse needs of today's classroom. First, we discuss the exceptionalities you are likely to encounter among your students, laws governing special education, and services available.

Choosing tools for diverse needs

P RINCIPLES AND PRACTICE   Technology as a Tool

Many researchers and writers in the field of educational technology propose that computers should be viewed as a "tool." What do they mean by this?

If you envision a tool, you might first think of a hammer or screwdriver—an instrument you would use to build or repair something. As educators, we broaden our idea of a tool: pencils, pens, paintbrushes—these are tools children (and teachers) use to express themselves and show what they know. Computers can also be this sort of tool.

In this sense, computers are not a specific curricular focus of the curriculum, but instruments that students use to express ideas, tell stories, give answers, and ask questions. Kids learn keyboarding much as they learn penmanship, and they use both of these skills in more and more sophisticated ways as they grow and learn. Mastering the use of computers and technology in general helps children move toward the larger goal of learning.

AN OVERVIEW OF EXCEPTIONALITIES

According to the National Information Center for Children and Youth with Disabilities (NICHCY), five million U.S. children receive some sort of special education services each year (NICHCY, 1999). In the 1999–2000 school year, 11.2 percent of all students enrolled in public schools (grades K–12) received services in federally supported programs for children with disabilities, up from 8 percent in 1977 (U.S. Department of Education, 2000). These students have a range of differences, from specific learning disabilities to severe restrictions of movement or communication.

We all have strengths in some areas and weaknesses in others. A student may have severe problems in math and science but be a gifted public speaker with a talent for learning foreign languages. A student may be an intelligent, creative learner in all academic areas but may be hampered by a wheelchair that makes many locations and activities inaccessible. You may, for example, have students like these in your classroom:

- Jason, a tall fifth grader, can throw a baseball at eighty miles per hour yet cannot hear.

- Michael, an excellent mountain climber, cannot see.

- Susan, whose drawings and paintings show a sophisticated understanding of composition and color, reads two years beneath her grade level.

As a teacher, you must carefully evaluate each child's strengths and weaknesses. The process of "assessing" a child's learning needs includes (1) evaluation and screening by psychologists and therapists, and (2) determining the child's day-to-day specific needs in academic, social, and creative realms. Deciding whether a student needs special education services rests on the degree to which a disability interferes with normal functioning. We all mix up left and right now and then, but that does not mean we have a learning disability or dyslexia.

Defining exceptionality

A child who has an **exceptionality** has some area of functioning in which he or she is significantly different from an established norm. This definition includes both students with disabilities and those with special gifts or talents. For example, an average score on a standardized intelligence test such as the Wechsler Intelligence Scale for Children–III (WISC-III) is 100, with a standard deviation of 10 points. If your IQ score is between 80 and 120, you are considered of "normal" intelligence. If your IQ score is above 120, you may be identified as "gifted," and if your IQ score is lower than 80, you may be labeled "developmentally disabled" or "mentally retarded." Of course, intelligence tests are not always accurate, and educators consider further measures of ability and achievement before placing a child in a special category.

The same holds true for exceptionalities in other areas, such as emotional development, amount of leg movement, white blood cell count, and so forth. Any behavior or performance outside the "normal" range is exceptional. If an exceptionality interferes with normal functioning across various situations, educators consider "labeling" a student as exceptional in order to provide services. For all disabilities, the process of screening, identification, and labeling includes numerous evaluations and observations.

Although some see the act of giving a person a label as unfair and insensitive, current laws governing U.S. schools require that a student be identified as exceptional in order for the school or treatment center to receive funding to support that child's education. That is the main reason for classifying students by exceptionality. As you read this book, keep in mind that your teaching tools and methods should be based on each child's individual needs, not on the child's label.

● The Individuals with Disabilities Education Act

The **Individuals with Disabilities Education Act (IDEA)** is the principal federal law providing for special education services. Originally passed by Congress in 1975 as the Education for All Handicapped Children Act (Public Law 94-142), it was reauthorized most recently in 1997 and is up for reauthorization in 2002.

IDEA requirements

IDEA requires that special needs students be incorporated into the public school system. It further states that all students, regardless of ability, are entitled to a *free, appropriate education* in the **least restrictive environment.** Prior to this law's enactment, children with disabilities had no legal right to an education, and parents frequently paid for their children to be placed in private institutions or else kept them at home.

IDEA requires that students be classified according to their primary disability. Table 1.1 lists and describes the typical categories used in special education. (Later chapters will explore these categories in more depth.) The table also indicates percentages of students in each category—the percentage relative to the overall school population and the percentage among students receiving special education services. You can see, for example, that between 5 and 10 percent of school-age children are considered to have a "learning disability," and this category comprises more than half of the students in special

Disability	% of School-Age Population	% of Special Education Population	Description
Learning disabilities	5–10%	50.8%	Students with learning disabilities have normal IQ scores but fail to perform well in the classroom, as measured by achievement tests. More precisely, IDEA defines a learning disability as a "disorder in one or more of the basic psychological processes involved in understanding or in using spoken or written language, which may manifest itself in an imperfect ability to listen, think, speak, read, write, spell or to do mathematical calculations."
Speech and language impairments	10%	19.4%	Students with these impairments have problems in communication and related areas such as oral motor function, including both expressive language (articulation) and receptive language (understanding).
Mental retardation	1%	11.0%	People with mental retardation lag in development and have trouble learning and making social adjustments. The IDEA regulations provide the following technical definition: "Mental retardation means significantly below average general intellectual functioning existing concurrently with deficits in adaptive behavior and manifested during the developmental period, that adversely affects a child's educational performance."
Emotional and behavioral disorders	1%	8.4%	Many terms describe emotional, behavioral, or mental disorders. IDEA uses the term *serious emotional disturbance,* defined as "a condition exhibiting one or more of the following characteristics over a long period of time and to a marked degree that adversely affects educational performance: (A) An inability to learn that cannot be explained by intellectual, sensory, or health factors; (B) An inability to build or maintain satisfactory interpersonal relationships with peers and teachers; (C) Inappropriate types of behavior or

● TABLE 1.1   Types of disabilities and frequency of occurrence for students ages six to twenty-one

Disability	% of School-Age Population	% of Special Education Population	Description
			feelings under normal circumstances; (D) A general pervasive mood of unhappiness or depression; or (E) A tendency to develop physical symptoms or fears associated with personal or school problems."
Physical and health impairments	0.6%	5.5%	The federal government distinguishes between orthopedic impairments, other health impairments, and traumatic brain injury. In this book we will treat these as a single category that includes a wide range of conditions from mobility impairments to AIDS.
Multiple disabilities	0.2%	1.9%	A combination of disabilities from other categories.
Hearing impairments	0.1%	1.3%	Loss of hearing, ranging from mild deficit to total deafness.
Visual impairments	1.2%	0.5%	The terms *partially sighted, low vision, legally blind,* and *totally blind* describe students with various levels of visual impairment.
Deaf-blindness	0.003%	less than 0.1%	As the term implies, this indicates a combination of severe hearing loss with severe visual deficit.
Autism/ developmental disorders	0.08%	1.2%	Autism and other types of developmental disorder are usually evident by age three. These neurological disorders affect a child's ability to communicate, understand language, play, and relate to others.
Attention-deficit/ hyperactivity disorder	5%	*	Attention-deficit/hyperactivity disorder (ADHD) is characterized by inattention (an inability to focus on a task or activity) and/or impulsiveness and hyperactivity (a high level of activity and acting without thinking). The older term *attention deficit disorder* (ADD) still receives frequent use, especially when the child displays no symptoms of hyperactivity.

*Few students diagnosed only with ADD or ADHD receive special education services. Some who do are classified as having "other health impairments."

Source: Adapted from U.S. Department of Education, *Twenty-second annual report to Congress on the implementation of the Individuals with Disabilities Education Act.* Washington, DC: Government Printing Office, 2000, Table II-3; Code of Federal Regulations, Title 34, Section 300.7(b)(9).

education. As either a special or general education teacher, you can expect that the majority of your students served under IDEA will have a learning disability.

Here are three other points about the IDEA system of categorizing students:

1 Although students rarely receive special education unless they are placed in one of the IDEA categories, some students "on the borders" receive special services in inclusive classrooms, discussed later in this chapter.

2 Although IDEA does not deal with gifted and talented students, special education teachers sometimes also work with these students. Gifted and talented students will be discussed in detail in a later chapter.

3 A particular challenge to those who work in the field of special education is that many students have more than one disability. For example, an estimated 60 percent of students with learning disabilities also have some form of attention-deficit/hyperactivity disorder.

● Individualized Education Programs (IEPs)

For the most part, children with exceptionalities are not unlike so-called normal children. However, IDEA requires that each child who has been identified as having a disability have a specially designed instructional program, called an **individualized education program (IEP)**. An IEP identifies the educational goals, outcomes, and objectives for the student with a disability. It is evaluated and revised on a yearly or semi-yearly basis.

Developing an IEP

The team that develops an IEP typically includes the regular education teacher, a special education teacher, parents, the school psychologist and other specialists, school administrators, and, in many cases, the student. The IEP is designed to identify educational priorities for serving the exceptional student, but the IEP does not dictate *how* a child should be taught. Teachers—both special education teachers and regular education teachers—must select instructional methods that best match the student's needs.

● Inclusion: Exceptional Students in the Regular Classroom

As mentioned earlier, IDEA specifies that all students are entitled to a free and appropriate public education in the *least restrictive environment*. This element of the law has been interpreted in many different ways, but essentially it means that students should be placed in settings that allow them to have the greatest amount of contact with their nondisabled peers. This has led to a trend in special education known as **inclusion** or **mainstreaming.** In an inclusive model, the child with an exceptionality stays in the regular education classroom all or most of the school day.

The inclusive model

The inclusive model supports the idea that exceptional children can learn a great deal from their nondisabled peers—and that nondisabled students should have the opportunity to learn about human diversity and to accept differences. Its advocates believe that the inclusive model gives the school population a more diverse feel and produces an environment closer to real life, in which adults with a wide range of abilities must learn to work together. Its critics contend that the inclusive model does special needs students a disservice because regular classroom teachers lack the preparation to teach them. Further, the inclusive model often puts a strain on the regular education teacher and can be distracting to regular education students. A student with an exceptionality may demand more time and energy than other students, time and energy lost to the rest of the class. In other words, students at risk for academic failure may thrive in an inclusive model in which the teacher both uses a wider range of techniques and has special education teachers in the classroom to provide additional help to children who need it.

Unfortunately, many students miss out on special education services until they are two or three years behind. The inclusive model may help catch students in need of assistance before they get so far behind. Imagine, for example, that "Joey," a student with a learning disability, is placed in Mrs. Smith's regular third grade class. Mr. Jones, a special education teacher, comes in three days a week during math time to help Joey. During the unit on fractions, two or three other students (who have not been identified as having learning disabilities) seem to be having trouble understanding the material. Mr. Jones and Mrs. Smith decide to create small groups of students. Mr. Jones takes the "weakest" students to work intensively on visualizing fractions, while Mrs. Smith takes those who are working on adding fractions, and a parent volunteer takes the third group, who are working on fractions and division. In this setting, the special education teacher can use specially designed techniques to help the struggling students over the hurdle of fractions.

Thinking inclusively as a teacher

This is an ideal vision of how the inclusive model could work. In reality, most schools have only one special education teacher, and he or she cannot possibly be in a particular classroom every day. As a teacher, you can think inclusively by attempting to adjust your lessons both for more advanced students and for those who need more support. In this way, all students will receive appropriate instruction, even if they are not labeled as having a special learning need. Although this process takes more planning time and more classroom time, it helps each child to succeed and creates a better learning environment for all your students.

Research has been inconclusive on how inclusion affects the academic achievement of disabled and nondisabled students. Philosophical opinions differ on whether or not inclusion "works," and the debate between advocates and critics continues. Even so, the inclusive model has become the norm in most school systems. This trend springs from various reasons, including financial constraints, the desire to make schools more democratic, and advocacy by parents and other organizations interested in the welfare of children.

● Other Placement Options

Despite the trend toward inclusion, IDEA regulations do provide for other options in placing a child who needs special services. As the IEP team considers a child's placement, it must evaluate the fit between the child's needs and the available programs. Placement is not simply determined by disability or by a team's point of view about the ideal setting for all students. Instead, a continuum of placements should be available.

The following list describes the typical continuum of placements, in order from the most inclusive to the least. Figure 1.1 illustrates these options.

Variety of placement options

- *Regular education classroom.* The student works with peers in a regular classroom with no additional support. A child who uses a wheelchair but has no other special needs may be given such a placement.
- *Regular education classroom with consultant.* The student works with peers in a regular classroom, but a special education teacher serves as a consultant to the classroom teacher.
- *Regular education classroom with itinerant teacher.* The student remains in the regular classroom, and the special education teacher comes in to assist the student during class time. For example, the special education teacher might come in during math time to help a child with a learning disability primarily in mathematics.
- *Regular education classroom with resource room support.* The student leaves the regular classroom for a portion of the day and goes to a special education classroom, most often known as the resource room. For example, the student may leave during reading time in order to receive intensive reading support. Students with similar needs from different classes may go to the resource room at the same time.

● FIGURE 1.1

The continuum of special education placements

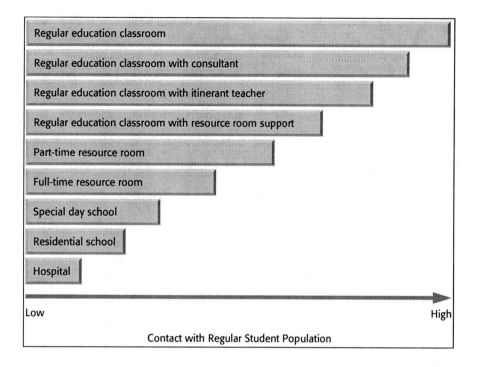

Regular education classroom

Regular education classroom with consultant

Regular education classroom with itinerant teacher

Regular education classroom with resource room support

Part-time resource room

Full-time resource room

Special day school

Residential school

Hospital

Low ⟶ High

Contact with Regular Student Population

- *Part-time resource room.* The student spends approximately half of his or her day in the resource room receiving intensive instruction from the special education teacher.
- *Full-time resource room.* The student spends all of his or her day in the special education classroom.
- *Special day school.* In this case, the student attends a school other than his or her neighborhood school and receives intensive services all day. The student may be placed at this special school for a semester or for his or her entire school career. For example, at the Phoenix Day School for the Deaf, some students attend long enough to learn sign language and then return to their home school. Other hearing-impaired students attend this school from kindergarten through high school.
- *Residential school.* In this type of placement, the student lives at the school. The student receives academic support during the daytime and support services at night. For example, a child with a severe behavioral disorder may live in a group home at a residential treatment facility and attend the on-campus school during the day.
- *Hospital.* A hospital is unfortunately another setting in which some exceptional students must be placed. For example, a child with cancer must be placed in a setting where his or her health care can be the primary focus.

● FIGURE 1.2

Percentages of students with disabilities served in different educational environments (1997–1998 school year)

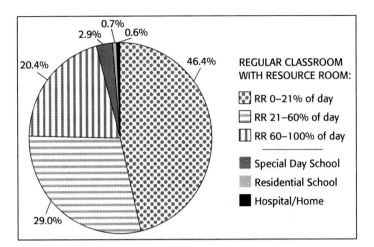

Source: U.S. Department of Education, *Twenty-second annual report to Congress on the implementation of the Individuals with Disabilities Education Act.* Washington, DC: Government Printing Office, 2000, Table III-1.

Some hospitals staff special education teachers trained not only in providing individualized instruction, but also in helping students understand their health situations. For example, a hospital with a program for terminally ill children might include a classroom and playground scaled and designed for children with health problems.

As shown in Figure 1.2, only a small percentage of students with disabilities attend special day or residential schools. Almost 96 percent attend a regular classroom for at least part of the day, although many spend substantial parts of their day in a resource room.

● Impact of the Standards Movement on Students with Disabilities

The recent **standards movement** in U.S. education has been establishing for each academic discipline guideposts or criteria that all children should meet by a particular grade or age. Standards set forth by organizations such as the National Council of Teachers of Mathematics, the National Council of Teachers of English, the American Association for the Advancement of Science, and the National Council on Social Studies, as well as states and local school districts, establish specific desired outcomes for students. Teachers are responsible for helping students meet these educational objectives, and student learning is regularly measured.

The standards are similar in some ways to the objectives in an IEP. However, differences in ability or mental age render many such standards inappropriate for students with exceptionalities. In 2000, an Oregon student failed to pass the competency test for high school graduation after receiving none of the accommodations specified on his IEP. This case established a nationwide controversy about the use of competency testing for students with all types of disabilities.

Standards can be helpful when they emphasize higher-order skills and forego standardized tests. Students with learning disabilities, for example, may fail a standardized math or physics test but may be able to apply principles of geometry to the task of building a boat. The issue—as it has always been in special education—is whether to force special education students to learn basic skills to pass tests, making skill remediation the primary focus of instruction, or to use a strategic approach by teaching techniques that will help students learn.

Accommodations for standardized testing

The 1997 Reauthorization of the Individuals with Disabilities Act (ADA) requires that students with disabilities participate in large-scale assessments and that each student's IEP include a statement of the individual modifications required to administer assessments. In response, most states are now developing and implementing assessment models that include all students. Numerous school districts are already using **testing accommodations,** and a few are developing alternative assessments, but the majority of school districts are receiving this new mandate with concern and confusion.

Although many states allow for special testing conditions and accommodations, proper use of the term *accommodation* has become an issue. Accommodation policies vary from district to district and state to state, making it almost impossible to compare student performances. For instance, one district might allow students to use a calculator or provide someone to read students the test questions, while another district might specify that students can have extra time. Implementing accommodations varies widely across disability groups, too. Accommodations for students with physical or sensory disabilities routinely gain approval, whereas students with cognitive or behavioral difficulties encounter more obstacles.

Curriculum-based measurement

University of Oregon professor Gerald Tindal (1995) believes that testing accommodations should take into account the learner's needs, the task demands, and the purpose of the accommodation. Tindal stresses the need for a sound decision-making process, such as curriculum-based measurement. **Curriculum-based measurement** (CBM) can be defined as measuring student progress and performance through continuous (for instance, weekly) use of classroom-based measurements.

Tindal has been working with practitioners in Oregon to embed CBM in the IEP process and to relate a student's performance as measured by CBM to performance on large-scale assessments. A pilot group of teachers has been working to consider standards in math and reading for their students, identify benchmarks, determine the appropriate assessments and accommodations, and write these into the IEP (Tindal and Nolet, 1995).

TECHNOLOGY TOOLS FOR STUDENTS WITH DISABILITIES

Technology provides only one possible avenue of instructional methods for children who have disabilities. Technology choices should follow the same principles that guide other instructional choices: matching the technique to the intended learning objective. All caregivers who work with children with exceptionalities must evaluate available resources and choose the tool that best fits the student's needs. The challenge is to be creative and flexible in instructional techniques, including the use of technology.

● The Variety of Educational Software

Educational software has grown into a multimillion-dollar industry aimed at a market that includes both parents and teachers. Today's software comes in a bewildering variety. JumpStart Kindergarten (Knowledge Adventure), for example, teaches the alphabet and colors with computer-driven lessons. In this application, children see the letter A, hear the letter A, and are asked to point to the letter A on the screen. In the program Where in the World Is Carmen Sandiego? (Learning Company) children ages seven to twelve can participate in a worldwide search for the evil villain Carmen while rehearsing geography facts in a quiz-show environment.

Most educational software falls into one of three categories:

Categories of educational software

- Applications that tutor the student in a particular process or skill
- Applications that provide practice sessions to reinforce previously learned skills
- Applications that simulate a learning environment, such as a program that replicates a science experiment

Throughout this book, you will see examples of all three types.

Integrated learning systems

The educational software market also includes **integrated learning systems.** In addition to providing personalized, computer-based tutoring, these systems monitor daily progress and performance and provide teachers with detailed reports on a student's skills and development. The Jostens Learning System, for example, allows high school students to practice reading and mathematics skills in a remedial environment.

Some types of software have impressive and realistic graphics, sound, and animation but lack grounding in learning theory. In fact, educational software is rarely matched to any national curriculum standards, and it rarely matches precisely what the teacher would like the student to learn. In addition, most educational software is designed for an audience either too broad or too narrow and therefore rarely meets the diverse needs of students in today's classrooms. No amount of artificial intelligence can endow an educational software application with the skill to identify subtle differences in students' rates of understanding.

||||▶

Integrating technology into your own teaching

As a teacher, when you select technology, you'll want a strategy that most closely matches your chosen instructional approach for each individual student. Good teachers can adjust and redirect student learning by observing the student as he or she listens to an explanation, works on a problem, or asks a question. Because such talents and flexibilities are not part of the software repertoire, you must integrate technology into your own teaching, not build your teaching around the technology.

Many teachers who want to integrate technology into their curriculum face the challenge of designing their own computer-based materials. Fortunately, applications such as test-making software and templates (preformatted documents or "shells" for inputting information) allow almost any teacher to use computers for numerous tasks with minimal effort. A plethora of web pages can help you point students to research resources, and email offers a convenient communication system between teachers and parents, professional organizations, and students.

T ECHNIQUES FOR YOUR CLASSROOM

Three Points to Help You Choose Technology

1 Teachers rarely have the time to personally give individual students all the practice and reinforcement they need in basic skills.

2 The computer can do work or create effects that you cannot easily manage in your classroom, such as administer individualized lessons or produce engaging sounds and images and animation.

3 Students can feel empowered when they use computer applications to "show off" their skills—that is, to demonstrate their knowledge in innovative ways.

● Technology for Students with Exceptionalities

When we think of technology for persons with disabilities, we often think in terms of *assistive* and *adaptive technologies.* Assistive and adaptive technologies can be anything from wheelchairs to specially designed computer systems.

Assistive and adaptive technologies

Assistive and adaptive technologies are tools that enable a person with a disability to do something more easily or quickly. **Assistive technology** tools such as specialized keyboards, switches, or a special mouse give a disabled individual easier access to equipment, thus improving functional capabilities and expanding independence. **Adaptive technology** modifies traditional tools, much as a shoulder rest makes a telephone receiver easier to hold. Together, assistive and adaptive technologies can range from high-tech and expensive (a voice-activated home environment) to a simple tool such as a "special" spoon. Federal regulations require that technology be considered along with a disabled student's other educational needs (see the feature "Assistive Technology and the Law").

Assistive and adaptive technologies are not the only tools available to students with exceptionalities. State-of-the-art word processors, voice-activated computers, graphical user interfaces, and multimedia authoring applications, though not designed with the exceptional student in mind, often provide enormous benefit. For example, they can help a learning disabled student in a regular classroom understand complex concepts, express ideas more clearly, and gain personal pride in his or her work.

Remedial technology

Software applications designed for special education students often are known as **remedial technology.** Although children in special education often need no specialized adaptive or assistive tools, they do have academic needs different from those of their peers. Remedial instruction is designed to address a child's educational deficits, and remedial technologies include software programs that provide intensive practice, present a topic in a different way, or break the topic into small parts (task analysis). One remedial software program, Access to Math (Don Johnston Incorporated), allows children to make their own worksheets for specific areas of mathematics. For instance, the student can engage in extended practice on addition of two-digit numbers without regrouping.

Universal Design for Learning

Another useful theoretical framework is the **Universal Design for Learning.** This theory relies on the ideas that student differences fall on a continuum rather than in distinct groups and that teachers should adjust for learning differences among *all* students (Rose & Meyer, 2000). In this model, curriculum materials, assessment techniques, and instruction should be varied and diverse.

P RINCIPLES AND PRACTICE | Assistive Technology and the Law

The following summarizes principles reflected in a policy letter from the Office of Special Education Programs (OSEP) of the U.S. Office of Special Education and Rehabilitative Services (OSERS). The summary helps clarify assistive technology for students with disabilities.

1 Assistive technology needs must be considered along with the student's other educational needs.
2 Needs for assistive technology must be identified on an individual basis.
3 Assistive technology can involve special education or a related service.
4 Assistive technology can also be a form of supplementary aid or service used to help a student benefit from education in a general education environment.
5 If participants in the evaluating team determine that a student with disabilities needs assistive technology in order to receive a free, appropriate education, the student's IEP must include a specific statement of such services, including their nature and amount.

Article 7, Rule 6, Section 5(d) of the Individuals with Disabilities Education Act (IDEA) states the following:

The public agency shall provide instructional equipment and augmentative or assistive devices and services if necessary for a student with unique special needs to participate in the educational program on parity with other students identified as disabled under this Article or non-disabled students, as appropriate.

In addition, IDEA provides that "assistive technology devices and assistive technology services be added to the list of early intervention services" for infants and toddlers.

The Americans with Disabilities Act (ADA) provides for accessibility to public places for all individuals. This means that not only should public buildings offer restrooms accessible to people with disabilities, but also that schools should be made accessible to all students beyond simple retrofitting of the physical space. ADA also mandates adaptation of responsibilities, so that a child with a physical disability may not be "required" to pass a physical education class, and a child with a developmental disability may be excused from taking the statewide standardized test.

In a Universal Design for Learning classroom, students are encouraged to use a wide range of techniques in learning about a topic, and they are given options for how they will be assessed. For example, you might provide students with your lesson outlines, and students who thought they needed this assistance would use the outlines to take notes. You might give students the option of reading a book or hearing it read by the computer. As their final project, students might be allowed to produce either a paper report or a multimedia HyperStudio stack.

In such an environment, you would have many options, some of them technology based, for teaching and assessing your students. The concept of universal design extends beyond classrooms to areas such as architecture and construction. Some buildings constructed according to universal design principles have all doors wide enough for a wheelchair and all restrooms accessible.

Universal design aims to make options available to everyone. If you watch people entering a building that has both steps and a ramp, you'll see that most people take the ramp, whether or not they use a wheelchair. The ramp is easier on your knees and usually more convenient.

● How Effective Is Technology Use?

Many studies have attempted to gauge the effectiveness of technology in teaching and learning. To date, the results for students with special needs have been more promising than for the school population at large. Although the question is clouded by the fact that the available technology changes as fast as it can be studied, the following sections summarize important information about technology's effectiveness.

Effectiveness in General Education ● Early studies (for instance, Papert, 1980) established a body of evidence suggesting that technology can positively affect several dimensions of students' educational experiences. A meta-analysis (a study of studies) conducted by James Kulik (1994) found that computer-based instructional materials have a positive effect on student performance but not in all areas. Research conducted by the Apple Classrooms of Tomorrow (ACOT) group (1996) found that using technology resulted in higher levels of cooperative learning and reasoning, but it had no impact on students' test scores in reading, math, and vocabulary.

Technology's impact is based on many factors

Some studies have found that various factors affect technology's impact: the specific student population, software design, teacher practices, student grouping, and the form of access to technology (Software Publishers Association, 1996). By the mid-1980s, people began to understand that we could fully understand technologies' effects on teaching and learning only as part of multiple interacting factors in the complex life of schools (Hawkins & Honey, 1990; Hawkins & Pea, 1987; Newman, 1990; Pea, 1987; Pea & Sheingold, 1987).

In nationwide studies of technology's effect on student learning as measured by scores on standardized tests, technology seems neither to harm nor to help. This lack of evidence for a positive or negative impact has been called the "no significant difference" effect by Thomas L. Russell, Director of the Office of Instructional Telecommunications at North Carolina State University. His work, summarizing findings from research reports, summaries, and papers from 1945 to the present, contends that technology-driven education methods yield results no better and no worse than traditional classroom instruction (Russell, 1999). It may be that technology is simply a new medium, and techniques of instruction have remained the same. It may also be that the impact of technology is not easily measured with standardized tests. Many advocates of technology claim that it allows students to gain higher-level thinking skills that are not measured by standardized tests.

The use of technology in school has many critics. For example, Clifford Stoll, in his book *Silicon Snake Oil* (1995), warns that today's classroom use of technology resembles the use of the filmstrip in previous decades—an inadequate substitute for education. Stoll suggests that technophiles are isolating students at their keyboards and throwing them into the chaos of cyberspace.

Despite such criticisms, technology has become such a part of our everyday lives that children must become fluent users of computers and other technological tools in order to meet their educational and social-emotional goals. Today's second-grader must learn to compose writing on a computer in addition to handwriting cursive script. High school students require the

---

PRINCIPLES AND PRACTICE   Medical Advances and Technology

If we think of technology as including all types of tools that enable society to progress, then advances in medical research and biotechnology have implications for people with disabilities as well. For example, laser surgery can allow us to permanently improve our vision. Cochlear implants may improve the hearing of deaf children. Nanotechnology that stimulates cell growth may make organ transplants safer, using a person's own cellular structure rather than risking rejection of donor cells. Gene research, such as cataloging the human genome, may help scientists identify chromosomal abnormalities that result in disabilities.

Many of these medical technologies are still in the developmental stage. Nevertheless, parents, teachers, and society must examine the moral and ethical elements of medical testing and research. For example, cochlear implants require major surgery that may have to be performed repeatedly in young children. Many participants in deaf culture who use sign language as their primary means of communication oppose these implants, especially for children. They consider them an insult, a threat to their culture, a condemnation of deafness, and an attempt to fix something not in need of fixing. Thus the decision to receive a cochlear implant is a personal one, to be made carefully by a deaf adult or the parents of a deaf child. The same situation is true for many disabling conditions that medical advances may someday eliminate. As educators, we must be supportive and protective of parents' rights while we retain our focus on the education of children with exceptionalities.

skills to search online databases and to distinguish reliable web sources. As a teacher, you will help students develop these skills.

Effectiveness for Students with Disabilities   ●   Research on technology's effect shows clearer and more positive results with special needs students than with the general school-age population. Most obviously, technology affords greater access and more individualized instruction for students with exceptionalities. For example, screen readers, which convert text on a screen into spoken language, allow students with visual impairments to better join in on reading education. By the early 1990s, college students with visual problems and learning disabilities displayed an increase in grade-point averages and graduation rates when they used a screen reader (Hilton-Chalfen, 1991).

Clear benefits of technology for students with special needs

The current influx of technology in schools appears to significantly help students at risk for academic failure. A team at Vanderbilt University studied at-risk inner-city kindergartners for three months and found that a group that learned in a computerized, multimedia language arts environment showed significantly superior gains in auditory, language, decoding-in-context, and story-composition skills, compared with a control group that did not use the computer (Cognition and Technology Group, 1991). Similarly, the Peabody Literacy Program (PLP), a program designed for English-as-a-second-language (ESL) students, nonreaders, and slow readers, uses video and text to promote reading comprehension; students in the program doubled their reading and comprehension scores over five years (O'Riordan, 1999). In another study, Bialo (1997) looked at two groups of elementary-age learning-disabled students. One group received traditional classroom instruction, and the other used software with video vignettes designed to simulate classroom instruction. Bialo found that the video-using students showed less anxiety toward math, were more likely to see math as relevant to everyday life, and were better able to appreciate complex challenges.

One way to look at technology's effectiveness is to examine its potential to provide alternative representations and multisensory experiences. A frog dissection simulated on CD-ROM is not only cleaner than the traditional laboratory method, it also allows the student to slow down the pace of instruction, view the activity from different perspectives, and review steps that would otherwise be "gone." A student with a learning disability could match such a simulation to his or her learning style, perhaps starting from the inside and moving toward the outside of the frog, rather than the traditional dissection from the outside in.

Computer simulations also allow students to see what they cannot otherwise see, like a three-dimensional model of the space shuttle interior or the inside of the human brain. Computer simulations differ from television simulations in that the student controls the pace and order of the presentation.

Technology and Active Learning ● The greatest promise of technology lies in giving students control over the computer and allowing them to be creators. As educators integrate technology into special education they can move beyond using software to "treat" a problem. Future uses should focus on using technology to allow students to express what they know. We know that people learn best when they actively participate in learning. Think about it: you didn't learn to ride a bike by watching a video or by listening to your parents tell you what to do. You gathered information from watching and listening and then tried it yourself. You didn't assume you could ride because you passed a written test, you *proved* you knew how to ride the bike by riding it. Classroom students must be active participants in the learning process, too; they require opportunities to "do" what they are learning about and to talk about it with others.

Using technology as a tool for active learning

Thinking about active learning with technology returns us to the idea of technology as a tool. You can use technology to watch someone perform, to listen to a lecture, or as a vehicle to show your understanding. For example, you can read about the rotation of the planets in the Encarta CD-ROM encyclopedia, which shows you a three-dimensional model of the planets in motion. To really understand how rotation works, however, you can use Apple QuickTime Virtual Reality to create your own model of the rotating planets, then put this into a PowerPoint presentation that you give to a class. In the process, you have actively incorporated the idea of rotation into your understanding and into your own words and model.

Figure 1.3 offers examples of technology use along a continuum from passive (such as watching a movie on a VCR) to active (creating a multimedia project). What other examples can you think up at each level? This book will discuss technologies throughout the continuum, with an emphasis on those that encourage active learning.

● FIGURE 1.3

The continuum of technology use, with examples

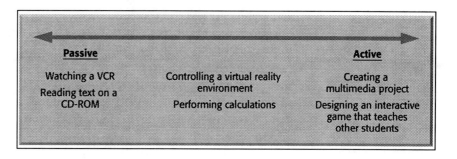

Passive		Active
Watching a VCR	Controlling a virtual reality environment	Creating a multimedia project
Reading text on a CD-ROM	Performing calculations	Designing an interactive game that teaches other students

Four Core Principles: A Way of Thinking About Technology Use

The following principles form the foundation of how we will discuss incorporating technology into the education of children with exceptionalities. For more information on the general uses of technology in education, please refer to Cindy and Mark Grabe's *Integrating Technology for Meaningful Learning* (2001).

Principle 1: Technology Is an Instructional Tool ●

The first principle of integrating technology into special education is to view technology as one instructional tool on an entire tool belt of teaching strategies. Given this perspective, you, the teacher, guide technology use through your selection of the role it will play in your classroom and the types of technology you will use. You can choose to use technology as a tool for information retrieval, for communication, for display of knowledge, for skills practice, or for any combination of these.

This view also defines what technology is not. We don't bring technology into the classroom just to learn how to use it. Although students must learn how to use the tool (be it a calculator or film-editing software), the focus should stay on their academic objectives.

Principle 2: Fit Technology Choice and Use to Students' Individual Needs ●

Selecting technology should be a **diagnostic process**. First, we carefully assess a student's learning needs. Then we evaluate available technology.

As a teacher, you are responsible for knowing your students and selecting the best technology for them. No application is right for every child's instructional needs.

Principle 3: Use Applications in Different Ways with Different Students ●

All software applications have different degrees of flexibility and usability in the classroom. Some students will benefit from certain aspects of a program and others will not. A word processor is the perfect tool to help some students begin the writing process. Other students find a blank computer screen just as intimidating as a blank paper. For some students, the software program Inspiration (Inspiration Software, Inc) (which allows the user to create concept maps) is the perfect tool for brainstorming. For other students, Inspiration's most useful feature is its built-in templates that allow the user to view the structure of an essay.

Schools have limited resources for obtaining technology. It's often up to teachers to figure out what they can have and how creatively they can use it.

Principle 4: Avoid Overreliance on Technology; Balance Benefits and Drawbacks

● Any intervention should enable the student to learn the lesson's targeted skill or objective. Sometimes overreliance on an intervention can result in the student's using that technology as a "crutch." As a teacher, you must decide, for example, how important it is for a student to memorize multiplication tables. One student may make better progress using a calculator than relying on memorization, but another student may come to depend too much on the calculator.

Making decisions about the amount of technology to use can be difficult. But decisions of this type are not new to educators, and you are not alone in the process. A team of parents, evaluators, specialists, and administrators can work toward the best choices for each child.

SUMMARY

Students with exceptionalities are much like other students, but they have been identified as having special instructional needs because they differ in some way from established norms. The Individuals with Disabilities Education Act (IDEA) requires that students with special needs be given a free, appropriate education in the least restrictive environment. To help identify students' needs, the government specifies categories in which students are classified according to their primary disability. The process of labeling a student with a category name, such as "learning disability" or "visual impairment," is sometimes seen as unfair and insensitive, but it is required in order for the school to receive special funding for the child's education.

When a child is identified as needing special services, a team of educators and specialists, including the classroom teacher, devises an individualized instruction program (IEP). Accommodations must also be made in standardized testing and other assessment procedures.

The trend toward inclusion means that children with exceptionalities are often placed in the regular classroom for all or most of the school day. In this model, the classroom teacher might be assisted by a special education consultant or by an itinerant special education teacher who comes in for part of the day. The child may also receive special education services in a separate resource room for part of the day.

As a teacher, you may have children who bear various disability labels, but you should always base your teaching tools and methods on each child's individual needs, not on the child's label. Within any disability category the students may have vastly different academic skills and needs. There is no "one size fits all" in special education. In the process of selecting instructional settings and methods for children with exceptionalities, teachers must make decisions one student at a time.

Although technology in education remains a somewhat controversial subject, research indicates that students with disabilities do benefit from appropriate uses of technology. Assistive and adaptive technology, ranging from simple pieces of equipment to complex, high-tech systems, can help a disabled person to work more easily or quickly. Many disabled students also profit from technology designed for remedial instruction. Beyond these options, however, lies a wide range of other useful technologies, including mainstream software applications. Technology can provide alternative representations and multisensory experiences, and it can encourage students to become active learners.

According to the Universal Design for Learning concept, student differences fall on a continuum rather than in distinct groups, and teachers should adjust for learning differences among *all* students. In classrooms that follow this model, teachers encourage all students to use a wide range of techniques in learning about a topic—some technological, some not—and give students assessment options. This approach allows every student in the classroom to proceed in the way that he or she learns best, using technology in any way appropriate to the goal.

This book is based on four basic principles for using technology with students who have exceptionalities: (1) Technology is an instructional tool, one of many at the teacher's disposal. (2) Technology should be selected and used in a way that suits each student's individual needs. (3) Technological applications can and should be used in different ways with different students. (4) Technology's benefits should be balanced with its potential drawbacks, such as the possibility that a student may come to depend too much on a technological aid.

KEY TERMS

exceptionality (p. 4)
Individuals with Disabilities Education Act (IDEA) (p. 5)
least restrictive environment (p. 5)
individualized education program (IEP) (p. 8)
inclusion (p. 9)
mainstreaming (p. 9)
standards movement (p. 12)
testing accommodations (p. 13)

curriculum-based measurement (p. 13)
integrated learning systems (p. 14)
assistive technology (p. 16)
adaptive technology (p. 16)
remedial technology (p. 16)
Universal Design for Learning (p. 16)
diagnostic process (p. 22)

RESOURCES FOR FURTHER INVESTIGATION

Ability OnLine.
http://www.abilityonline.org/
> Ability OnLine provides a place where parents and students with special needs can connect and begin talking via email. It also offers links to activities and other information. You must register to access many areas of the site.

Alliance for Technology Access.
http://www.ataccess.org/
> This organization acts as an advocate for technology use for persons with special needs and has a great database of products and resources.

Center for Applied Special Technology.
http://www.cast.org/
> This center provides information about technology use for persons with exceptionalities. The site has a detailed section on Universal Design for Learning, as well as many resources and tools for using technology in the classroom.

Closing the Gap: Computer Technology in Special Education and Rehabilitation.
http://www.closingthegap.com/
> Closing the Gap is an organization founded to provide information on technology for persons with special needs. The site includes a searchable database of software and hardware, information about the annual Closing the Gap conference, and ongoing forums about technology use.

Council for Exceptional Children.
http://www.cec.sped.org/
> This is the main website for the Council for Exceptional Children, the main professional organization for special education teachers. It provides many useful links to information about specific exceptionalities, information for parents, careers in special education, and the annual meeting.

ERIC Clearinghouse on Disabilities and Gifted Education.
http://ericec.org/
> The ERIC Clearinghouse on Disabilities and Gifted Education, part of the Educational Resources Information Center database, has great mini-data sheets on various exceptionalities, as well as information about relevant laws and the U.S. Department of Education.

Exceptional Parent Magazine.
http://eparent.com/
> This magazine offers great resources and current information about various exceptionalities. It also has an excellent technology section with information about the current state of special education technology.

IDEA Practices.
http://ideapractices.org/
> This website provides a great deal of information about the Individuals with Disabilities Education Act, including a searchable index of the law itself, activities related to the law, and other information about special education practices.

National Information Center for Children and Youth with Disabilities.
http://www.nichcy.org/
> This website provides helpful fact sheets (in English and Spanish) on many exceptionalities, as well as links to valuable resource sites.

Special Education Resources on the Internet.
http://seriweb.com/
> This site includes a collection of links to resources and information about special education careers, laws, organizations, and specific exceptionalities.

2

SELECTING TECHNOLOGY
FOR THE CLASSROOM

FOCUS QUESTIONS

As you read this chapter, think about the following:

- What should I consider when selecting software for classroom use?

- What sorts of technologies are available for students with special needs?

- In what ways will the student's IEP guide technology decisions?

- How will I learn about using computers?

- Who will assist me in applying technology to educating students with special needs?

hoosing technology for classroom use requires a means of evaluation. In this chapter we present a method for evaluating technology for use with exceptional learners. No single criterion governs this process. Each decision, whether it involves common hardware or software or assistive/adaptive technologies, must take into account the particular needs of the child—both the instructional objectives and the student's technical capabilities—as well as the available materials. Examining a technology's features and matching them to the child's needs will help you select the best tool for enhancing instruction.

Ⓜ️AKING CHOICES ABOUT TECHNOLOGY: A FRAMEWORK

Choosing computers and other types of technology can be challenging. The process requires thoughtful and purposeful consideration of financial, logistical, and curricular issues. In financial terms, technology can commandeer a significant percentage of the available budget, whether that budget belongs to a school district or an individual school. Logistical questions include whether to set up computer labs or place a few computers in each classroom. Curricular issues are perhaps the most fundamental of all, for they involve the basic question of what teachers and students are going to *do* with the technology once it is available to them.

Because technology choices begin at the school and school district levels, let's take a brief look at large-scale issues before turning to the selection of technology for individual students.

● Selecting Technology for the School or School District

For more than a decade, U.S. schools have invested heavily in desktop computers, computer software, and computer networks, as well as in teacher training. But software and hardware selection has not always been based on students' needs or even particular program requirements. Too often the planning and evaluation required to make appropriate choices have been neglected. Frequently, principals or technology directors select technology to meet an immediate need or concern, spending little time assessing long-term needs of the students, program, or school.

Although many schools and districts have developed technology plans and adopted technology curricula, it appears that these plans are rarely used as decision-making guides (Kinnaman, 1999). Instead, both hardware and software tend to be purchased when other technology becomes broken, lost, or outdated. Such "reaction" decision making has obvious drawbacks. Yet many schools lack the administrative structure that would allow individual programs and teachers to make proactive decisions about purchasing technology.

This results in one of the most troubling situations with regard to integrating technology into the curriculum—teachers with little training or support are given technology tools that are poorly "researched" and poorly matched to the school's curriculum and to any individual student's educational needs and IEP goals.

Although school decision makers rarely receive a windfall of surplus time to devote to technology, a proactive approach to technical purchasing decisions and budget development is well worth the investment. Here are three points to consider:

Principles for technology planning

1 Business and industry models for technology upgrades are neither appropriate nor realistic for schools. For example, many industry technology experts recommend upgrading computers every two to three years. This schedule is simply unrealistic for the majority of schools. Educational decision makers must select hardware and software that will remain useful four to five years for a variety of students with a wide range of learning needs. This means that hardware and software selections must be made at times when operating systems and upgrades are compatible.

2 Technology planning, like all school initiatives, benefits from a high level of structure and the input and support of the school community. As a teacher, you form part of that community, and you can help by making your voice heard.

3 A well-organized written plan is a powerful tool to communicate technology priorities to parents, upper-level administrators, and outside groups.

● Selecting Technology for Individual Students

The best time to plan and select technology use for the individual student with an exceptionality is while developing the individualized education program (IEP). The IEP team should examine the school's technology curriculum (if one exists), determine which objectives are appropriate for the student with special learning needs, and then decide how to meet those objectives. Often, the objectives listed in a school or district technology curriculum can support other academic, social, and physical goals for the student. For example, a student with a learning disability may benefit from learning a keyboarding program or having access to a laptop. Understanding the school's technology plan and curriculum can help the IEP team make informed decisions about requirements for the student with an exceptionality.

By law, however, the chosen technology must relate to the student's individual needs, not just to the school or district's technology plan. The IEP team can use an in-place plan to identify types of technologies currently available and can seek to complement the schoolwide plan by selecting appropriate tools from that group; nevertheless, if the tools at hand fail to meet student needs, the team must recommend adoption of new technology.

As part of IEP development, an occupational or physical therapist will do a diagnostic evaluation to determine which assistive and adaptive technologies the student may need. Beyond that, teachers of children with special needs should look for tools that not only will motivate the child with enticing graphics and sounds but also will have long-term educational usefulness.

Begin with the student's needs

Figure 2.1 presents a model for a diagnostic approach to technology selection. Notice especially where the model begins—with the needs of the student. Formal techniques for assessing students' instructional needs include evaluations by special education teachers, school psychologists, and educational assessment specialists. These are supplemented by the input of classroom teachers and parents, who often comprehend the student's specific learning needs and academic strengths and weaknesses. Once a student's needs have been established, the team can begin to select appropriate technology.

Figure 2.1 divides students' needs into four basic types:

Types of student needs

1 *Mobility and accessibility* combine into one fundamental area of need. Students who have limited use of or control over their bodies benefit from technology that allows them greater access, not only to a computer but also to everyday normal activities for their age. Mobility and accessibility aids can include devices such as wheelchairs, switches, voice-activated systems (to control the computer or other machinery), and adaptive utensils (for eating, writing, computer access, and so forth). Many students with mobility needs have other needs as well.

2 The second area of student need concerns *adaptability and input tools*. As with tools to increase mobility, students use these tools to enter a wider range of activities. Unlike mobility tools, though, these focus on a stu-

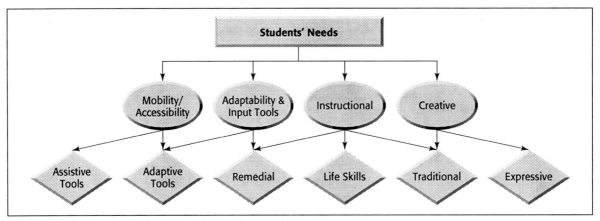

● FIGURE 2.1   Framework for technology decision making

dent's cognitive needs. For example, a student may have difficulty with keyboarding not because of motor difficulties but because of a language deficit, such as letter-sound correspondence. If a student doesn't understand the relationship between letters and the sounds they represent, an adaptive keyboard will not help, but voice-activated software, specialized keyboards, or word-prediction software may be appropriate.

3 Most *instructional* objectives for students with exceptionalities relate to one of three instruction subtypes: traditional skills, remedial skills, and life skills. Traditional skills are those taught to other students in the same age group and at the same level, such as reading, mathematics, science, and social studies. Remedial skills are those "missing" from a student's repertoire, such as an inability to perform a math subskill such as subtraction or to perceive differences in letter formation. Life skills include abilities such as writing résumés and counting back change—skills that prepare the student for independent living and work.

4 Students also need *creative* outlets. These outlets, which allow a student to express ideas and understanding, range from verbal expression to opportunities for artistic or original thinking. Fulfilling these needs leads to learning experiences that increase motivation. Motivated and engaged students are encouraged to produce knowledge they can share with others.

Though designed as a general guide, Figure 2.1 is not all encompassing. Students' often have needs more complicated than the chart can show. In reality, the framework for selecting any instructional technique for the special education student is three-dimensional. The third dimension includes the social and environmental factors that influence how and where a child can receive instruction and special education services. The environmental conditions in which a child learns affect the types of technology that child can use and how she or he can use them. For example, in an inclusion model, in which the student is taught in the regular classroom, it might be difficult to use specialized software or specially designed devices. These tools might be noisy, cumbersome, or embarrassing to the student.

The following sections discuss different types of technology, beginning with the kind you may find most difficult to appraise—educational software. If any of the computer terms puzzle you, consult the definitions in Table 2.1.

● Evaluating Educational Software

Before selecting software, teachers must understand that software has limits that constrain its use as an exclusive teaching tool. Software, no matter how sophisticated it may be, does not make connections to what the student knows

Bandwidth	The amount of information moved over a telecommunications line, measured in bits per second (bps). Bandwidth can also refer to the speed of a transmission.
CD-ROM drive	A compact disk (CD) drive that reads CDs but can not save new files on them.
CD-RW drive	A drive that can read and write data to compact disks (CDs). (CD-RW disks can have data written to and erased from them multiple times; CD-R disks allow data to be saved on them once.)
Central Processing Unit (CPU)	The CPU is the main part of the computer that houses the processor.
Floppy disk drive	This drive reads and writes on small, removable disks that allow you to move files from one computer to another.
Frames	Independent sections into which web page content is divided.
Hard drive	The permanent storage unit on your computer. Files or programs you install or save to your hard drive will remain there until you remove them.
Hardware	The physical parts of the computer, including the CPU, monitor, and keyboard, as well as peripheral devices such as digital cameras and CD-ROM drives.
Interface	The look and format of a software program or website—what a user sees.
Memory	The working space a computer uses to run programs and to process and store information. The amount of memory determines the number of processes a computer can do at a time.
Modem	A modulator-demodulator (modem) allows a computer to send and receive information through a telecommunications line or via wireless transmission.
Monitor	The computer screen that displays information. Monitors come in different sizes and resolutions, as well as in flat and tube screens.
Networking capability	A network is a system of interconnected computers. Networks have many uses; for example, networked computers can share a printer, access to the Internet, and files. A computer's networking capability is determined by the ports (e.g., Ethernet port) it has available. (Ports are the plugs or slots on the back of the CPU.)
Operating system	The underlying language that runs and formats your computer. The two most common operating systems are Windows and Macintosh.
Processor	The processor "drives" your computer as fast as it can go. Processors vary by speed, which is generally measured in megahertz (MHz). The more MHz, the faster the computer can operate.
Random Access Memory (RAM)	RAM refers to memory the computer uses to help execute programs. This memory is not permanent; when the computer is turned off, all information in RAM is lost.
Software	The applications that are installed on a computer, such as word processors and Web browsers, that allow it to perform different functions.
Zip drive	A drive that accepts a Zip disk, which is a removable disk that holds 100 or 250 megabytes of data.

● **TABLE 2.1**   Common computer terminology

and deals with in daily life. Teachers, parents, tutors, and peers can make these connections if they participate with the learner as he or she interacts with the program. Technology is a tool, as we discussed earlier. Software works best when teachers and students talk about the experiences and material presented in programs. An ongoing dialogue allows you and the student to develop greater understanding and wider application of the program's information.

IIII➤

The teacher's role in software evaluation

You may wonder why you as a classroom teacher will need to be concerned with evaluating software. Won't specialists do that for you, or at least provide a step-by-step method for you to use? The answer is yes and no. Often school districts have a procedure for general software evaluation, but students in special education may have learning needs that demand additional or adapted procedures. You will often rely on your own efforts to technology that matches a student's specific needs, that will help keep the student on target within the curriculum, and that helps meet the student's IEP. For this reason, researchers such as Lahm and Nickels (1999) stress that it is essential for all teachers to know how to determine whether a software program or assistive device can benefit a particular student or class.

T ECHNIQUES FOR YOUR CLASSROOM

Collaborating on a Technology Evaluation Guide

If you think that technology evaluation is easy to discuss and much harder to practice, you're right. The vast array of software options in particular marketed to schools and teachers is overwhelming. For that reason, considering pooling your knowledge and expertise with that of your fellow teachers.

To begin, you and your colleagues can create an evaluation guide that builds structure into the technology selection process. A collaborative evaluation guide also provides consistency across the curriculum and across disciplines and helps you compare and contrast similar software. As you put your guide to use, you'll begin to develop a shared and growing database of valuable information.

Many checklists or rubrics for evaluating software address broad, generalized use. Most attempt to describe the technical aspects of a piece of software, information that is necessary but not sufficient for education purposes. For teachers, as Smith and Vokurka (1990) point out, software selection should be "grounded on the principles of functional utility . . . and not on the creation of 'window dressing.'" The same researchers suggest that an effective evaluation instrument ought to meet the following criteria:

- It is easy to use by evaluators.
- It is organized in understandable and legible format.
- It is detailed enough to present a reasonable determination of a program's value and short enough to encourage use
- It includes an overview that, at a glance, indicates the evaluator's recommendation

Figure 2.2 provides a software evaluation form that you may want to use as a starting point.

The Web carries a great deal of information about many software packages. Software publishers often list the curriculum areas and academic levels for which their products are useful. National organizations dedicated to individuals with special needs also have websites that provide software evaluations and suggestions. Websites such as Kids Domain (**http://www.kidsdomain.com/**) offer reviews of educational software and downloads of demonstration versions of software. At this site, you can find out more about popular software designed for students at different ages and across the curriculum.

Often, however, the most important step in software evaluation is to put it to a first-hand test. You may want to sit down with a student who understands his or her instructional needs and carefully go through the process together while you talk about the software program. The idea of "talking out" while learning encourages the student to evaluate his or her understanding of an academic procedure. In particular, this process can encourage students to analyze how well a software program is helping them. Such interactions give you a good idea of how well the software program works and how well a student or group of students understands the directions and processes of instruction. At the same time, you will help students develop evaluative and communication skills essential to the IEP goals of many special needs students.

The software evaluation form in Figure 2.2 is designed to be a simple tool for you to use and adapt. Feel free to copy it and share it with other teachers or with parents who are willing to evaluate software for you. The following list discusses the items on the form.

Points to note when evaluating software

1 *Name, price, and software publisher.* In any evaluation, it is important to keep track of the name, publisher, and price of the program, as well as the date the evaluation was completed. Because software programs are available in many formats, and different programs may have similar titles, this basic information is essential to a useful evaluation—not to mention the fact that, if you list the name and publisher accurately, you will be able to locate the program if you decide to use it.

2 *Hardware requirements.* From a technical standpoint, the simplest question with regard to choosing technology is "Will it run on my computer?" Many of the newest programs require state-of-the-art computers, with a great deal of capacity and memory.

3 *Content area for which the software is designed.* When selecting a program, most of us look first at the title and packaging to determine what skills and content that program is designed to teach. As with other products, however, you cannot always judge the product by how it is packaged. As an evaluator, you must determine whether the packaging accurately describes the program. For instance, is it really a math program, or is it a

video game with a few numbers thrown in? Another reason to investigate the software content is that programs designed to teach one area of the curriculum often prove useful in other areas as well. For example, SimCity from Maxis, a popular software package designed to be an experience in city planning and organization, is used primarily in social studies, but it can also be a great tool in a social skills curriculum or a math classroom.

4 *Type of knowledge the program addresses.* Within the general content area, what particular skills does the program address? To make this assessment, it can help to classify learning outcomes according to one of these well-known systems:

- Gagné's (1985) learning hierarchy: memorization underlies concept learning, which underlies principle learning, which underlies problem solving. Looking at the software, you can think about where the program "fits" in terms of memorization of basic facts, understanding principles, or solving problems.

- The task analytic approach, which breaks a complex task into its component or prerequisite skills. Does the software break down the skill into small enough steps? Do activities build on the previous ones? (See chapter 3 for a discussion of task analysis.)

These two systems of classifying learning events can help identify the next step in a student's learning. For example, the task analytic approach can help you determine that a student needs specific instruction on borrowing from the tens column in subtraction, or needs practice with sounding out words with the "sh" sound.

Special education teachers have been trained to analyze an instructional objective, breaking it down into the subskills and strategies that make up the larger instructional goal. Then, in designing instruction, special education teachers assess which subskills and strategies the student has and teach to the specific point of need. This is known as "precision teaching" (Lindsley, 1972), a process that most teachers go through without even thinking about it. The same process applies when selecting a software package.

Bloom's taxonomy (Bloom et al., 1956) offers another way to think about the type of knowledge being targeted. Most teachers are familiar with this way of analyzing types of skills, and it is easy for others to understand. As shown in Table 2.2, Bloom divides learning into three domains: cognitive, affective, and psychomotor. The cognitive domain has six categories, ordered hierarchically and referred to as levels of intellectual objectives. These range from knowledge (the lowest level; for example, recalling information) to evaluation (the most complex level; for

---

Date: _____   Evaluation completed by: _____

1. Name of software: _____

   Price: _____   Publisher: _____

2. Hardware requirements (include RAM and ROM needed): _____

   _____

3. Content area for which the software is designed: _____

   _____

4. Type of knowledge program addresses: _____

   _____

5. Process and type of instruction: _____

   ❐ Discovery

   ❐ Drill and practice

   ❐ Simulation

   ❐ Other: _____

   Rate items 6–14 with a score (5 = excellent, 4 = good, 3 = fair, 2 = poor, 1 = unsatisfactory, 0 = not applicable) and a written description.

6. Ease of use (clear instructions, installation), independence for students, and interface: _____

   _____

   _____

7. Age appropriateness: _____

8. Degree of active learning on the part of student (vs. passive learning): _____

   _____

9. Degree of open-endedness and flexibility: _____

   _____

10. Clear documentation and good support: _____

    _____

11. Adherence to principles of learning:

    • Matched to instructional level of students: _____

    • Appropriate vocabulary: _____

● **FIGURE 2.2**   Software evaluation form

- Ability to engage students: _____
- Expanding complexity: _____
12. Technical soundness: _____
    - Animation: _____
    - Colors: _____
    - Sound: _____
    - Printing: _____
    - Saves student's work: _____
    - Uncluttered, realistic graphics: _____
    - Consistent operation: _____
13. Diversity: _____
    - Mixed gender and role equity: _____
    - People of diverse cultures: _____
    - Diverse family styles: _____
14. Opportunities for transfer: _____
    _____
    _____
15. Recommendations: _____
    _____
    _____

example, using previous learning to determine the worth or merit of a problem). Higher-level tasks subsume tasks at the lower levels, so students engaged in an evaluation task must also demonstrate all the lower-level skills. Table 2.2 shows the breakdown of skills, from simplest to most complex, in each domain. Remember that some students will need specific instruction in tasks outside the cognitive area.

Of course, you will probably use other theories of learning to guide your instructional practice, such as constructivist, generative, brain-based, and differentiated-learning theories, to name just a few. You should bring your knowledge of all these learning theories and an appropriate skills analysis to your choice of software for each student.

● TABLE 2.2

Bloom's taxonomy

Cognitive Domain	Affective Domain	Psychomotor Domain
1. Knowledge	1. Receiving	1. Reflex movements
2. Comprehension	2. Responding	2. Fundamental movements
3. Application	3. Valuing	3. Perceptual abilities
4. Analysis	4. Organization	4. Physical abilities
5. Synthesis	5. Creating	5. Skilled movements
6. Evaluation	6. Characterization by value	6. Nondiscursive (expressive) movements

5 *Process and type of instruction.* This item refers to the methods the software uses to engage the learner. For example, you may want to choose software that emphasizes discovery learning, in which students actively explore, question, and try out their ideas. Other common software approaches include simulation and drill and practice. Finding a good fit between the instructional process and the student will go a long way toward ensuring an engaging learning experience.

6 *Ease of use, independence for students, and interface.* How easily can you load, start, run, and use the program? Will the student be able to run the program independently? Are instructions clear and readily available? Is the **interface**—that is, the aspects of the program experienced and used by the student—clear, logical, and appealing? If a software program fails to provide clear instructions or is difficult to use, it will not be an effective technology tool.

7 *Age appropriateness.* For what age level is this software designed? Consider the vocabulary, graphics, layout, and design. You want to make sure that the software package is age-appropriate for your student. This can often be a challenge. For example, older students frequently find remedial software programs to be "babyish" because they are targeted toward younger students. If the student is unable to connect to the level of instruction, the program cannot be beneficial.

8 *Degree of active learning on the part of student.* In evaluating any software package, ask yourself how the user participates. Does the program engage the student mentally, physically, and emotionally? Or can a person simply point and click through the program, without actively interacting with the software? Research shows that the more time a student is involved in active learning, the more knowledge and understanding he or she will develop.

9 *Degree of open-endedness and flexibility.* How much flexibility do students have in using the program? Can students produce an original creation or must they follow defined templates? Consider, for example, Storybook Weaver (The Learning Company) and HyperStudio (Knowledge Adventure). Both are popular programs that allow a user to create his or her own story or presentation. In the Storybook Weaver software, you select the background, pictures, and sounds from a collection of preinstalled options. With HyperStudio, the selection of sounds, images, animations, and other add-ons goes well beyond the options that come installed in the program. You can include photos you've taken, images from the Internet, and your own vocal track. Thus, Storybook Weaver allows for limited individual creativity, while HyperStudio opens the door to many individualized variations.

Storybook Weaver is a great program when you want your students to have instant success in story writing. HyperStudio has more options, but it can be confusing at first. The point is to examine the number and kinds of options, decide if these are appropriate for your students, and evaluate the short- and long-term benefits.

10 *Clear documentation and good support.* Is the software documentation clear? Is technical support available to take care of problems with the software? How and when is the technical support available? Support or documentation that you can't locate or understand may render the software useless.

11 *Adherence to principles of learning.* Do the instruction and the vocabulary match the student's age and academic level? Vocabulary that is either too difficult or too simple will turn the student off. It's also important for students to be engaged by the software; you don't want them to be bored if they work with it on a regular basis. Finally, does the program have different levels of difficulty so that the student's work can expand in complexity? That is, once a student has mastered a desired level, can the software provide continuing challenge?

12 *Technical soundness.* Looking at technical aspects of the software, are the animation, colors, and sound vivid, enticing, and appropriate? Are the animations realistic? Do the sounds relate to the task or simply distract? Are the layout and design consistent so that students can find their way around the program? Watch out for distracting graphics or color schemes that may be counterproductive, drawing attention away from the material and from an active learning process. Does the program allow students to save their work or to save their place so they can resume work at a later time? Some students may need this feature to use the software. Can you print student work or progress reports, and if so, are the pages readable? Is the software consistent in operation so that it works the same way every time?

13 *Diversity.* Is the software free of gender or role biases? Does it make assumptions about the user's knowledge based on sociocultural background or living environment? For example, some children may not know what a "subway train" is; is the term explained in the software? Does the program assume that all children are living in homes with two parents, or does it incorporate more diverse and realistic images of family lifestyles?

14 *Opportunities for transfer.* This standard examines the degree to which the program gives students an opportunity to transfer the skills they have learned to another setting. A math software program should not only provide skill and drill, it should show how those skills would be applied in a more "natural" setting. For example, if a student practices identifying coins, he or she should also be able to practice counting back change.

15 *Recommendations.* This is a place to list any recommended uses of the program or ideas about what could make the program more user friendly. Suggestions for software revisions could also be included here.

WEB-BASED LEARNING ENVIRONMENTS

As more and more classrooms connect to the Internet, educational uses of the World Wide Web are increasingly available. A true educational website has something more than a self-serving purpose; it presents new and valuable information (Bailey & Bagby, 1998). You can evaluate a website with the software standards just described, but you should also take into account other factors as well.

● Elements of Educational Websites

In examining a website for possible student use, be sure to look at the following elements:

Website elements to evaluate

1 *Site overview and objectives.* The site should include a brief overview and clearly stated learning objective.

2 *Information about the author, as well as the date the site was completed or last updated.* Who created the site? When was it first created and last updated? Is the material fresh or outdated? What is the author's authority for the information?

3 *The population for which the site is designed.* Visitors should be able to find out easily for whom the website is intended. Elementary kids? High school students? Adults? Teachers? Dancers? Artists? Parents?

4 *Creative and useful graphics that can be viewed via a dialup connection.* Keep in mind the bandwidth of the Internet connection your students will use, especially when you are asking them to access a website from home. **Bandwidth** refers to the connection speed of a website visitor's computer. Your school may have a large-bandwidth, high-speed connection that allows data to be transferred at speeds of more than two megabytes (or two thousand kilobytes) per second. Many home users, however, use a *dialup connection,* which relies on an ordinary phone line and which currently is limited to 56 kilobytes per second. Large and detailed graphics will take much longer to load via a slower connection. Six seconds is generally the tolerated wait-time for a web page or picture to load. Thus, if a site's graphics require a longer time, your students are likely to feel frustrated.

5 *Interactive menu or graphic.* Look for a menu or graphic that visitors can use to navigate the site.

6 *Nonlinear/hypertext instruction or presentation.* A well-designed site should allow visitors to view the various pages in a nonlinear order; they should have the option of skipping around among pages. A "next" or "back" button is rarely sufficient.

7 *Thorough, useful presentation of the topic.* Make sure a student can actually learn from the site.

- *A method for the user to interact with the information.* The visitor should be able to review the information and test his or her knowledge.

- *A complete sequence of instructional activities, including examples and practice.* An instructional site should have a complete presentation of the information, plus activities that help the visitor actually learn or do what the site is teaching.

- *Specific and meaningful feedback.* Look for sites that provide as much information as possible to help students understand what they are doing right or wrong when they interact with the site.

8 *Consistent design and instructional method.* The site's design should allow the user to easily become familiar with the colors and locations of buttons on the page. This familiarity will help students focus on the content as they navigate through the site.

9 *Links to other resources for more information.* An educational site should provide at least a few links that lead visitors to other sites that either relate to the topic or provide further information.

TECHNIQUES FOR YOUR CLASSROOM

Are They Safe Out There?

Whenever we talk about using the Internet, the issue of security emerges. Can students see pornographic or violent images or text by clicking on a button? These issues must be addressed before students start surfing around. Inappropriate content is easy to encounter.

Here are three methods for making the Internet "safe" for students:

1 Start students off on the Internet with a website that has links to sites you've already previewed. Avoid letting students use search engines when you don't know what they will find. You can do a quick Web search to find appropriate resource websites, and then bookmark these for use by students.

2 Use a filtering device. Programs such as Net Nanny (Net Nanny Software), Cyber Patrol (SurfControl), and CYBERsitter (Solidoak) scan web pages for words and pictures that have been identified as inappropriate. They include different levels of security (such as a filter for children under 5). In addition, the network manager for your school or district may have installed a **proxy server,** which acts as a filter for all computers on the network.

3 Find out if your school system's connection to the Internet has a *proxy server.* A proxy server is a piece of software that runs at the school's (or school district's) main Internet connection server and blocks out web addresses known to be inappropriate for children. A *firewall* is a piece of equipment or software that blocks people (hackers) from getting unauthorized access to the schoolwide network.

All of these methods are useful, but none is more effective than the most basic method of keeping students safe on the Internet: supervise them! If you think of the Internet as the ultimate library and resource center, you know that you would never send a student off on this field trip without supervision. For more specific recommendations, refer to the Handbook of Resources at the back of this book.

---

10 *A method by which the user can access the webmaster.* If you or your students have trouble with the site, it ought to provide you with a way to contact the web designer, either by email or by other correspondence.

● Accessible Web Design

The above criteria focus on educational websites in general. Further criteria come into play for a person with special needs such as low vision, hearing impairment, or difficulty in reading large amounts of text. You've probably visited sites that welcome you with busy, complicated graphics or movies. Imagine how difficult these would be for a person who couldn't see or didn't understand what was happening on the screen.

To make sure a website is accessible to a wide variety of learners, look for the following features:

Features of a fully accessible website

- *A text-only or low-graphics option on the site's main page.* This can also help viewers with slow Internet connections who want to avoid tedious downloads for pictures and animated images.
- *"Alternative text" for all images.* That is, words that describe the images for users who cannot see them.
- *Absence of frames.* **Frames** create, in effect, multiple web pages on a single screen. Often the screen shows text on the right and a menu list on the left. A site with frames frustrates users with a screen reader or text-to-speech program; they cannot read how to move around the site.

Ⓢ ELECTING ASSISTIVE AND ADAPTIVE TECHNOLOGIES

As noted in chapter 1, assistive and adaptive technologies cover a wide range of possibilities. Some low-tech devices include pencil grips, picture boards, and taped instructions. Higher-tech devices include calculators, notetaking cassette recorders, word processors, and various communication devices. **Optical character recognition (OCR)** systems use a scanner and software to recognize text and convert it to electronic information for computer use. **Voice recognition** programs allow the user to control a computer or other device through voiced commands. **Screen readers** read aloud the text displayed on a screen. Using such technologies, children with disabilities can participate in regular education.

In selecting assistive and adaptive tools for classroom use, follow the same process stressed throughout this chapter: evaluate the usefulness of a technological tool on the basis of the student's specific needs. Keep in mind that the ultimate goal of assistive technology is to enhance instruction and to modify the way in which a child takes in, responds to, or implements the instructional process.

Lahm and Morrissette (1994) identify seven areas in which assistive or adaptive technology can be helpful for students with mild disabilities:

Seven uses of assistive and adaptive technology

1. *Organization.* Teaching students how to organize their thoughts and materials.
2. *Note-taking.* Helping students effectively organize written material.
3. *Writing assistance.* Word processing tools to help with spelling and grammar.

4 *Productivity.* The use of calculators, spreadsheets, and databases for work requiring number manipulation, categorizing, or grouping information.

5 *Access to reference materials.* Using telecommunications and CD-ROMs to gather and synthesize information in a nondistracting environment.

6 *Cognitive assistance.* Tutorials, drill and practice, and problem-solving software, as well as reading assistance using multimedia CD-ROMs.

7 *Materials modification.* Adaptation of standard materials, often involving the use of video clips, animation, and digitized pictures that make learning more efficient and more active.

Table 2.3 lists common types of computer-based assistive and adaptive technologies, some of which have been mentioned in other parts of the chapter as well.

Alternative input devices	These include specialized keyboards, on-screen keyboards, keyboards with pictures, as well as alternative mouse and joystick options.
Optical character recognition (OCR)	Optical character recognition systems use a scanner and software to recognize text and convert it to information that a computer can use. The user can display printed text on a screen, magnify the text, or read it with a screen reader.
Screen magnification	Screen magnification tools enlarge print and images on a computer screen.
Screen readers	A screen reader will read the text of a screen aloud in an electronic voice. Examples include JAWS (Henter-Joyce), Window-Eyes (GW Micro), and text-HELP! (HumanWare).
Voice (or speech) recognition	Voice or speech recognition programs allow the user to dictate to the computer through a microphone and to control the computer and other devices through the voice. Examples include Dragon NaturallySpeaking from Scansoft and ViaVoice from IBM.
Word prediction	Word prediction tools, used with a word processor, offer the user a list of options of possible words that begin with a certain letter or series of letters. For example, if the student types *ca,* the word prediction software may suggest *cat, can,* and so forth. Word prediction may help students with a range of communication and reading difficulties. Examples include textHELP! (HumanWare) and Co:Writer (Don Johnston).
Word processors	Common word processors, such as Microsoft Word and WordPerfect (Corel), allow text input; simplify organization, editing, and formatting; and supply spelling and grammar checking. Can be used in conjunction with voice recognition and screen readers.

● TABLE 2.3   Common types of computer-based assistive and adaptive technologies

LOCATION AND NUMBER OF COMPUTERS

Integrating technology into your educational program requires a careful look at the number of computers in your school or classroom and where they are placed. Take the simplest case, in which you have a single computer located in your classroom. Mostly likely it will be designated for teacher use, but if you have a television in the room, you may be able to connect the computer to the television for group instruction or presentations. Small groups of students might use the computer for Internet research or word processing. You can do as many teachers limited to one computer do and set up "digital recess," in which students use the computer during free time or as a reward for good behavior. Remember, too, that if it is determined that a student with special needs would benefit from computer use, the school district is legally required to provide that resource.

When teachers have two to four computers in the classroom, they most often use them as "learning centers," in which students go to a particular learning center for work on a specific subject or project. Students must learn to collaborate and work together efficiently, because time on the computer will be limited. Students should be prepared before they come to the computer in order to make good use of their time.

Options for placing computers

Many individual schools and programs have to decide whether to put computers into classrooms or into a lab setting. If you have input into such a decision, ask yourself and the other teachers in your school how you intend to use the computers. Will computer use be integrated into the current curriculum? Do teachers have the necessary skills to integrate technology into their classrooms? What are your instructional goals?

Other options involve the use of laptop computers. Many schools and school systems have been requiring students to purchase laptops. This system allows students to have instant access to a computer and to the campus network via a wireless network. Some schools, rather than making each child responsible for a computer, utilize classroom sets of laptops. Some teachers believe that when each child has a laptop, the students benefit from instant access and "just-in-time" learning. Other teachers, however, feel uncomfortable with the laptop computers and believe they are being pressured into using them. In any case, the wider use of laptop computers in classrooms may require you to think explicitly about the computer's place in your curriculum. For the student with an exceptionality, easy access to a laptop can be a great way to incorporate the use of appropriate technology.

COLLABORATING WITH SPECIALISTS

To achieve the IEP goals of special needs students, you will find yourself collaborating with various kind of specialists. Typical *related services,* as they are known in the field of special education, include speech therapy, occupational therapy, physical therapy, psychological or psychiatric support, social work and family resource support, and legal services. For your students to gain the maximum benefit from these services, you'll need to develop your skills of diplomacy and facilitation, especially when a specialist is working in your classroom.

Roles of various specialists

Occupational and physical therapists often have the most significant input on technology use. Occupational therapists (OTs) assist the student with skills, strategies, and devices that allow them to operate in the environment more successfully. The OT may help a child with a physical impairment develop a strategy for dressing him- or herself, or may help a child with a learning disability with keyboarding and organization. The physical therapist provides the student with specific physical interventions that matched IEP goals, perhaps helping a student with fine- or gross-motor development. For example, a student may spend physical therapy time doing exercises with a medicine ball to encourage sensory development.

Some school systems have a technology specialist, although the parameters of this person's job (and exact title) differ from school system to school system. In some districts, this person may be responsible for network administration and assistance. In others, he or she may run a computer lab and help repair computers in the classrooms. In still other districts, this person may be an administrator in the district office who is responsible for making decisions about software and hardware purchases. Where one is available, the IEP team would consult a technology specialist about what equipment and software is available and what may be needed to meet the student's learning needs.

Finally, some children are under the care of professional medical specialists, such as a nurse or physician who may be directing medical treatments for the child. The IEP team makes sure that the child's health and physical well-being are supported by any academic and social objectives that are established.

SUMMARY

Although a teacher and an IEP team making technology decisions for a student with an exceptionality can gather initial ideas from the school- or districtwide plan for integrating technology into curriculum, the process should focus on each student's individual needs. For most purposes, a student's needs can be divided into four basic categories:

mobility/accessibility, adaptability and input tools, instructional objectives, and creative outlets.

Often the process of selecting technology will include evaluating software. You as the teacher must carefully preview what is available and decide whether it is educationally useful. A thorough software evaluation should consider, among other factors, hardware requirements; content area and type of knowledge the program addresses; process and type of instruction; age appropriateness; degree of active learning for the student; degree of open-endedness and flexibility; adherence to sound principles of learning; and opportunities for transfer of knowledge. You may want to collaborate with fellow teachers on a software evaluation guide and enlist parents or volunteers to help with evaluations. All software choices must be based on the student's IEP goals.

Educational websites require similar previewing and evaluation. Be sure that a website offers up-to-date information from a reliable author or institution. It should also provide a thorough presentation of its subject, meaningful activities and appropriate feedback, a consistent instructional method, and links to additional resources. Its graphics should be clear, useful, and appropriate for an ordinary dialup connection. To be fully accessible to all students, a website's interface should be free of frames and should offer a text-only or low-graphics option.

Common assistive and adaptive technologies include screen readers, voice recognition programs, optical character recognition systems, screen magnifiers, word prediction tools, and alternative input devices. These technologies can aid the student in activities ranging from organization and notetaking to productivity and cognitive activities.

Your selection of technology for students will also depend in part on the number and location of the computers available to you. If you have some control over the placement of computers, base your choice on how you will integrate them into the curriculum.

Finally, part of your task will be to collaborate with specialists, such as occupational and physical therapists, technology experts, and medical practitioners. Because all of these people can provide crucial assistance for your students, you must be prepared to work with them in a cooperative and mutually supportive fashion.

KEY TERMS

interface (p. 38)
bandwidth (p. 41)
frames (p. 43)
optical character recognition (OCR) (p. 43)

proxy server (p. 42)
voice recognition (p. 43)
screen reader (p. 43)

RESOURCES FOR FURTHER INVESTIGATION

Online Resources

Alliance for Technology Access.
http://www.ataccess.org/
　　The Alliance for Technology Access is an organization of resource
　　centers and vendors that provide technological support for persons
　　with disabilities.

Assistive Technology Industry Association.
http://www.atia.org/
　　On this site you'll find a listing of technology companies (under the
　　"Members" link) that sell a wide range of assistive and adaptive technology
　　as well as instructional software.

EASI's K to 12 Education Technology Center.
http://www.rit.edu/~easi/ak12/k12.html
　　At the Equal Access to Software Information (EASI) website you will find
　　a set of links to EASI's resources on using educational technology (includ-
　　ing adaptive and assistive technology), descriptions of products, and re-
　　source sites for students and adults. Under the heading "The Basics of
　　Adaptive Technology," you will find some great information about tech-
　　nology terminology as well as contact information for vendors.

Evaluation Rubrics for Websites.
http://www.siec.k12.in.us/~west/online/eval.htm
　　This site, from Loogootee Elementary School West in Loogootee, Indiana,
　　provides a useful set of rubrics for evaluating websites for students at dif-
　　ferent age levels. The site also has a set of links to resources on using web-
　　based materials.

Kids Domain.
http://www.kidsdomain.com/
　　In addition to software reviews, this site offers a newsletter and many
　　other resources for teachers, children, and parents.

Product Resources

HyperStudio. Torrance, CA: Knowledge Adventure.
http://www.hyperstudio.com

NaturallySpeaking. Peabody, MA: Scansoft.
http://www.lhsl.com/naturallyspeaking/

SimCity. Walnut Creek, CA: Maxis.
http://thesims.ea.com/us/ and http://www.sc3000.com/

Storybook Weaver Deluxe. Novato, CA: Learning Company.
http://www.learningcompany.com/

part

II

The Students

Specific technology tools can provide much needed access to information and provide opportunities for learning
(© Michael Zide)

3

TECHNOLOGY FOR STUDENTS WITH LEARNING DISABILITIES

FOCUS QUESTIONS

As you read this chapter, think about the following:

- What are learning disabilities?

- How do students with learning disabilities differ from other students in my classroom?

- What sorts of educational needs will these students bring?

- What sorts of approaches work best for the student with learning disabilities?

- How can technology play a supportive role in teaching students with learning disabilities?

 n this chapter we discuss fundamental information about learning disabilities. After a brief overview of instructional techniques that have proven successful (such as task analysis and project-based learning), we will discuss various types of technologies, including software applications and special keyboards. We also profile a student with learning disabilities, describing his use of technology.

As you read through this chapter, keep in mind that most students encounter some academic difficulties. The techniques and technologies described here can help you find teaching strategies for students with disabilities and for those with mild learning problems who have not been formally identified as learning disabled.

This chapter does *not* provide a prescriptive or complete list of software applications matched to different types of learning disabilities. Far too many software programs fit into the curriculum for students with learning disabilities to list them all here. The main idea to grasp is that teachers must evaluate the features of technology and match them to students' needs and IEP goals.

ⓉHE BASICS OF LEARNING DISABILITIES

Learning disabilities are most often defined by describing a discrepancy between ability and performance. Children with learning disabilities are of average to above-average intelligence (or IQ), but performance assessments and standardized tests indicate that their classroom achievement fails to match their evident ability. Because learning disabilities relate specifically to classroom performance, they are rarely identified before a child enters school and confronts academic instruction.

It can be difficult to determine the cause of a learning disability, and the matter is often confusing for both parents and teachers. Learning disabilities are frequently identified when no other reason for academic failure can be found, such as a hearing or visual problem, behavioral problem, or mental deficiency.

● A Working Definition

Many professions have contributed to a working definition of learning disabilities: educators, psychologists, psychiatrists, social workers, linguists, and lawyers. Defining and describing learning disabilities are matters of ongoing discussion in the field of special education. Some researchers are committed to finding a neurobiological basis for the condition, whereas others believe that learning disabilities are, for the most part, environmental in origin. Although this debate will certainly continue, as teachers we can be most effective when we agree on a broad definition that allows us the greatest amount of flexibility. The National Joint Committee on Learning Disabilities defines learning disabilities in this way:

A definition of learning disabilities

> A general term that refers to a heterogeneous group of disorders manifested by significant difficulties in the acquisition and use of listening, speaking, reading, writing, reasoning or mathematical abilities. These disorders are intrinsic to the individual, presumed to be due to central nervous system dysfunction and may occur across the life span. Problems in self-regulatory behaviors, social perception and social interaction may exist with learning disabilities but do not by themselves constitute a learning disability.

Using this definition, a teacher has the flexibility to recommend that a student be screened for a learning disability once it is determined that other variables—such as poor eyesight, hearing problems, and environmental factors—are not responsible for the child's struggles in the classroom.

● Categories and Prevalence of Learning Disabilities

Even if educators agree on a definition like the one just offered, the term *learning disabilities* covers a wide variety of academic and psychological difficulties. To put it another way, a learning disability can affect a considerable range of cognitive abilities that children need to develop preacademic skills and to succeed in school in general (Chalfant & Van Dusen, 1989; Smith, 1995). Students with learning disabilities have been found to lack skills in visual perception, visual discrimination, auditory processing, and other areas of language use and communication. They can have difficulty understanding numbers, making sense of letters on a page, or understanding cause-and-effect relationships. They may face obstacles in just one area of academics or in several, seemingly unrelated, areas. Thorough evaluation is necessary to understand each child's unique set of learning challenges.

Students with learning disabilities often experience academic failure in school. The national dropout rate for students with learning disabilities during the 1998–1999 school year was about 27 percent (U.S. Department of Education, 2000). By comparison, the dropout rate for nondisabled youth is about 11 percent (National Center for Education Statistics, 2000). According to the Office of Special Education and Rehabilitation, 30 percent of students with a learning disability graduate from high school with a traditional diploma, versus 77 percent of nondisabled youths (National Center for Education Statistics, 2000).

The learning-disabled population is the largest group of students with disabilities. Referring to Table 1.1 in chapter 1, you can see that an estimated 5 to 10 percent of all U.S. school-age students have learning disabilities. Other sources place the figure even higher or lower—3 to 15 percent of the total school-age population (National Center for Education Statistics, 2001; National Center for Learning Disabilities, 2001). Because the term *learning disabilities* includes such a wide range of disabling conditions, the exact meaning of the percentages is often difficult to determine.

The federal government, along with many special educators, uses the term *specific learning disabilities*—a helpful reminder that giving a child the label "learning disability" does not help unless we can specify the condition more exactly. At least six categories of learning disabilities have been identified:

Categories of learning disabilities

1 *Auditory-language.* An auditory-language difficulty is a perceptual problem in which a child may take a long time to comprehend or follow directions. The student with an auditory learning disability is physically able to hear, but "hears" in a different way.

2 *Visual-spatial.* Some visual-spatial disorders involve an inability to understand color or see a difference between the foreground and the background. A student may also have trouble visualizing directions in space, and this can significantly affect the ability to learn to read. For example, the letters *b, d, p,* and *q* are all formed in essentially the same way. Those who lack a sense of spatial relationships and directionality are unable to tell these letters apart.

3 *Motor-related.* A child with motor-related learning disabilities has difficulty with either fine or gross motor coordination or both. The student is unable to perform isolated, coordinated movements. This problem is evident in many settings—in the classroom, on the playground, at home, and elsewhere. In using technology, the child can have difficulty with handwriting, keyboards, and mouse control.

4 *Organizational.* A student with an organizational learning disability may have trouble locating the beginning, middle, or end of an assignment. Drafting an outline is difficult because the child cannot narrow down and organize information. Such weaknesses make it difficult or impossible for the student to assemble materials for papers or for oral presentations.

5 *Academic difficulty.* An example of academic difficulty is a student in math class who has problems with order and placement of numbers or who switches processes, such as long division and multiplication. Another example is a history student who has difficulty with the concept of time and cannot understand the order of events in relation to their dates of occurrence. Academic-specific learning disabilities are common among students with learning disabilities. Special education teachers often see students who are, for instance, gifted in mathematical calculation and reasoning but have significant deficits in written language and spelling.

6 *Social skills disorders.* The student with a social skills disorder has trouble with skills such as taking turns and understanding how to effectively interpret facial expressions. Such children are unable to perform social activities consistent with their chronological age and intelligence. Although social skills are not typically seen as being within the realm of the classroom teacher, these difficulties can significantly impair a child's ability to succeed in the classroom.

INSTRUCTIONAL TECHNIQUES

Because learning disabilities cover a wide range of functional and learning difficulties, you will need a full spectrum of instructional techniques and strategies to teach effectively. These students have such varied sets of perceptual and communicative skills that no "one size fits all." A student may understand how to perform a fractions problem but needs a "rhyme" to remember how to add two numbers with regrouping.

Need for creativity, flexibility

When you teach a student with a learning disability, your lesson designs must be especially innovative, creative, and flexible. You must understand and respond to the unique nature of each child's learning disability—and be prepared to change a lesson plan in midstream if it is not working. Every lesson, therefore, should include the opportunity to monitor for understanding and provide ongoing feedback to students on their performance.

Techniques that have been proven to work with students with learning disabilities include the remedial approach, the task analytic approach, project-based learning, direct instruction, multisensory and interdisciplinary techniques, and experiential learning approaches. The best learning environment for any student (with or without a learning disability) is one that combines these techniques appropriately. For a more detailed description of instructional techniques for students with learning disabilities, read Janet Lerner's book, *Learning Disabilities: Theories, Diagnosis, and Teaching Strategies.*

Now we take a brief look at four of the above techniques—the remedial approach, task analysis, project-based learning, and direct instruction. We'll also discuss the use of technology with each.

⬤ The Remedial Approach

Teaching the student with a learning disability can be described as an intervention process. The instructional activities must mediate the student's difficulties using a variety of tools and techniques. During school-based intervention, teachers attempt to reduce the student's learning difficulties and to include him or her in the normal planned curriculum as much as possible. Intervention involves determining both what the student must learn and how to teach it, on a day-to-day or lesson-by-lesson schedule.

Teaching students with learning disabilities has also been called **remedial teaching.** When Samuel Kirk (1963) first described learning disabilities, he discussed remedial teaching as involving ten steps:

Steps in remedial teaching

1 Discover the special needs of the child.

2 Develop annual goals and short-term objectives.

3 Analyze the tasks to be taught.

4 Begin instruction at the child's level.

5 Decide how to teach.

6 Select appropriate awards for the child.

7 Provide the opportunity for the student to experience success.

8 Give time for extended practice.

9 Provide the student with feedback.

10 Continuously measure the student's progress.

Technology for the Remedial Approach ● A good example of remedial technology is Fast ForWord, created by Scientific Learning (**http://www.scilearn.com/**). Students start using this application by taking a pretest to assess their reading skills. They proceed through short lessons focused on the objectives missed in the pretest. The lessons are short, about ten minutes each. Based on the student's performance, the program then moves on either to a more challenging lesson or to an equivalent lesson within the same subskill. If the student begins to have trouble with a previous skill, the program reverts to work on that skill. The software constantly assesses the student's performance and can print out reports showing which specific reading tasks gave the child difficulty.

Using an application such as Fast ForWord

● Task Analysis

Deciding *how* to teach a lesson to a student with learning disabilities is as important as determining *what* to teach. Many teachers still follow Samuel Kirk's recommendations regarding the remedial approach, often going through this process without thinking about the individual steps.

You may have noticed, however, that the third step in the remedial process involves analyzing the tasks to be taught. Here the **task analysis** approach may become essential. Task analysis involves breaking down a task into its smallest subtasks and strategies. For example, if you were to "task analyze" brushing your teeth, you might come up with the following subskills and strategies:

Task analysis: breaking down a task into small subtasks

1 Hold the toothbrush in your dominant hand, with your thumb on the base of the brush and all fingers on the handle.

2 Hold the toothpaste in your other hand and squeeze from the bottom of the tube onto the brush portion only. (Substrategy: Determine how much toothpaste to use, given mouth size and number of teeth.)

3 Rinse the brush with tap water (optional).

4 . . .

You can see that task analysis can be quite tedious, but it is useful because the teacher can pinpoint exactly which part of the task is giving the student difficulty. Those committed to the task analysis approach believe that a child who is missing a subskill is learning on a shaky foundation. Although the student may be able to perform the skill through memorization, he or she will never fully understand it.

Scope and sequence charts, often published in classroom textbooks or school curricula, provide an insight into the task analytic approach. If you look at a scope and sequence chart, you will see a breakdown of the skills and the order in which they should be presented. Figure 3.1 shows a scope and sequence chart for objectives related to probability and predictions. This chart was created for students in third through sixth grades using the Pennsylvania state curriculum. According to the chart, third-grade students should be able to predict the likelihood of outcomes of an experiment; by the end of sixth grade, students should be able to compare experimental results with theoretical probability. Note how the chart illustrates both the scope (upper and lower boundaries) and the sequence (order) of the objectives.

As another example of the task analysis approach, consider multiplication skills and strategies. Multiplication involves many subtasks and strategies related to addition, subtraction, and organization. The teacher using a task analysis approach can determine the exact source of a child's problem, teach to the problem, and then build on those skills to reach the greater multiplication objective.

Technology for the Task Analysis Approach ● "Skill-and-drill" software typically takes a remedial/task analysis approach. These programs require students to complete a series of subtasks until they have mastered a skill under a variety of conditions and over a period of time. In Math Munchers (Learning Company), for example, the student must guide a creature through a maze while "eating" all the correct answers to a mathematics problem. The JumpStart series by Knowledge Adventure includes games that follow the skill-and-drill process. While playing JumpStart Kindergarten, for instance, children must click quickly on the letter that makes the sound they hear. In Reader Rabbit (The Learning Company), students perform matching and categorizing tasks.

"Skill-and-drill" software

Spelling, letter-sound relationships, word recognition, and all areas of mathematics are popular content for skill-and-drill software programs. These tasks require step-by-step, repeated instruction, and programs that can respond to a mouse click or a keyboard stroke by giving appropriate feedback are fairly easy to produce. You should note that although skill-and-drill software is helpful for practicing certain step-by-step tasks, that is all it does. Sometimes the process of answering yes/no, right/wrong questions can frustrate students with learning disabilities, so use programs of this type with caution.

	Grade Level Content Objectives			
School Level Standards	Gr./Course __3__	Gr./Course __4__	Gr./Course __5__	Gr./Course __6__
Grade 3 Predict and measure the likelihood of events and recognize that the results of an experiment may not match predicted outcomes.	Predict and measure the likelihood of events and recognize that the results of an experiment may not match predicted outcomes.	Predict and perform probability experiments based upon equally likely outcomes using spinners.	Predict and determine why some outcomes are certain, more likely, less likely, equally likely, or impossible.	Compare experimental results with theoretical probability.
Design a fair and unfair spinner.	Design a fair and unfair spinner.	Explain all possible combinations on a fair and unfair spinner.	Determine the fairness of the design of a spinner.	Explain the likelihood of independent events related to spinners.

Subject Area __Mathematics__   Strand __2.7 Probability and Predictions__   **Grade Levels** _____
(primary/inter./MS/HS)

Cisek, Lurant & Wilt/Berks County Intermediate Unit

● **FIGURE 3.1**   Sample scope and sequence chart

Source: Pennsylvania Department of Education, http://www.pde.psu.edu/connections/currdevl/res2-d.htm.

● Project-Based Learning

As any teacher knows, learning and knowledge are more than a simple combination of tasks and skills. You must be able to process what you have learned, and you need some idea about what steps to take toward a goal. These applications reach far beyond schooling. Being a member of any society requires the reasoning ability to choose an appropriate time and place to use the skills you possess.

Project-based learning rests in the idea that we as teachers must give students more than basic academic skills. We must teach children how to think, how to solve problems, and how to ask questions. Project-based learning

A project as the basis for lessons

involves using a project or problem as the central component of a lesson or series of lessons. This one central project leads to sublessons in other curricular areas, thereby tying the curriculum together and providing "real-life" opportunities for application. Fundamental to the project-based learning model is the idea that authentic learning must be student centered and meaningful and must foster engagement in real-world experiences (Dede & Sprague, 1999).

Imagine that students in the Miami area decide that they want to study Cuba and the peoples of Cuba. They might determine that the final product of their study will be a television commercial for tourism in Cuba. They will research Cuba by finding facts and figures in the library, input those facts on a spreadsheet, and analyze them through graphs and charts. Students can also interview local people who have lived in Cuba. To produce their video commercial, they will begin with storyboarding and continue through filming, editing, and distribution. This large project can be continued over a long period of time. Of course, any such project should have realistic objectives and methods of assessment.

Project-based learning helps motivate students to learn, and this is a key factor for students with learning disabilities. They must see the "why" of academic tasks, and they need opportunities to be creative and to follow their curiosity.

Technology for Project-Based Learning ● A multimedia authoring tool, such as HyperStudio, described more fully later in this chapter, can be useful in project-based learning. Students can employ such a tool to produce and present their final product, as well as to exhibit and discuss their work along the way.

Websites for project-based learning

Numerous websites now offer long-term learning projects. At **MayaQuest. com,** for example, students and teachers follow real-time expeditions through places like the Amazon and Africa. While following the expeditions, students can log on to the site and read about children who live in these regions, about currency and weather trends, about culture and geography. Through such projects, students learn about other regions of the world while tracking a real-time adventure with real people. The website includes lesson materials for teachers and parents and many supplementary resources.

Software for project-based learning

Project-based learning can also take place with stand-alone software programs. Kids Culture, a learning series created by Pierian Springs, is an example of a CD-ROM project-based learning package. Kids Culture: The Great Explorers explores history, culture, geography, reading, math, and science as they relate to the lives of explorers such as Amelia Earhart, Ferdinand Magellan, the Islamic traders of North Africa, and the crew of *Apollo 11*. Students can view diagrams of Amelia Earhart's airplanes that can be printed out, cut apart, and built into models. In other Kids Culture software packages students learn about Northwest Indian culture, Polynesia, and ancient Greece.

● Direct Instruction

Direct instruction: carefully engineered tasks, rapid pacing, choral responses

Direct instruction teaches through rapid pacing and choral group responses. The theory behind direct instruction is that students can learn well when they are exposed to carefully engineered tasks. The process of designing these tasks is extremely time-consuming, so the majority of direct instruction teaching uses scripted sets of instructional materials, published primarily by SRA/McGraw-Hill, in the areas of reading, remedial reading, spelling, math, writing, and language. In theory, teachers using the packaged programs can learn the design theory while they teach and go on to extend and modify the programs or apply the theory to instruction for other content. Most teachers who use direct instruction do create additional activities so that students can have independent practice and small-group work.

Technology for Direct Instruction ● Technology use in the direct instruction approach is somewhat limited. Earlier specifically designed lessons do not currently have software matched to the technique.

One form of technology currently in development is the Study Buddy, a wireless keyboard with a small LCD screen along the top. Students using the Study Buddy type responses during choral lessons, and the teacher receives all the responses on his or her own computer. With the Study Buddy software, the teacher can immediately see which students have responded correctly to the questions. Because each direct instruction lesson is prescripted, the teacher can download each set of questions onto students' Study Buddies where they read the questions as the teacher asks them.

ADVANTAGES OF TECHNOLOGY FOR STUDENTS WITH LEARNING DISABILITIES

The preceding discussion suggests that students with learning disabilities can profit from a variety of technologies integrated into a range of instructional methods. Indeed, technology can afford opportunities for success the students might not otherwise achieve.

Table 3.1 lists three basic advantages that technology offers students with learning disabilities: (1) more individual attention and feedback; (2) interesting,

Advantage	How and Why?
Computers make individual attention possible.	One-on-one instruction is ideal, but rarely possible. With twenty to thirty students in a classroom, the teacher cannot always design specific lessons for each child. A computer-based lesson, though not a substitute for the teacher, can focus the student on a specific skill or task.
Computers present students with tasks that interest and engage them.	The computer isn't inherently more interesting than the teacher, but by individualizing a lesson, the theme can be one the student finds engaging, such as dinosaurs or a recent election. In addition, even in this day of technology saturation, students are still interested in computers because they are fun. This might also be the only area in which students can successfully compete with the teacher for mastery!
Computers give students greater control over their learning and encourage more risk taking.	The student works one-on-one, at his or her own pace with the computer. Mistakes can be made without fear of ridicule. This is important, because risk taking is vital for meaningful learning. If a student is afraid to ask a question in front of peers because of the possibility of being laughed at, often he or she simply won't ask.

● **TABLE 3.1**   Three advantages of technology for students with learning disabilities

engaging tasks; and (3) greater student control over learning. The following sections present examples of technology use in classrooms and evidence of these advantages.

● Example 1: Talking Books

The book form of *Little Red Riding Hood* consists of text and illustrations, an excellent format for people who can read and who have the background knowledge necessary to understand the story. Nonreaders, however, require a mentor to help with reading and comprehension. This is not a problem where there is one mentor (such as a teacher or parent) for every one or two students. In typical classrooms, however, teachers rarely can help all children as much as they would like.

Talking books can help create reading situations that provide many of the resources of an experienced teacher. The "Arthur" stories in the Living Books Series, for example, display the printed story and illustrations on the computer screen. The screen display looks like a regular book with pages. The student can select from the following options: (a) have the book read aloud in its entirety (relevant text is highlighted as the reading progresses); (b) have any word or phrase pronounced (the child reads all other printed text); (c) have key vocabulary words defined as needed; and (d) have words, sentences, or entire texts translated into another language.

Options for using talking books

● Example 2: Math Practice and Problem Solving

Extended practice is an important component of mathematics instruction, and the computer is a tireless tutor. Math drill software can be individualized, and it is repetitive and systematic. The software controls the rate of presentation, allows the proper time to solve problems, and provides students with personalized, immediate feedback. Such a positive reinforcement system can enhance student motivation.

Students control their learning

Students with learning disabilities, armed with computers, can take greater control over their learning. Andrea Gooden, who has worked with the Apple Classrooms of Tomorrow program, says that computers, video laser disc players, LCD projection panels, and CD-ROMs enable youngsters "to work around their disabilities" and allow them to participate in content appropriate to their age level. They more willingly take risks in problem solving, engage in computer-generated simulations and experiments, exhibit understanding through creation of multimedia products, visualize abstract concepts, and conduct independent and collaborative research using electronic communications (Gooden, 1996).

● Example 3: Collaborative Learning in the Inclusive Classroom

The movement toward inclusion has benefited from development of a wide range of technology that gives teachers greater freedom to bring together students with and without learning disabilities. Besides helping teachers individualize instruction, technology can permit students "to work cooperatively to create a quality product, and allow students with special needs to contribute at their level of competence and be supported by peers" (Holzberg, 1997). Table 3.2 indicates that, as of 1997, 90 percent of teachers in inclusive classrooms were using computers at least weekly for student learning; the percentage is undoubtedly higher by now.

Technology to aid collaboration

Teachers report that mainstreamed students can successfully use computers with their peers in the regular classroom or school computer lab (Lewis, 1993). Working with peers, students are much more eager to learn and, as a result, develop greater self-confidence, regardless of their learning needs. In such peer-directed learning, students support and guide each other, for they are pursuing similar academic understanding (Schank, 1998).

The next section focuses on specific technology applications for use in particular content areas. Remember that these technologies can be useful for many students, not just those with identified learning disabilities.

● TABLE 3.2

Teacher-reported frequency of student technology use in the inclusive classroom (1997)

Technology	Percentage of Teachers Using Technology at Least Weekly
Computers	90%
Special input devices	18%
Speech synthesizers	14%
Modems	13%
Special switches	7%
Voice input devices for computers	6%
Scanning devices	5%

Source: Adapted from A survey of technology in the inclusion classroom, by J. Gange, 1997, *Advanced Technologies in Education Monograph*. Washington, DC: American University.

TECHNOLOGY IN CONTENT AREA LEARNING FOR STUDENTS WITH EXCEPTIONALITIES

This section covers only some of the ways in which teachers can integrate technology into the curriculum for students with learning disabilities. Rather, we aim to start you exploring the wide range of possibilities and stimulate your creative planning on behalf of all your students. Be sure to check the section "Choosing Technology by Content Area" (page 261) to find a match up of software applications and the particular skills they are designed to teach.

● Reading

Many consider reading the most important academic achievement. Indeed, reading is an essential skill for success in school on any level. But the process of learning to read is complicated, to say the least. Think back to your earliest memories of reading: you may recall turning pages or recognizing letters, but you are less likely to be able to pinpoint the moment you learned to read. Reading researchers and curriculum designers have long been investigating this process, and many programs and materials "teach" reading by methods that range from phonics-based instruction to the whole-language approach.

Students with learning disabilities can find learning to read especially frustrating. At the beginning of this chapter we defined learning disabilities. Think about the problems a child with these difficulties might have in learning to read. Imagine the struggles of a child who has trouble with visual discrimination (such as reversing letters), poor attention to details, or lack of auditory processing skills (such as recognizing the differences among sounds).

No single method always works best for developing reading skills in any student, and this same pattern holds true for students with learning disabilities. Children come to school with a variety of reading experiences, and as a teacher you should plan to use a variety of methods to introduce the initial stages of reading.

Computer products that can support the process of learning to read range from those designed to teach letter/sound recognition to those that claim to teach reading comprehension. In the classroom, you should know which skills the software is designed to develop, and match those to the specific needs of your students. For example, with Accelerated Reader (Advanced Learning Company), a literature-based program, students read simple basal texts on paper and respond to comprehension questions about that short story or text on the computer. But a child still working on letter-sound relationships can find reading comprehension difficult. Students often work so hard at sounding out words that by the end of the sentence they have forgotten the meaning of what they have read. Therefore, you might want to save Accelerated Reader for more successful readers and consider some of the following programs instead.

Useful reading programs

- Reading Blaster (Knowledge Adventure) is a skill-and-drill software application that allows students to practice spelling and letter-sound relationships.

- The Living Books Series (The Learning Company) includes CD-based books that read stories to children in a normal (human) voice and help them gain "book sense"—the ability to read from left to right and understanding of written text patterns and punctuation concepts. Because software programs of this type highlight words as they are read, they can be especially helpful for the student with limited reading skills.

- The Scholastic Company produces a commercial version of the highly successful Peabody Learning System called READ 180, originally developed by the Cognition and Technology Group at Vanderbilt University specifically for students (and adults) with reading difficulties. The student begins each lesson by viewing a video that provides background knowledge on a particular topic. The student then reads texts about the same topic, with "clickable" vocabulary words. During writing activities students can refer to an online tutor for help with organizing their thoughts, structuring a report, designing graphics, and adding music and video clips.

- Fast ForWord (Scientific Learning), mentioned earlier, is a popular program for teaching reading to students with extremely limited reading skills.

- Earobics (Cognitive Concepts) is a software application designed to teach phonemic awareness through a series of activities and games. The program teaches skills such as letter-sound relationships, sequencing, and patterning. Students with language-based learning disabilities find this program helpful with specific language skills.

We'll continue to discuss further examples of software applications focused on reading in later chapters.

● Written Language

Many children with learning disabilities who have poor fine-motor control and difficulty attending to detail struggle with the manual process of writing. Word processing can help these students put thoughts to paper. Simply using the keyboard as a word-input tool—the first computer skill most of us learn—can be the most important technology use for students with poor fine-motor control because it enables them to produce readable material.

Uses and limitations of spell checkers

Most modern word processors include spelling and grammar checkers. These allow the user to gain confidence, but may have the unintended consequence of reducing spelling acuity and grammatical skill. For example, using a spell checker gives the student the correct spelling of the word *perceive,* but doesn't remind him or her of the rule "*i* before *e* except after *c.*" Nor does the spell checker point out a mistaken use of *their* for *there.* Most grammar checkers and spell checkers offer a "correct" solution that the student will usually accept without thinking about it. Students must be reminded to reread their text to make sure that the words and phrases they have chosen make sense.

Contemporary word processors also allow the user to select a dictionary appropriate to that person's vocabulary. Teachers and parents can download specific word lists and dictionaries from the Internet and integrate them into the software program. Specific dictionaries can provide a more limited vocabulary list that gives the student fewer options to rule out when running the spell checker. Specialized dictionaries also include words that might otherwise be counted as misspelled, such as *website* or *remediate.*

Editing tools

The editing tools of a standard word processor can also aid students with learning disabilities. Not only do actions such as "cut" and "paste" allow the student to reorganize his or her thoughts, but programs such as Microsoft Word include features that allow teachers to provide specific feedback directly within the document. Figure 3.2 shows editing marks made in Microsoft Word on an early draft of this very paragraph. Consider the value of being able to make written comments and also insert voice comments into your students' text.

● FIGURE 3.2

An example of editing tools in Microsoft Word

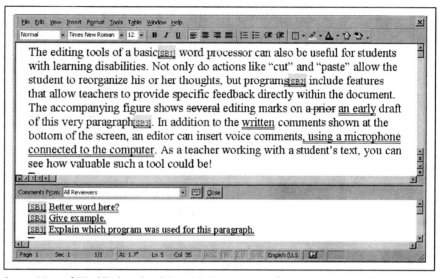

Source: Microsoft Word Trademark and Copyright © 2002 Microsoft Corporation. Screen shot reprinted by permission from Microsoft Corporation.

● Keyboarding

Although students with poor fine-motor control often find typing less frustrating than handwriting, they do need to develop keyboarding skills. Most schools today include keyboarding instruction in their curriculum; for the student with learning disabilities these lessons should be consistent and frequent. Most software applications designed to teach keyboarding (such as Type To Learn by Sunburst Communications and Mario Teaches Typing by Brainstorm) are appropriate for students with learning disabilities, but scheduling matters. Ten minutes of keyboarding instruction *every* day at the same time are more effective than two forty-minute lessons per week.

Software to teach typing

The standard keyboard layout familiar to most computer users, known as the QWERTY layout, emerged in 1867 as a typewriter layout. Christopher Latham Sholes designed the configuration to reduce mechanical jams when typing letters in quick succession. Unfortunately, the QWERTY keyboard has many limitations for students with learning disabilities. The seemingly unorganized layout of the keys can confuse students who have difficulty noticing differences and details. Alternative keyboards and keyboard layouts, such as colored keys and keyguards, allow distractible students to see and feel the different letters more clearly.

Keyboard overlays

The IntelliKeys system, created by IntelliTools, is a touchpad that responds to multiple overlays. The overlays, which look and feel like plastic placemats, are set into the touchpad for the student to type on. Students with learning disabilities benefit from the system's more logical arrangement of keys and options for individualization. We'll have more to say about uses of the IntelliKeys keyboard in other chapters.

● Word Prediction, Voice Recognition, and Text to Speech

Word prediction software, voice recognition products, and text-to-speech technologies hold great promise for students with learning disabilities, particularly those who have difficulty reading and writing. This section describes each of these technologies and then discusses particular applications.

Text to Speech ● **Text-to-speech software** uses an algorithm to produce a specified letter sound when the letter is encountered. When the letter *v* occurs in the text, for instance, the computer makes the *v* sound. Screen readers use text-to-speech technology to read aloud the words on a computer screen. Some devices, such as the handheld Reading Pen (WizCom Technologies), also allow the user to scan words in printed text and hear them pronounced.

Technology that reads text aloud

Text-to-speech technologies are making rapid advances. Many produce sounds that increasingly resemble human speech, although you may think it sounds strange. This occurs for two reasons: first, the set of tones and octaves that the computer can produce is limited; second, and more significantly, English, and all other spoken languages, have idiosyncrasies that go beyond a simple letter-sound correspondence.

Nevertheless, this second limitation can be turned into a tool for teaching students the rules of letter-sound correspondence and the exceptions. The strange sound the computer is making offers an opportunity for the teacher to talk about reading, to illustrate the distinction between reading and "word calling," and to show students how punctuation makes the flow of written words more logical. Listening to computer speech, students hear the basic pronunciation of letters and letter combinations. Watching the computer sound out words, they see a model of this process. Overall, the computer modeling builds students' familiarity with the reading process.

Word Prediction ● The computer can use a **word prediction** process to guess the word you are typing on the basis of the letters you have already typed. You may be familiar with this feature from using a web browser. As you type in the first few letters of the web address, the rest of the address suddenly appears. In a word processor, you might be typing the date (or the beginning of your name or anything you frequently type) and the computer will make a prediction, giving you the option to press a key and have that word or phrase

Predicting a word from a few letters

inserted. For the student with learning disabilities, word prediction can help with "word finding" problems, spelling, and with basic grammar.

As this "intelligent" technology advances, you may have to type fewer and fewer words to produce documents bearing your writing style. Your next word processor may be able to recognize that you are composing a letter to someone you frequently write as soon as you type the first few letters (such as "Dear Dr. Jones"). The word processor may also help you format the page and insert phrases or words that you use frequently.

Voice Recognition ●

Voice recognition, as mentioned earlier in the book, enables your computer to recognize and respond to your voice. For example, the Macintosh operating system (versions 9.0 and above) can respond to voice commands like "Computer, take me to Google" by opening Netscape Navigator to your favorite search engine.

Converting speech to text

Voice recognition can also be used to import spoken words into text in a word processor. For instance, Dragon NaturallySpeaking (Scansoft) allows the user to speak to the computer and have the words appear on screen. However, this process is not as simple as installing the program, putting on your microphone headset, and starting to talk. The computer must be "trained" to recognize the tone and pitch of your voice. This training process can be especially frustrating for students with learning disabilities, because of the quantity of text that must be read and the requirement to speak with the same tone and pitch every time you use the program. (Don't get a cold or go through puberty!)

In addition, normal speech patterns are not as linear and organized as even the roughest of written drafts. For the student with learning disabilities, therefore, speech-to-text is a demanding process, requiring a carefully prepared mental outline and the ability to keep that outline in mind as he or she speaks—a challenging memory task for anyone!

Software Applications ●

Co:Writer and Write:OutLoud, both designed by Don Johnston Incorporated, use word prediction and text-to-speech technology. Because the needs of students with learning disabilities often cluster around problems with producing and processing written text, using these programs together can be helpful for many students.

Using Co:Writer

Co:Writer is a word prediction program that allows a student to begin typing a word and then offers its best guess as to the word intended. If the student types in the letter *t*, the words *the, them, to,* and *Thursday* may come up as choices. At this point, instead of typing the entire word, the student can choose the number 4 key (temporarily assigned to the word *Thursday*), saving the time and effort of finding the remaining seven letters. Students with poor skills in sounding out words find this software helpful, because it narrows the options for encoding the word they are typing. Unfortunately, students may find themselves over-relying on Co:Writer to "write" the sentence for them. They might, for instance, see a choice in Co:Writer's prediction list that they hadn't thought of, like the way it sounds, and in that way allow the software to make a more "interesting" sentence than they would have produced on their own.

Write:OutLoud is a text-to-speech application that reads back a letter (or word or sentence, depending on the settings) after it has been inputted, giving the student immediate feedback on the writing. Using Co:Writer and Write:OutLoud together allows students to have immediate success and feedback on writing projects. Keep in mind that some students become overly dependent on these programs, so they are best used on a limited basis.

The Kurzweil system

Kurzweil is a well-known name in the area of technology for people with disabilities. Ray Kurzweil invented and produced the Kurzweil Reading Machine that, in 1976, gave blind people easy access to printed text for the first time. The Kurzweil 3000, distributed by Kurzweil Educational Systems, is an advanced text-to-speech system that allows the user to scan in text and have it read aloud using high-quality voices that are included in the program. A teacher can scan in page after page of text, save the text, edit and insert comments; students can then listen to the text over and over again. High-functioning students with learning disabilities—those who have excellent perceptual and organizational abilities but lack simple decoding skills—find the Kurzweil a useful system. The system's reading speed can be increased to its highest level, and students can quickly gather information that would have taken them painfully long to read on their own. However, many students with learning disabilities find the system cumbersome and tedious, and many teachers and principals find it simply too expensive (close to two thousand dollars for a single-unit color system, not including the computer or scanner).

● Speech and Language Skills

Speech-language therapists often use software to work on a range of communication problems, from stuttering to difficulties with oral comprehension. We'll explore some specialized types of communication software, including augmentative and adaptive communication technologies, in the chapter on communication disorders. For students with learning disabilities related to speech and language, there are far fewer specialized programs available.

For example, a program entitled SpeechViewer III, by IBM, improves students' phonological skills and their voice and articulation abilities. Using a microphone, students speak into the computer as a visual impression of their

Software for learning speech skills

speech appears on the screen. This visual impression looks something like the volume lights that go up and down with the sound of the music on a stereo system; as the sound level increases, the lights go higher. Using SpeechViewer the student completes on-screen activities that must be controlled with his or her voice. A student whose voice is too quiet can work on increasing or decreasing vocal loudness as a balloon inflates or deflates. The student with difficulty controlling the volume of his or her voice can work on modifying vocal pitch as a character moves up and down through an obstacle course. A student with a lisp controls the on-screen character while pronouncing different pairs of sounds (such as *s, st,* and *sh*) as a canoe traverses a river or a monkey climbs a tree. The SpeechViewer program allows the therapist to individualize lessons to address each student's unique educational needs.

Other programs popular with speech and language therapists include Earobics, Daisy's Castle, WordMunchers Deluxe, and Muppets: Beginning Sounds, all of which focus on letter-sound relationships.

● Mathematics

Students with learning disabilities may have trouble with mathematics because of difficulty understanding spatial relationships and symbols and because of problems with visual perception. The term *dyscalculia* has been used to describe these specific difficulties with quantitative elements and mathematical comprehension. Unfortunately, the software for teaching mathematics is not as well developed as that for reading instruction.

Most mathematics applications are skill-and-drill remedial programs, and they are often limited by the fact that they are marketed to the general school population. Because most addition and subtraction programs are designed for young children, older students with learning disabilities are unmotivated by and embarrassed about using these "kiddy" programs. A few software packages manage to avoid this problem. Their graphics, animations, and reinforcements make Math Blaster (Knowledge Adventure) and Math Munchers (The Learning Company) popular software programs. Both have versions designed for students from kindergarten through sixth grade. Math Arena (Sunburst Technology) is a nice program for older students who need to brush up on the basics. It is not too childlike (a sports theme helps), and it has a timing element that helps increase mastery for students who are ready for it.

Useful math applications

Traditional productivity tools such as spreadsheets can also help a student learning about mathematical concepts. A spreadsheet program such as Microsoft Excel allows you to organize numbers and information in table form and can perform basic and advanced calculations. Spreadsheets can be a valuable tool in data collection and analysis. For the student with learning disabilities, a spreadsheet can assist in organizing information into categories. In addition, spreadsheets help students look at relationships and patterns in numbers and numerical transformations.

Access to Math (Don Johnston Incorporated) is a worksheet production tool that offers a breakdown of specific mathematical subskills. A teacher can create an on-screen worksheet that focuses on a narrow set of mathematical concepts (such as two-digit subtraction without regrouping). The program is designed so that students can log on and complete the worksheets specifically designed for them right on the screen. It includes targeted feedback and space for students to type in "borrowing" numbers, as well as color-coding and a simple, nondistracting layout.

The Logical Journey of the Zoombinis (The Learning Company) is a logical-mathematical thinking application that students with learning disabilities find compelling because of its engaging content and graphical interface. The program focuses on mathematical concepts, rather than basic math facts, and presents these concepts in a dynamic, enticing way.

The use of calculators is a contentious issue for many teachers. During math time, students will often ask, to the teacher's dismay, "Can't we just use our calculators for this?" Many students and adults rely too much on calculators. The ease of using a calculator reduces the perceived need to be able to do math "in your head." However, students do need the skills of estimation and basic mathematical reasoning to use a calculator in the first place. In making the decision to use calculators with students with learning disabilities, consider carefully the difficulty of removing this helper tool. Again, you must remain committed to the best interests of the student with regard to both immediate and long-term IEP goals.

If you do decide to allow students with learning disabilities to use calculators, you may want to provide instruction in using the calculator's ten-key keypad. Keypad skills can make students much more proficient with their calculators. Teaching the ten-key keypad is similar to teaching basic keyboarding. Programs such as Touch Key by Fantasy II Software can help.

● Study Skills and Organization

Students with learning disabilities are notorious for messy backpacks, for forgotten and misplaced assignments, and for responding, "Oh . . . nothing," when asked what they have for homework. Students with learning disabilities frequently wait until the last minute to study for tests. They often have difficulty determining the main point of a set of information.

Researchers in the field of learning disabilities have looked at how technology tools can help students become more organized. Lynne Anderson-Inman at the University of Oregon has found that concept-mapping software can help high school and junior high students gain study skills, improve attitudes toward school, and decrease test anxiety. **Concept mapping** is the process of using a visual diagram to illustrate the relationships among words, facts, or other pieces of information.

Figure 3.3 shows a screen from Inspiration, a concept-mapping program created by Inspiration Software. With this software, students can create a web of ideas or concepts and connect these ideas to one another visually. This process of using illustrations to show the relationships between concepts or words allows brainstorming to become a valuable step in the writing process. Besides providing a tool for students with learning disabilities to visually organize their ideas, the Inspiration program includes templates that allow students to visualize how they might organize ideas in a compare-and-contrast essay or another writing process. Inspiration has proven especially valuable in helping students with learning disabilities comprehend the abstract concepts involved in composing and understanding written material.

Software for concept mapping

● FIGURE 3.3

A screen from Inspiration

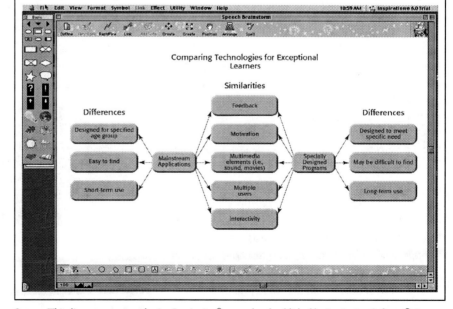

Source: This diagram was created using Inspiration®, created and published by Inspiration Software®, Inc. Reprinted with permission.

Other organizational tools, such as the Encarta Researcher in Microsoft's Encarta Encyclopedia, can help students conduct research and organize sources. Outliners and notetaking programs also help students with learning disabilities better identify main ideas and important information. Students in early grades benefit from color-coded calendars and checklists at home and school.

Personal digital assistants (PDAs) are handheld electronic devices that include calendars, address books, and other organizational tools. The Palm Handheld (**http://www.palm.com/**) and the Visor by Handspring (**http://www.handspring.com/**), two of the most popular PDAs, allow the user to

ⓣECHNIQUES FOR YOUR CLASSROOM

Notetaking Options

A **notetaker** is an accommodation often recommended for students with learning disabilities. Traditionally, a notetaker is a person in the student's class assigned to take detailed notes and share them with the student with learning disabilities. Tools such as minicassette recorders often replace the human notetaker.

The idea of using laptops to help the student with learning disabilities take notes has also been tested, because the student may have difficulty with handwriting and organizing ideas. Imagine that every student in your classroom has a laptop computer. What sort of picture immediately comes to mind? Do you see all your students working away, staring at their screens? Or do you picture students finding new ways to become distracted?

Laptops can indeed be useful tools for notetaking and organization, but if you've ever brought one to a workshop or meeting, you know how difficult it can be to stay on task. Distraction is even more of a problem for learning-disabled students. Teachers must establish rules for laptop use *before* any student uses the machine in the classroom.

The AlphaSmart keyboard can serve as an intermediate alternative to having laptops for every student. An AlphaSmart is a small, lightweight keyboard with a small LCD screen that shows about four lines of type. This durable piece of equipment runs on batteries and is appropriate even for young students. Files can be saved on the AlphaSmart and transferred to the classroom computer for editing or incorporation into another program, such as a word processor or authoring program.

An AlphaSmart keyboard
(Photo courtesy of AlphaSmart, by Intelligent Peripheral Devices, Inc.)

access the Internet and communicate with other PDAs without wires, send faxes, and read email from any location. PDAs can also act as cell phones and perform a wide array of other functions, such as those of an MP3 player, digital camera, or video game station. A student with learning disabilities can have a PDA programmed to provide reminders and alarms when he or she needs to be somewhere. If a classroom or school uses a similar PDA system, teachers can organize calendars for students and have students regularly "sync-up" to the teacher's computer to get updates and assignments. As advances in microtechnology continue, PDAs are likely to help students with learning disabilities in many other ways.

How PDAs can assist students

● Interdisciplinary Activities

Project-based learning, described earlier in this chapter, involves students in meaningful projects that tie together various elements of the curriculum. Students' motivation is increased because they have some degree of control over their work. Applications like authoring programs and web-design tools can provide similar advantages. They allow students not only to show that they have learned academic facts and skills, but also to showcase their creative and technical skill.

Using authoring tools

An **authoring tool** is an application that enables the user to design a stand-alone product, such as a presentation or report, with multimedia or hypermedia components. *Multimedia* means the incorporation of several different kinds of media, such as text, sound, pictures, and animations. **Hypermedia** refers to multimedia that allows the user to move in a nonlinear fashion from one segment of the product to another (Grabe and Grabe, 2001). Web page links that allow you to click on a word to go to a new section or new page are examples of hypermedia.

HyperStudio (Roger Wagner Publishing) is an authoring software package available for Windows and Macintosh computers that allows the user to manipulate text, graphics, sounds, and animation. The final product in Hyper-Studio is called a stack because it resembles a computerized version of a stack of cards. User-designed buttons connect the cards to take the viewer from screen to screen. Designed to be "kid-friendly," HyperStudio includes basic drawing tools, such as paintbrushes, shapes, and colors. It allows students to import text from other programs or to write directly in the program. Students can also animate anything on the screen, add their own sounds, and record their voices. In this way, the student with learning disabilities has the opportunity to demonstrate and present his or her knowledge in a way that allows multiple modes of expression.

Zachary Winters

A screen from Zack's
HyperStudio project
on space

T he accompanying picture is a screen shot from a HyperStudio
stack created by Zachary Winters, a student with learning disabilities. During a space study unit, Zachary worked with a team of his
peers to create a project showing an imaginary adventure in which
the children take the school bus into space and visit each of the planets.
Along the way, the students present facts they have learned about space and
planetary science.

For this particular screen, Zack took a digital picture of himself, cut out
his face, and pasted it digitally onto the image of a spacesuit he found on
the Internet. He then added the background, drew in the satellite and the
moons, and added a button to move on to the next screen. In addition, if
you click on Zack's face, you will hear him say, "Many moons and satellites
rotate around the planet Jupiter."

According to Zack's mother, he had a normal early childhood, and when
his teacher recommended that he stay an extra year in pre-kindergarten because of his "poor processing ability," she was stunned. After much turmoil
in kindergarten, Zack's first grade teacher recommended that he be tested
for learning disabilities, and the school psychologist found that he had major difficulties with perceptive and receptive language. The psychologist
found Zack's verbal intelligence to be normal, but his performance IQ was
in the eighth percentile, meaning that his score was well below average.
During testing, Zack couldn't recall a word list, but he was able to answer
questions about a story read to him. He was found to have difficulties with
fine motor skills, as well as language problems that included an inability to
recognize some sounds.

Halfway through the first grade, Zack started seeing a speech therapist at
the school, and he began visiting the special education teacher three times a
week for help with reading. Although his speech and language seemed to
improve, his reading did not, and he continued to fall behind. In second

PROFILE CONTINUED

grade, the special education teacher and Zack's mom decided to keep Zack in the special education class all day, so that he could have the intensive help he needed. Yet Zack continued to be frustrated by reading, spelling, and writing, and he also started to have difficulties in mathematics.

The lack of progress frustrated Zack's mother, who knew that Zack had great skills in building things and in sports as well as good problem-solving and communication skills. Zack, too, was depressed and frustrated, and he told his mom that he hated school and wanted to drop out. At the end of second grade, Zack's mom met with the special education teacher, the school psychologist, and the school principal and decided to find out whether Zack could transfer to a special school for students with learning disabilities. Beginning in the third grade, Zack started attending such a school. At first, he was quiet and unassuming, and hesitant to speak. But soon his progress was evident.

Zack's class has nine other students with problems similar to his. The class is led by a special education teacher and a teacher's assistant. The school has an arts-based curriculum, but other subjects are not neglected. A tutor comes in every morning, and the students work in small groups on reading and mathematics. During reading time, Zack uses the computer to listen to a story and answer questions, although he enjoys reading books like those in the Harry Potter series without any technological assistance. In his classroom he uses an AlphaSmart keyboard to work on writing projects while continuing to refine his penmanship. Zack also uses Co:Writer and Write:OutLoud to input text into the computer, and as a twelve-year-old he has had his first success at producing stories. His technological supports have allowed him to demonstrate his excellent comprehension and writing skills while still receiving remedial help with decoding and spelling. Zack's occupational therapist taught him how to use the 10-key pad for math. Now he is much quicker doing calculations on the computer or on a calculator because he can use just one hand. In the afternoons, Zack goes to science class (where he created his HyperStudio project) and to one of his art classes. Zack also takes a woodworking class to help him with his fine motor skills and drama to help him with his communication skills.

Overall, Zack is much happier now. He is improving in his language skills, and he is now—as you can see—an artist. Instruction keyed to his specific needs, plus the careful integration of technology into his daily learning, has helped him achieve these successes.

Using authoring tools such as HyperStudio lets you create instructional units to address particular content area deficiencies. These units can be designed for and, more importantly, *by* individual students. When the student uses hypermedia he or she is in control of the screen and the "look" of the final product, which can also improve students' focus and attention. Moreover, you will appreciate the ability to create portfolios of students' work that include more than writing and pictures on paper.

Video editing tools such as iMovie (Apple) and Adobe Premiere can take the idea of authoring to another level. With these tools, students can create video-based (or DVD-based) productions of their work.

When you allow students with learning disabilities to use such high-tech tools, you motivate them to perform and produce at the highest level. Students with learning disabilities are experts at creating alternative paths to a goal, be it reading a sentence or animating a computer-generated robot. The challenge in using these types of technologies with students with learning disabilities is to carefully explore the larger goals of the student's IEP and to focus on the long-term impact this type of undertaking will have.

SUMMARY

Learning disabilities, the most prevalent type of disability, are usually defined as a discrepancy between ability and actual performance. They can involve auditory-language, visual-spatial, motor-related, organizational, academic, or social skills problems—or any combination of these. Because the students vary so widely, no "one size fits all" approach works. When you have a student with a learning disability in your classroom, you must be innovative, creative, and flexible, and willing to alter your lesson plans as necessary to accommodate the student.

The most common approaches to instruction for students with learning disabilities are the remedial approach, task analysis, project-based learning, or direct instruction. Technological applications are useful in each of these approaches. But these are not by any means the only methods you may find yourself using. You must first examine the student's specific skills and needs, and then select instructional approaches and technology accordingly.

Using technology offers three basic advantages for students with disabilities: more individual attention and feedback; interesting, engaging tasks; and greater student control over learning. Today's software programs offer these benefits in a variety of subject areas, including reading, writing, math, and study skills. Authoring tools can be used in interdisciplinary projects that give students the chance to show off their creative talents *and* their academic knowledge.

Remember that the technologies discussed in this chapter are not only for the student labeled as "learning disabled." Designing new teaching and learning experiences around sufficiently adaptable technologies can help you include all your students in active exploration. Also remember that students with learning disabilities are intelligent and capable. Your belief and interest in their success may be the encouragement they need in order to progress.

KEY TERMS

learning disability (p. 53)
remedial teaching (p. 56)
task analysis (p. 57)
project-based learning (p. 59)
direct instruction (p. 61)
talking books (p. 62)
text-to-speech software (p. 68)
word prediction (p. 68)
concept mapping (p. 73)
personal digital assistant (PDA) (p. 74)
notetaker (p. 74)
authoring tool (p. 75)
hypermedia (p. 75)

RESOURCES FOR FURTHER INVESTIGATION

Online Resources

Center for Applied Special Technology: Tools for Individualizing Curriculum.
http://www.cast.org/udl/index.cfm?i=392
This area of the CAST website offers recommendations of software applications and discussion of how those applications can be used in the regular classroom to individualize instruction.

Center for IT Accommodation.
http://www.itpolicy.gsa.gov/cita
This site has a collection of links to programs using technology to give people more access to information and help them become more useful in the workplace. The site offers helpful information on legal issues as they relate to technology and persons with disabilities.

Council for Exceptional Children: Division of Learning Disabilities.
http://www.dldcec.org/
The Division of Learning Disabilities of the Council for Exceptional Children is an active group of researchers and teachers who discuss many of the important issues facing students with learning disabilities. At the website, you'll find information about their publications and annual meetings.

Easy Access to Software and Information.
http://www.rit.edu/~easi/

> Here you will find a wealth of information about technology tools and suggestions for using these tools in your classroom. EASI holds regular online conferences (known as "webcasts") about special education technology and publishes guidelines for accessible web design. If you click on the link that says "K-12 Center," you'll find a resource guide to specific technologies to use with students with learning disabilities and attention deficit disorders.

LD OnLine.
http://www.ldonline.org/

> LDOnline, a website with a vast set of resources about learning disabilities in general, has a great technology guide with information about products that might assist a student in your classroom. LDOnline also has research articles, a bulletin board where parents and teachers can connect with one another, and a Kid Zone with material just for children with learning disabilities.

The National Academy for Child Development.
http://www.nacd.org/

> This international organization of parents and professionals is dedicated to helping children and adults reach their full potential.

Product Resources

AlphaSmart. Cupertino, CA: AlphaSmart, Inc.
http://www.alphasmart.com/

> This portable keyboard can provide an affordable way for students to input text.

HyperStudio. Torrance, CA: Knowledge Adventure.
http://www.hyperstudio.com/

> This is the website for the authoring software discussed in this chapter. The site includes sample projects that you can download, lesson plans, and product support.

Inspiration. Portland, OR: Inspiration Software.
http://www.inspiration.com/

> Popular software for concept maps and semantic webs.

IntelliKeys Keyboard. Petaluma, CA: IntelliTools.
http://www.intellitools.com/

> An alternative keyboard with transparencies that you can place over the keypad for different functions.

Don Johnston Incorporated. Volo, IL.
http://www.donjohnston.com/
> Publishers of various applications, including Co:Writer and Write:Out-Loud as well as Access to Math.

Laureate Special Needs Software. Winooski, VT: Laureate Learning Systems.
http://www.laureatelearning.com/
> Laureate offers software geared toward various students with special needs, from the developmentally disabled to those with mild language-learning deficits. With the software, students can work on visual cues using an alphabetical approach.

SpeechViewer III for Windows. Armonk, NY: IBM.
http://www-3.ibm.com/able/snsspv3.html
> Software to aid students with phonology, voice, and articulation.

Print Resources

Dockrell, J., & McShane, J. (1983). *Children's learning difficulties.* Oxford: Blackwell. A concise overview of the child with learning disabilities, this volume is a quick and easy reference.

Kirk, S. A., & Chalfant, J. C. (1984). *Academic and developmental learning disabilities.* Denver: Love. This book discusses learning disabilities from birth on. It offers a concise overview of the historical perspective, the definition, and intervention methods for teachers, parents, and students to use.

Lerner, Janet. (2000). *Learning disabilities: Theories, diagnosis, and teaching strategies,* 8th ed. Boston: Houghton Mifflin. A key textbook on types of learning disabilities and specific techniques used with students.

Smith, Sally L. (1995). *No easy answers: The learning disabled child at home and at school.* New York: Bantam Books. Professor Smith's book offers a unique look at the child with learning disabilities and gives examples of the types of approaches that work best.

West, Thomas G. (1997). *In the mind's eye: Visual thinkers, gifted people with dyslexia and other learning difficulties, computer imaging, and the ironies of creativity.* Amherst, NY: Prometheus Books. West discusses the ways in which advances in computer imaging are making learning easier for visual-spatial thinkers.

Organizations

Abledata: National Rehabilitation Information Center
8630 Fenton Street, Suite 930, Silver Spring, MD 20910
http://www.abledata.com/
    Abledata offers a database of products for learning disabilities.

American College Test Administration
Box 168, Iowa City, IA 52243
(319) 337-1332
    This organization allows those with learning disabilities to make special
    arrangements during tests.

ERIC Clearinghouse on Disabilities and Gifted Education Council
for Exceptional Children
1920 Association Drive, Reston, VA 22091-1589
(703) 620-3660
http://ericec.org/
    Free publications include the *Digest on Learning Disabilities* and an anno-
    tated bibliography called *Digest on Reading About Learning Disabilities*.

The International Dyslexia Association
Chester Building, Suite 382, 8600 LaSalle Road, Baltimore, MD 21286
http://www.interdys.org/

Learning Disabilities Association (LDA)
4156 Library Road, Pittsburgh, PA 15234
http://www.ldanatl.org/
    This nonprofit organization serves to advance the education and general
    welfare of children and adults with learning disabilities.

National Center for Learning Disabilities
381 Park Avenue South, Suite 1401, New York, NY 10016
http://www.ncld.org/

TECHNOLOGY FOR STUDENTS WITH DEVELOPMENTAL DELAYS

FOCUS QUESTIONS

As you read this chapter, think about the following:

- What are developmental delays? Are they the same as mental retardation?

- What academic and behavioral activities will a child with developmental delays do in school?

- What support will a child with developmental delays receive outside the regular classroom?

- How can technology play a supporting role in the education of students with developmental delays?

- What happens after a student with developmental delays leaves school?

echnology has many applications for students with developmental delays. Although the term *mental retardation* is used for many of these children, they actually have a wide range of disorders. Technology can be an important tool for them both to learn basic life skills and to become engaged in the curriculum.

After a brief overview of the types of developmental delay likely to be represented in a special education program, this chapter discusses technologies teachers can use with these students, ranging from software programs designed to teach life skills to remedial programs that help students learn math and language.

WHAT ARE DEVELOPMENTAL DELAYS?

Any discussion of students with developmental delays requires a clarification of terminology. The terms *mental retardation* and *brain damage* are still in common use, but they bring up stereotypic images of children who will never be able to function in "normal situations" because of behavioral idiosyncrasies or an inability to learn. Special educators and researchers know that this simply is not the case. Children with developmental delays *can* learn. However, they take much longer to grasp ideas or finish tasks. Therefore, *developmental delay* (or, at least, *developmental disability*) is the term many educators prefer because it conveys the idea that children with such difficulties are worth the challenge of providing educational experiences that engage and encourage them. Nevertheless, use of this term to describe children with mental retardation is still controversial, and when the Individuals with Disabilities Education Act (IDEA) was reauthorized in 1997, its provisions allowed states and local education agencies to come up with their own definitions and eligibility criteria for this category.

Broadly speaking, people with developmental delays are those who develop at a rate significantly below average and who experience difficulties in learning and social adjustment. According to the Developmental Disabilities Act of October 2000, the current federal definition of developmental disability is as follows:

> The term *developmental disability* means a severe, chronic disability in an individual five years of age or older that
>
> **1** Is attributable to a mental or physical impairment or a combination of mental and physical impairments
> **2** Is manifested before the person attains age 22
> **3** Is likely to continue indefinitely
> **4** Results in substantial functional limitations in three or more of the following areas of major life activity:
> - self-care
> - receptive and expressive language
> - learning
> - mobility
> - self-direction
> - capacity for independent living
> - economic self-sufficiency
> **5** Reflects the individual's need for a combination and sequence of special, interdisciplinary, or generic services, supports or other assistance that is of lifelong or extended duration and is individually planned and coordinated

Preferred term: developmental delay

Defining developmental delay

In practice, consistently low scores on intelligence tests, in combination with poor academic functioning and a lack of adaptive skills, usually indicate that a child has a developmental delay. Delays in motor development and in receptive and expressive language skills are also typically present.

● Identifying Children with Developmental Delays

Children with developmental delays often are identified early in life, because they fall significantly behind their age-mates in meeting developmental "milestones." For example, a young child may be slow to roll over, to understand his or her name, or to exhibit fine motor skills. Parents of infants often worry when their second child takes longer than the first to display a specific ability. In fact, the range of ages within which an infant should be able to perform any given skill is broad. Differences in personality can also result in variations in developmental progress. Nevertheless, special educators and medical doctors find that the behaviors and abilities of children who have developmental delays are well outside the age ranges for almost every developmental benchmark.

Identifying a child with a developmental delay involves going through a set of evaluative processes, including intelligence tests, developmental scales, adaptive behavior evaluations, and tests of general knowledge. Evaluation tools such as intelligence tests and behavioral scales are "normed" on a large sample of the population over a long period of time, and the scores from these sample assessments are distributed along a curve, offering a picture of how the measured attributes occur in the general population.

The bell curve

Figure 4.1 illustrates a *bell curve* (or *normal curve*), the graphic shape that depicts scores on any standardized measure. On such a curve, the mean (average) score falls in the middle, and a statistical measure called a *standard deviation* is used to indicate the distance of a given score from the mean. When educational evaluators describe children with developmental delays, they are talking about children whose assessment scores fall at least two standard deviations below the mean. As you can see from the figure, this means that the children's scores are lower than those of 95 percent of the population used to establish the norms for the test.

● Causes and Prevalence of Developmental Delays

The primary cause for developmental delays in school-aged children is genetic abnormalities. For example, **phenylketonuria (PKU)** is a single-gene disorder

● FIGURE 4.1

The bell curve

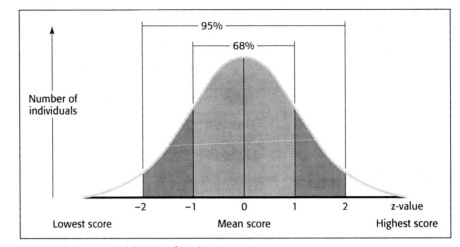

Note: Z-values are standard deviations from the mean.

Genetic abnormalities

also referred to as an "inborn error of metabolism." PKU leads to mental retardation and other developmental delays if untreated in infancy because the body is unable to produce proteins or enzymes needed to convert certain toxic chemicals into nontoxic products or to transport substances from one place to another (Glanze, 1996). Infants with untreated PKU appear to develop typically for the first few months of life, but by twelve months of age most of them will have a significant developmental delay and will be diagnosed with mental retardation before they start school.

Down syndrome is an example of a chromosomal disorder. Chromosomal disorders happen sporadically and are caused by too many or too few chromosomes or by a change in structure of a chromosome. In the case of Down syndrome, the children have recognizable physical characteristics and limited intellectual endowment because of the presence of an extra chromosome 21.

Similarly, **fragile X syndrome** arises from a single gene located on the X (female) chromosome. It is the leading inherited cause of mental retardation.

Other causes of developmental delays include these:

- *Problems during pregnancy.* Use of alcohol or drugs by a pregnant mother can cause mental retardation and developmental delays in the child. Research suggests that smoking also increases the risk of developmental delays. Other risks include malnutrition, certain environmental contaminants, and illnesses of the mother during pregnancy, such as toxoplasmosis, cytomegalovirus, rubella, and syphilis. Pregnant women who are infected with HIV may pass the virus to their child, leading to future neurological damage.

- *Problems at birth.* Although any birth condition of unusual stress may injure the infant's brain, prematurity and low birth weight predict serious problems more often than any other conditions.
- *Problems after birth.* Childhood diseases such as whooping cough, chicken pox, measles, and HIB disease (which may lead to meningitis and encephalitis) can damage the brain, as can accidents such as a blow to the head or near drowning. Lead, mercury, and other environmental toxins can cause irreparable damage to the brain and nervous system. It is important to note that some children with developmental delays have problems caused by abuse or neglect. Although accidents and injuries can result in brain damage, it is often difficult to determine whether the child's problems existed prior to the accident.

Measured by both intelligence and adaptive behavior measures, approximately 1 percent of the general population has developmental delays. According to states' data reported to the U.S. Department of Education, in the 1997–1998 school year approximately six hundred thousand students between the ages of six and twenty-one were classified as having developmental delays and received services from public schools. This figure does not include students reported as having multiple disabilities or those in noncategorical special education preschool programs.

● Types of Developmental Delays

Developmental delays are disorders, not diseases, and should not be confused with mental illness. Many educators and researchers agree that people with developmental delays develop in the same way that people without a developmental disorder do, but at a slower rate. Others suggest that persons with developmental delays have difficulties in particular areas of basic thinking and learning such as attention, perception, or memory. Depending on the degree of impairment, individuals with developmental delays will follow different developmental pathways for academic, social, and vocational skills.

In an attempt to characterize and classify the varying degrees of difficulty these children experience, special educators often label children according to the type of services that they receive. In 1992, the American Association on Mental Retardation established a system of classification that is in wide use today. It includes the following four levels of intensity:

Four levels of intensity

1 *Intermittent.* Children who have developmental delays that do not cause day-to-day difficulties, but who need support occasionally and during transitions (for example, the transition from junior high to high school).

Jason Hunter

Jason and his teacher explore the Little Fingers Preschool software package.

Jason Hunter was born in 1996 with Down syndrome. He is the youngest of four children, and the only one of his siblings to have any special needs. He is outgoing and kind, and loves all types of robotic toys. He is a huge fan of radio-operated cars and boats, which he uses with his oldest brother, Mark.

While his mother was pregnant with Jason, she had a sonogram that showed some thickness in the back of the fetus's skull and wide eye-spacing. The results of an amniocentesis confirmed that Jason had Down syndrome, and his parents and siblings prepared for his difference in appearance and potential developmental difficulties before he was born.

After birth, Jason had no complications in the hospital, though many children with Down syndrome have heart problems and intestinal problems. Before he started a preschool program at age two and a half, Jason stayed home with his mom and participated in swimming lessons, gymnastic classes, and physical therapy in an effort to help him with motor development and fine-motor skills.

When Jason started school, he went through a long series of tests. Over a two-week period, he was tested just about every day to determine his cognitive abilities, motor skills, vision, hearing, and perception. In addition to being tested at the school, he was observed at home. The testing process was probably the most grueling experience Jason had ever had, according to his mother, and made him protest going to school at all. Jason's mother and siblings convinced him that this ordeal wasn't really school.

At the preschool program, an integrated program for both disabled and nondisabled children, Jason established his love of anything mechanical, and he became well known for taking apart the pencil sharpener and the remote control to the class television. Then, in the fall of 2001, Jason started kindergarten. He was eager to ride the bus to school with his siblings. He is

PROFILE CONTINUED extremely fortunate that his neighborhood school houses the special education program for children with developmental delays; some of the other students come from as far as twenty miles away.

Jason's IEP goals include working on his fine motor skills (hopefully he'll learn to put the pencil sharpener back together!) and identifying words. He uses technology applications to aid his progress. For beginning literacy skills and fine-motor skills, he uses Fast ForWord Basics (also known as Away We Go!) by Scientific Learning. This program helps him focus on learning shapes and sorting in preparation for learning letters and sounds. In mathematics Jason's teacher uses a simple program called LittleFingers Preschool (LittleFingers Software), which helps him practice recognizing colors and following directions. Jason also just started using a program called Monkeys Jumping on the Bed (Don Johnston Incorporated) that helps him use auditory cues to recognize numbers and counting. Jason uses an IntelliKeys modified keyboard with the physical and occupational therapist (see chapter 3), which helps him focus his fine-motor skills and develop keyboarding proficiency.

Jason's parents hope that he will learn to read and are encouraging him at home. He continues to be an excellent swimmer, and he is interested in becoming a race car driver when he grows up.

2 *Limited.* Children who have daily limitations but can achieve a good degree of self-sufficiency after education and training.

3 *Extensive.* Support for these children extends consistently throughout their lifetime, and they will not live independently.

4 *Pervasive.* Used rarely, this term describes children whose developmental delays prohibit them from most self-help activities. These children typically require support for life-sustaining activities.

● The Roles of Specialists

When you teach children with developmental delays, they usually receive a variety of special services from therapists:

Specialized therapies

- *Occupational and physical therapy.* Therapy can help children with motor skills (such as increasing range of motion and fine motor skills); perceptual skills (for instance, helping a child track an object in two- or three-dimensional space); and social-emotional skills (working in groups and

PRINCIPLES AND PRACTICE   Commitment by Teachers

The great majority of children with developmental delays can become productive and full participants in society. Through appropriate educational services that begin in early infancy and continue through the developmental period and beyond, children with developmental delays can develop to their full potential. Acting upon the idea that these children have the capacity to learn requires investing time and energy in incremental lessons and looking for small amounts of progress. Moreover, it requires maintaining the belief that the time and energy spent on instruction are worthwhile.

Teachers, psychologists, and therapists do encounter parents who feel defeated by comparisons between their child's rate of progress and that of "normal" children. We may be tempted to "let them off the hook" by prematurely reducing or eliminating our expectations for the child. But if we believe that these children can learn, we must remain committed to providing learning opportunities and investing time and energy in their development.

As with all education, modifying instruction to meet individual needs is the starting point for successful learning. Continuity between school and home also helps to ensure that learning gains are maintained. Parents of children with developmental delays should be an integral part of the planning and teaching team.

taking turns). Occupational therapy also focuses on the use of adaptive and assistive technologies.

- *Speech/language therapy.* This type of therapy can help children with articulation and expressive disorders; it also boosts receptive language skills.

- *Psychotherapy and psychiatric therapy.* Broadly speaking, psychological therapy helps children with the process of recognizing, defining, and overcoming psychological and interpersonal difficulties. School psychologists are also responsible for administering many of the assessment inventories mentioned earlier. Psychiatrists have medical credentials and are responsible for managing any medication therapy the child may receive for psychological issues, such as anxiety, depression, and sleep disorders.

Collaboration with these specialists is extremely important. Teamwork and communication ensure that the adults working to help a child are pursuing related or compatible goals; that they can support, inform, and inspire each other; and that problems or obstacles are identified as early as possible. Occupational therapists, for example, can often contribute creative and useful strategies for helping children with developmental delays become ready to use technology, as well as suggestions for appropriate technologies and programs to use in the classroom.

Educational, Social, and Life-Skills Needs of Students with Developmental Delays

In your study of children with developmental delays, take time to review some of the well-known theories of normal child development, such as those of Jean Piaget and Erik Erikson. (See Resources for Further Investigation at the end of this chapter.) Note, however, that children with developmental delays will not necessarily follow the same sequence of development as typical children. As a teacher, you may encounter a child with a developmental delay who has older-child cognitive skills such as conservation of quantity and some deductive reasoning, but, like a younger child, is still egocentric, with a limited capacity to shift perspective in order to understand or solve a problem. Some of these differences may be caused by environmental influences, because children with developmental delays are more likely than others to be in specially structured environments that in and of themselves affect the course of development.

Despite their differences, students with developmental delays have needs similar to those of other students. They are less likely, however, to take part in the regular curriculum than are children with learning disabilities or hearing or visual impairments. The challenge to the teacher is to provide materials that are developmentally appropriate and that offer opportunities to monitor small improvements or changes in performance.

Balancing needs: basic skills, social and language skills

Any teacher who works with children with developmental delays must balance the need for basic skills instruction with the children's need to learn age-appropriate social and language skills. Materials for these students should be concrete and should emphasize practice targeted to the child's developmental level and age level. Like seeking software for children with learning disabilities, finding applications that match both chronological age and specific learning objectives can be difficult. Although a student with a developmental delay may be learning simple addition and subtraction skills at age eleven or twelve, he or she should not be using a software program designed primarily for prekindergarten or kindergarten students.

Technology Applications for Students with Developmental Delays

Some of the most successful programs for children with developmental delays are simple skill-and-drill applications, such as Access to Math (Don Johnston Incorporated) and Fast ForWord (Scientific Learning). Programs like these provide basic, remedial instruction with effective use of reinforcement and without too many distracting or confusing graphics and animations. But children with developmental delays also need opportunities for expression and basic functioning. Programs such as Kid Pix (Broderbund) allow a child to both gain computer aptitude and explore being an "artist" without any right or wrong answers. You can build skills for daily computing functioning by incorporating productivity applications such as word processors and spreadsheets and equipment such as calculators into the life-skills aspect of the curriculum. The following sections discuss technology applications that you may find helpful in various areas of academic, social, and life skills.

● Readiness Skills

Effective use of technology requires many skills. Special education teachers and therapists (physical, occupational, speech, and others) have learned that introducing basic computing skills makes computers less complex for students with developmental delays to use (Rettig, 1987). Having these skills reduces a young child's natural tendency to bang on the keyboard, become frustrated, and lose interest in approaching the computer again. Basic computing skills can help children interact with the computer and see it as more than just a toy to react to. Instruction in basic input techniques, such as learning how to use a ten-key calculator or keypad, can help older students become more precise and expeditious in their work. Acquiring the skills necessary to use computers or assistive technologies is therefore part of the IEPs of many children with developmental delays.

Teaching basic technology skills

Generally, teachers, therapists, and parents introduce and teach basic computer and assistive technology skills using simple materials, such as simple, inexpensive toys and switches. Such toys can assist with the development of cognitive functioning (Doctoroff, 1996). Toys and switches are concrete objects that naturally motivate children with developmental delays. Many kinds of battery-operated toys help teach a young child basic manipulative skills, and any toy operated by batteries can be adapted for switch activation. The toys should be durable enough to stand this kind of everyday use—a child's occupational therapist can provide good information on their selection and use.

Children who have a physical delay or who are generally uninterested in manipulative toys can learn from battery-operated toys adapted to work with single switches. These can serve as tools for developing play skills with objects and with peers. They also provide children with physical disabilities increased control over the classroom and home environments (Musselwhite, 1986).

TECHNIQUES FOR YOUR CLASSROOM

Advice for Choosing Battery-Operated Toys

When choosing battery-operated toys for students with developmental delays, look for a variety of toys that reflect a range of sensory inputs. For example, toys with flashing and multicolored lights provide visual input; tape recorders, musical devices, and other noisy toys (for instance, ones that emit animal sounds or sirens) stimulate a young child's auditory senses. Toys should also provide a variety of movement patterns, such as horizontal, vertical, and circular movement. Examples include a drumming bear, a walking robot, a fireman going up and down a ladder, and small train or car track sets. Choose toys that incorporate easily into play routines (Musselwhite, 1986), match the motivational needs of the child, and are age appropriate (Greszko, 1988).

Learning readiness skills through games

Because children with developmental delays need opportunities to succeed, it is extremely important to match the switch or switches to the child's physical requirements. The child must be able to reliably make a motor movement that activates the toy. Consider using large buttons with plenty of space between them. Pressure-sensitive switches that require minimal movement are now on the market, and children with severe motor difficulties can even use an eye-blink switch or a puff switch to activate a device. One way to become more familiar with such adaptive technologies is to visit a technology center. The Alliance for Technology Access is a nationwide organization designed to help people locate assistive technologies in their communities. Visit the ATA's website at **http://www.ataccess.org/** to see if it has a center near you.

Once children have a variety of experiences with toys and switches, they are better prepared to interact successfully with the computer. But technology can assist in teaching other readiness skills as well. Simple web-based games such as Lemonade Stand (at **http://www.littlejason.com/lemonade/**) can teach goal setting, attention and concentration, and basic cause-effect relationships. This website takes the traditional lemonade-stand game and brings it to a web environment, offering instant feedback and simple graphics. Games for Nintendo systems and for the Sony PlayStation, such as NASCAR 2002 from EA Sports (**http://nascar2002.ea.com/**), provide environments in which children with developmental delays can learn about setting goals and tracking progress. Although the computer is not necessary to teaching these skills, it is often motivating and engaging to children with developmental delays. Helping a child play such a game, creating a chart that visually plots his or her progress, and setting short- and long-term goals, can help that child learn skills of metacognition and abstract thinking. The game consoles that children love can be used for other curricular areas as well; for instance, the Achieve Now series from Lightspan (**http://www.lightspan.com/**) offers a variety of reading and math programs that run either on a PC or on a Sony PlayStation.

● Life Skills

Software to develop fundamental life skills

Technology can aid in teaching and rehearsing life skills. As shown in Figure 4.2, students can review frequently performed activities at the computer. Many of these activities are easily organized to reflect a naturally occurring sequence—for example, washing hands, brushing teeth, flossing, using mouthwash. Teachers can then use printouts to rehearse complete activities in the classroom, to emphasize specific steps, and to provide picture cues at the actual location, like the bathroom or bedroom (either at home or in a residential facility). The Attainment Company (**http://www.attainmentcompany.com/**) produces a series of software applications to teach skills such as brushing teeth, going to a restaurant, shopping, organizing time, and solving conflicts.

● Social and Communication Skills

Children with developmental delays often (but not always) display behaviors inappropriate for their chronological age. They are more likely to have delayed speech or an articulation disorder and to speak in "baby talk," making

● FIGURE 4.2

A screen shot from Personal Success life-skills software

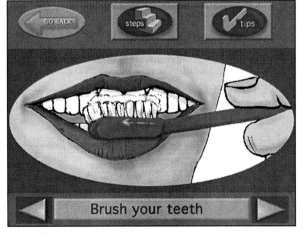

Source: Photo courtesy of Attainment Company, Inc.

them easy targets for teasing by their less sensitive peers. Part of their curriculum includes providing social skills instruction, which teaches a broad range of interpersonal skills such as ordering food in a restaurant, resolving conflicts, and understanding the physical space of others.

Social skills and communication deficits can include difficulties in areas such as these:

Types of deficits in social and communication skills

- *Kinesics:* the ability to understand the body language of self and others. Problems in this area include failure to respond to facial expressions of others, inability to "read" the feelings and attitudes of others, and incorrect use of gestures.
- *Proxemics:* the ability to understand how physical space communicates with others. People with difficulty here might stand too close in social situations, stare, avoid eye contact, or touch others inappropriately.
- *Vocalics:* the ability to understand how vocal volume and pitch communicate to others. Problems in this area include misinterpreting sarcasm, talking in a monotone, and talking too fast, too slowly, too loudly, or too softly.

The educational program for a child with developmental delays may include speech therapy, occupational therapy, and physical therapy, any or all of which will work on some aspect of social skills. Classroom teachers and parents can use various technology applications to contribute to and build on social skills instruction.

For example, decision-making applications help students observe social interactions and try to make sense of them. Students watch a video clip of an interaction and then help the character make the next choice. These applications give the child the opportunity to view the consequences of social decisions and actions under safe conditions. Albert Bandura, a researcher in educational psychology, found that people could learn through modeling and through watching others interact in reality-like situations and environments (Bandura, 1995). Children with developmental delays can learn how to handle interpersonal situations in real life by watching the interactions of others and the consequences of behavior. Teaching social skills with technology will be discussed more fully in the chapter on students with emotional and behavioral disorders.

Simple assistive technologies can help children with developmental delays understand and communicate about everyday activities. KidAccess, for example (**http://www.kidaccess.com/**), is a system of stickers and magnets with pictures on them that children use to make choices, understand expressions, and organize their day. Using these stickers and magnets (shown in Figure 4.3), a child can set up a calendar of daily activities such as dressing, eating breakfast, and planning playtime.

● FIGURE 4.3

Examples of the KidAccess stickers

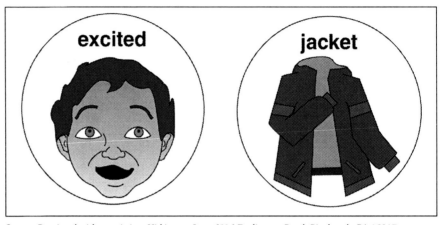

Source: Reprinted with permission, KidAccess, Inc., 6526 Darlington Road, Pittsburgh, PA 15217, www.kidaccess.com.

Communication boards

Communication boards can also benefit the child with developmental delays. A **communication board** is a simple, flat surface covered with buttons or pictures that the child uses to indicate his or her answer to a question or to make a request. Some communication boards include a speech option by which the selection is spoken aloud using a computerized voice. A child uses the assistance of a communication board to better express him- or herself and to interact with others. In helping him or her to communicate and to manage the environment, teachers, therapists, and parents can contribute to the child's growth and quality of life.

Electronic communicators, such as the Vantage sold by the Prentke Romich Company (**http://www.prentrom.com/**), work similarly to a communication board. Instead of a picture, an electronic communicator might have a synthesized voice that speaks for the student. He or she can select and play words or preprogrammed phrases via digitized speech. We'll have more to say about communicators in chapter 6.

You may find that children with autism benefit from communication boards or an electronic communicator, as well as from the IntelliKeys system mentioned in chapter 3. Under some labeling systems, autism is considered a developmental delay; others classify it as a learning disability, a communication disorder, or a behavioral disorder. See chapter 10 on students with other disabilities for further discussion of autism.

● Reading and Language Arts

For children with developmental delays, language development may be the most important educational objective in the child's IEP. Tools that break down the elements of reading and language into component parts are

Software to teach reading skills

particularly important, because they allow a teacher to carefully monitor specific skills.

A program such as Scientific Learning's Fast ForWord employs methods and systems that work for children with a variety of language and reading problems. This program succeeds because it strategically breaks down the reading process, provides immediate feedback, and is engaging to use. Its graphics and sounds are simple and not too distracting for a child focused on learning incremental elements of reading (see Figure 4.4). Sessions can be adjusted for short time periods as well. Hundreds of public and private schools have used Fast ForWord training for daily monitoring and feedback about a child's progress in learning basic language arts skills. The program has one major drawback—its significant expense.

The Start-to-Finish Books series, by Don Johnston Incorporated, is also designed to teach basic reading skills. These packages include a CD-ROM, a paperback book, and an audiocassette tape. Students can read the paperback book, hear it via the cassette tape, or watch and listen via the CD-ROM. The program provides students with multiple ways to "read" the book and encourages them to practice with the paperback book once they have heard it a number of times.

The Simon Skills Pack, also from Don Johnston Incorporated, teaches phonics and spelling skills. Within this package, the program Simon Sounds It Out (Figure 4.5) teaches phonics and phonological awareness through a friendly, patient, on-screen tutor. The tutor systematically introduces beginning sounds and word families and helps students use these sounds to

● FIGURE 4.4

A screen from Fast ForWord

Source: Photo courtesy of Scientific Learning, Oakland, CA.

● FIGURE 4.5

A screen from Simon Sounds It Out

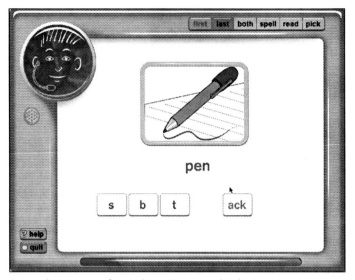

Source: Photo courtesy of Don Johnston Incorporated, Volo, IL.

successfully build increasing numbers of words. Pictures and animation provide word context. The tutor also tracks student progress and makes instructional decisions to optimize learning and prevent frustration. Through the tutor, the program offers positive feedback and automatically increases the difficulty level as each level is mastered. When students have mastered every level of Simon Sounds It Out, they can progress to Simon Spells for spelling instruction. The Simon Skills Pack thus takes your students step-by-step down the road to becoming successful readers.

● Mathematics

Computer software can be a good tool to reinforce basic mathematical skills for students with developmental delays. Computer work should be supplemented, though, by as much use of concrete manipulatives as possible. For example, with an addition game, a student should have access to Unifix cubes (small blocks) sitting next to the computer, or should have a good "counting-up" strategy. The cubes will allow the student to touch something concrete as he or she counts out numbers. A popular counting-up strategy is to have the student say the first number in an addition problem out loud, then use fingers to count up to the total. For example, if the student is adding four and three, he or she would say "four" and then touch three fingers to count up to seven.

Software for basic math skills and concepts

Access to Math (Don Johnston Incorporated) is an example of software that can help students with basic skills in four operations: addition, subtraction, multiplication, and division. This program looks like a worksheet, and you or your student can select specific mathematics skills as the focus: for instance, single-digit addition or subtraction with borrowing. The program provides prompts on the screen and immediate feedback.

Match Time (Attainment Company) teaches time concepts with four progressively difficult levels that feature both digital and analog clocks and increasingly challenging vocabulary. Another program from the same company, Basic Coins, helps students identify the correct value from an assortment of coins. Basic Coins is touch-screen and IntelliKeys compatible, features helpful for students who cannot use the keyboard.

TECHNIQUES FOR YOUR CLASSROOM

Freeware and Shareware

When you want simple programs that focus on a small element of mathematics or reading, look on the Internet for freeware and shareware, affordable alternatives to commercial applications. **Freeware** is exactly that—free software programs that you can either download or run on the Internet. **Shareware** is software that you can try out for free; if you decide to keep it and use it, you are supposed to pay a small fee, usually twenty-five dollars or less.

Probably the most popular types of freeware programs are games that can be played right on the Internet, using a web browser with the free Shockwave plug-in. The Shockwave website at **http://www.shockwave.com/** has games available that are worth looking at just to know what your students might be doing. However, the majority of these games can hardly be called educational.

Disney (**http://www.disney.com/**) also produces freeware programs that can be played on the company website. Board games, similar to Concentration, coincide with the Disney movies currently in theaters or video stores. Again, these programs may have limited educational use, but they can certainly help a student work on fine motor skills (while mousing) or on memory.

LittleFingers Software (**http://www. littlefingers.com/**), a company that provides affordable shareware programs (usually under twenty dollars), has several that can help with math readiness. Checkers' Playroom is a math readiness program in which students can practice shape recognition, counting, matching patterns, and ordering. Bone Appetit is a free program that gives students practice in identifying coins as they buy and sell bones. Space Worms teaches counting and identification. In this application, the student counts the number of birds, apples, or other objects until reaching the required number. The software requires the child to recognize numbers and has an option for an alphabet game as well.

● School-to-Work Transition Programs

Older students with developmental delays often have a major IEP focus on transition. The transition from the classroom to other environments can be a challenging time, and the student needs support and encouragement. Some students with developmental delays go on to work programs and vocational training, while others continue in a traditional academic program.

Learning computer job skills

Preparing for work often includes giving students basic computer and clerical skills. Learning to type, to use a word processor and other applications, and to operate a computer in general can be valuable job skills for the future. Transition programs designed to provide these skills might include the use of typing software, computer hardware instruction, and computer-based training. For example, the DO-IT program in Washington state (**http://www. washington.edu/doit/**) provides students with disabilities with computing skills and prepares them for employment in information technology professions (Burgstahler, Wild, and Smallman, 2000). The Attainment Company produces a program called Computers at Work that provides basic skills in data entry and order processing.

Type to Learn by Sunburst Technology (**http://www.sunburst.com/**) can be used with any student who is working on keyboarding. The simple layout and feedback provided in the program make it a logical choice for students with developmental delays.

SELECTING DEVELOPMENTALLY APPROPRIATE MATERIALS

Students with developmental delays have goals that range from readiness skills in reading and mathematics to vocational training in transition programs. Using technology to support these goals can provide individualized instruction and extensive opportunities for practice. Finding software that meets student needs, that matches educational goals, *and* that is developmentally appropriate, can be an exhausting task for the teacher or parent. Sometimes the most telling information comes from watching the child use the program and seeing what, if any, developmentally appropriate practices it encourages.

The task analytic approach (discussed in chapter 3) is an especially useful method for making specific decisions about how you will use different technologies for developmentally delayed children with developmental delays. Each form of technology should be a carefully calibrated tool that allows the child to have experiences specifically matched to cognitive, social-emotional, and physical needs. Remember that students with developmental delays have educational needs as varied as those of any other group of individuals. Some have no difficulties whatsoever with mathematics; others simply cannot perform calculation tasks. Therefore, a particular technology application may be perfect for one student and entirely inappropriate for another.

One of the four core principles stated at the beginning of this book is that teachers should use applications in different ways with different students. This is especially important for students with developmental delays because their cognitive, social-emotional, and physical needs vary so widely. Lemonade Stand, for example, can be a complex game or a simple cause-and-effect lesson. You can restrict the student's use of this game to manipulating one variable (such as the number of glasses of lemonade to make) or allow the student to vary elements as complex as advertising costs and price per glass. Similarly, Storybook Weaver (The Learning Company) can help a child create a story or serve as a more basic planning tool, using the scenes in the program to help a child organize his or her day.

As a teacher, you will have to decide how to focus the time of a student with a developmental delay. You can allow hours and hours of practice with letter-sound correspondence. You can focus on teaching life skills, such as counting back change. You can use technology that helps develop communication skills. You have many decisions to make, and for all such choices, you must understand each student's particular needs.

SUMMARY

Although we still often hear the terms *mental retardation* and *brain damage,* they bring up too many stereotypic images of children who will never be able to function in society. Many educators now prefer the term *developmental delay,* which suggests that these children can indeed become productive citizens if they are offered the right educational experiences.

In general, people with developmental delays are those who develop at a rate significantly below average and who experience difficulties in learning and social adjustment. On intelligence tests, they typically score lower than 95 percent of the population. Often they also show delays in motor development and in receptive and expressive language skills.

Occupational and physical therapy, speech/language therapy, and psychotherapy can all be useful for children with developmental delays. As a teacher, you will find it essential to work as a team with specialists in these fields.

Instruction for children with developmental delays should be balanced between basic skills and age-appropriate social and language skills. Technology applications can be useful in all of these areas.

Simple skill-and-drill applications often succeed with developmentally delayed children. Frequently, though, a child will need to develop readiness skills before using the technology; simple, inexpensive toys and switches serve as excellent teaching tools. Reading and language arts software can help students learn such basic skills as phonics and spelling as well as assist them with their expressive language. Math programs for children with developmental delays typically focus on a single area of mathematics, and many of these are available as shareware or freeware.

Technology can also help teach life skills and skills for social interactions. Children with communication difficulties can use communication boards and electronic communicators to express their ideas. School-to-work transition programs frequently use technology to help older students acquire basic computer and clerical skills.

KEY TERMS

developmental delay (p. 84)
phenylketonuria (PKU) (p. 85)
Down syndrome (p. 86)
fragile X syndrome (p. 86)
communication board (p. 96)
freeware (p. 99)
shareware (p. 99)

RESOURCES FOR FURTHER INVESTIGATION

Online Resources

Alliance for Technology Access.
http://www.ataccess.org/
This organization can help you find a local technology center.

The Arc.
http://www.thearc.org/
Formerly known as the Association for Retarded Citizens, this organization posts position statements related to mental retardation and provides information about education, training, and support for parents and teachers.

American Association on Mental Retardation.
http://www.aamr.org/
> This professional organization provides the federal definition of mental re-
> tardation, posts position statements, lobbies for the rights of people with
> mental retardation, and hosts research studies. Members include parents,
> teachers, and other professionals.

Assistive Technology Industry Association.
http://www.atia.org/
> Under the "Members" link you'll find a list of technology companies that
> sell assistive and adaptive technology and instructional software.

The Down Syndrome WWW Page.
http://www.nas.com/downsyn/
> A resource site containing information from the Down syndrome
> listserv, a worldwide email–based group of parents, teachers, and
> other professionals.

The Eunice Kennedy Shriver Center.
http://www.shriver.org/
> This division of the University of Massachusetts Medical School supports
> research to benefit people with disabilities and their families. The Shriver
> Center is home to one of the Mental Retardation/Developmental Delays
> Research Centers that examine the causes (and possible cures) of mental
> retardation and developmental delays. The Shriver Center also helps par-
> ents understand the diagnosis and treatment of children with developmen-
> tal delays.

Product Resources

Attainment Company. Verona, WI.
http://www.attainmentcompany.com/
> Publishers of MatchTime, Personal Success, Basic Coins, and Computers
> at Work.

Don Johnston Incorporated. Volo, IL.
http://www.donjohnston.com/
> Publishers of Access to Math, the Start-to-Finish Books, Monkeys Jump-
> ing on the Bed, and the Simon Skills Pack.

Scientific Learning. Oakland, CA.
http://www.scilearn.com/
> Publishers of the Fast ForWord suite of applications.

Print Resources

Gage, N. L., & Berliner, D. C. (1998). *Educational psychology,* 6th ed. Boston: Houghton Mifflin. An educational psychology text that offers a good introduction to developmental theories of Piaget, Erikson, Vygotsky, and others.

Gessell, A. (1950). *The first five years of life. A guide to the study of the pre-school child.* New York: Methuen. This book is about the developmental process of mentally retarded children for the first five years of their life.

Gessell, A., & Amatruda, C. (1941/1947). *Developmental diagnosis. Normal and abnormal child development: Clinical methods and pediatric applications.* New York: Harper & Row. This classic book is a comparison of the developmental progress of a normal child and an abnormal child. It also speaks about clinical methods and pediatric applications.

Lorton, J. W., & Walley, B. L. (1979). *Introduction to early childhood education.* New York: Van Nostrand. This book is about early childhood education for children with mental retardation.

Snowman, J., & Biehler, R. (2003). *Psychology applied to teaching,* 10th ed. Boston: Houghton Mifflin. Like the Gage and Berliner book, this is an educational psychology text with substantial sections on major developmental theories plus a chapter on the common physical, social, emotional, and cognitive characteristics of children at different ages.

TECHNOLOGY FOR STUDENTS WITH EMOTIONAL AND BEHAVIORAL DISORDERS

FOCUS QUESTIONS

As you read this chapter, think about the following:

- What do we mean when we speak of *emotional and behavioral disorders*? What types of conditions does this category include?

- What programs do students with EBD participate in?

- What academic goals does a student with EBD have in my classroom?

- In what ways can technology support the program for a student with EBD?

This chapter presents information on using technology to support the learning and behavioral objectives of students with emotional and behavioral disorders (EBD). Children with EBD can vary greatly in their behavior. An individual child may struggle with depressive symptoms such as sadness, negative self-evaluations, and social withdrawal, or display aggressive outbursts and other externalized behaviors. Some children will have a mixture of symptoms that interfere with learning and social relationships. Students with EBD have diverse learning and behavioral objectives and may be placed in either self-contained or inclusive classrooms.

Technology can help make school a more pleasant and successful experience for these students and their teachers. Technologies available today help monitor and treat emotional problems, provide alternative instructional strategies, and offer outlets for communication and creative expression.

WHAT ARE EMOTIONAL AND BEHAVIORAL DISORDERS?

Students with **emotional and behavioral disorders** have serious and persistent difficulties that can be described by a psychiatric diagnosis. When special educators identify a student as having an emotional or behavioral disorder, they are assisted by a psychologist or psychiatrist who conducts a thorough evaluation and makes a diagnosis of the disorder, using the categories listed in the *Diagnostic and Statistical Manual of Mental Disorders* (American Psychiatric Association, 2000). This medical manual, known as the DSM, groups behaviors in clusters corresponding to common clinical disorders.

Controversy about diagnosis and labeling

A great deal of controversy exists among those who work with children with behavioral disorders regarding the practice and method of diagnosis. Professionals disagree about whether and how to label children; some use a medical perspective and others prefer an ethnographic understanding of psychological and behavioral difficulties. Some researchers believe that almost all emotional and behavioral disorders can be traced to a difference in the chemical makeup of the child's brain and that such children need medication assistance. Others claim that the majority of psychiatric disorders result from environmental factors such as diet, abuse, neglect, or other traumatic experiences or relationships and that psychosocial and behavioral interventions can better resolve the student's difficulties. Most mental health professionals resolve this version of the "nature versus nurture" debate by referring to the ample evidence that biology and experience are equally powerful and mutually influential contributors to emotional and behavioral health. Although the specific cause(s) of a child's emotional and behavioral problems may never be identified, a combination of medical and psychosocial treatments helps many individuals.

In discussing emotional and behavioral disorders, the Individuals with Disabilities Education Act (IDEA) uses the term *serious emotional disturbance* and defines it as follows:

IDEA definition

. . . a condition exhibiting one or more of the following characteristics over a long period of time and to a marked degree that adversely affects educational performance—

- An inability to learn that cannot be explained by intellectual, sensory, or health factors;
- An inability to build or maintain satisfactory interpersonal relationships with peers and teachers;
- Inappropriate types of behavior or feelings under normal circumstances;
- A general pervasive mood of unhappiness or depression; or

- A tendency to develop physical symptoms or fears associated with personal or school problems. [Code of Federal Regulations, Title 34, Section 300.7(b)(9)]

As defined by the IDEA, the condition includes schizophrenia but does not apply to children who are socially "maladjusted."

Students who have behavioral or emotional disorders can exhibit widely varied types of behavior, including both internalized behavior (such as depression or an eating disorder) and externalized behavior (such as verbal outbursts). Other common characteristics and behaviors include these:

- Hyperactivity (short attention span, impulsiveness)
- Aggression or self-injurious behavior (acting out, fighting)
- Withdrawal (failure to initiate interaction with others; retreat from exchanges of social interaction, excessive fear or anxiety)
- Immaturity (inappropriate crying, temper tantrums, poor coping skills)
- Learning difficulties (academic performance below grade level)

Children with behavioral disorders do not necessarily have learning disabilities. Estimates show, however, that approximately 60 to 80 percent of students with EBD also have some form of learning disability (Weinberg et al., 1995).

Children with the most serious disorders may exhibit distorted thinking, excessive anxiety, bizarre motor acts, and abnormal mood swings. Medically, they are sometimes identified as having a psychotic disorder. Psychoses can range in severity from temporary and mild to recurring and severe (as in schizophrenia). Many children without emotional disturbances may display some of these same behaviors at various points in their development. However, when children have serious emotional disturbances, problematic thinking and behavior continue over a long period of time. Their behavior signals that they are not coping with their environment or peers; indeed, a child with a severe psychological disturbance will have great difficulty acting or interacting effectively.

TYPES OF **E**MOTIONAL AND **B**EHAVIORAL **D**ISORDERS

Defining and classifying emotional and behavioral disorders is a challenging task. The fourth edition of the DSM contains eighteen major classification areas, into which are grouped more than two hundred specific disorders. In the following sections we will discuss the emotional and behavioral diagnoses you are most likely to encounter as a teacher.

● Conduct Disorders

Types of conduct disorder

The diagnosis of *conduct disorder* is based on antisocial behavior, and it says little about the child's inner life, motives, and disabilities. The disorder is classified by type: aggressive versus nonaggressive, and overt (with violence or tantrums) versus covert (with lying, stealing, and/or drug use).

A distinction between "socialized" and "under-socialized" activity is common. For example, much serious adolescent misconduct takes place in street gangs, many of whose members are loyal to their friends and able to make a reasonable social adjustment as adults. The situation is much more serious when the misbehavior begins early and the child has no friends. Such children are more likely to develop "antisocial personality disorder" as adults, continuing a pattern of socially maladjusted behavior. Early symptoms include stealing, running away from home, habitual lying, cruelty to animals, and fire setting. As the child grows older, the pattern may develop into vandalism, malicious mischief, truancy, drug and alcohol use, and various forms of violence, from school bullying to robbery, assault, and rape.

Children, and especially adolescents, with conduct disorders seem callous, hostile, and manipulative. As students such children can present a real challenge to teachers, who often feel frustrated and angered by their noncompliance and disregard for others. The support of the school counselor is helpful, as well as that of school-based therapists or outside professionals who are involved with the child. Developing a working relationship with parents can be important, too.

● Emotional Disturbances

Subtle disturbances most common

Emotional disturbances can include eating disorders, depression, excessive stress reactions, and many others. Sometimes the disturbance is not readily visible. Emotional disturbances that manifest themselves in violence and similar extreme behavior occur less frequently than those with a more complex and subtle effect. And some disorders, such as eating disorders and substance abuse, are deliberately—and often successfully—hidden by the child. Some children develop a negative or maladaptive pattern of behavior and interaction that becomes deeply entrenched and seems to be part of their personality.

● Personality Disorders

The DSM defines a *personality disorder* as "an enduring pattern of inner experience and behavior that deviates markedly from the expectations of the individual's culture, is pervasive and inflexible, has an onset in adolescence or early adulthood, is stable over time, and leads to distress or impairment." The following descriptions of a few categories of personality disorder illustrate these maladaptive patterns:

Categories of personality disorder

- *Schizotypal personality disorder:* "a pattern of acute discomfort in close relationships, cognitive or perceptual distortions, and eccentricities of behavior."
- *Borderline personality disorder:* "a pattern of instability in interpersonal relationships, self-image, and affects, and marked impulsivity."
- *Dependent personality disorder:* "a pattern of submissive and clinging behavior related to an excessive need to be taken care of."

● Anxiety Disorders

Fearful, avoidant behavior

Anxiety disorders are a prevalent form of emotional difficulty, sharing with depression the dubious honor of most pervasive emotional disorder. Children with anxiety may be fearful, nervous, shy, and preoccupied, and they often strive to avoid the source of the anxiety—if there is a specific source.

Anxiety disorders include generalized anxiety disorder, phobias, panic disorder, obsessive-compulsive disorder, and posttraumatic stress disorder. Separation anxiety disorder specifically affects children and adolescents and can make separation from home and loved ones extremely distressing.

● ADHD

Doubtless, the most prevalent behavioral disorder in schools today is **attention-deficit/hyperactivity disorder (ADHD)**, sometimes referred to as **attention deficit disorder (ADD)**. According to the U.S. Department of Education (2000), approximately 3 to 5 percent of the school-aged population have ADHD. So what is ADHD? The official description in the DSM reads in part as follows:

ADHD defined

The essential feature of Attention-Deficit/Hyperactivity Disorder is a persistent pattern of inattention and/or hyperactivity-impulsivity that is more frequent and severe than is typically observed in individuals at a comparable level of development.

ADHD can include nine specific symptoms of inattention and nine symptoms of hyperactivity/impulsivity. Individuals with ADHD may know what to do, but do not consistently do what they know because of their inability to efficiently stop and think prior to responding, regardless of the setting or task.

The DSM describes four subtypes of ADHD: inattentive, hyperactive/impulsive, combined (showing both inattention and hyperactivity), and "not otherwise specified." See the feature "Types of ADHD" for a list of the specific symptoms for each type.

In most cases, the characteristics of ADHD become evident in early childhood. Children and adults who have ADHD are often restless and easily distracted, they struggle to sustain attention, and they are impulsive and impatient. These characteristics can result in serious social problems and

---

P RINCIPLES AND PRACTICE | **Types of ADHD**

The following list summarizes the four subtypes of ADHD as they are described in the DSM.

- *Inattentive type:* The individual experiences at least six of the following characteristics:
  1. Fails to give close attention to details or makes careless mistakes
  2. Has difficulty sustaining attention
  3. Often appears not to listen
  4. Struggles to follow through on instructions
  5. Has difficulty with organization
  6. Avoids or dislikes tasks requiring sustained mental effort
  7. Often loses things necessary for tasks or activities
  8. Is easily distracted
  9. Is forgetful in daily activities
- *Hyperactive/impulsive type:* The individual experiences at least six of the following characteristics:

  1. Often fidgets with hands or feet or squirms in seat
  2. Has difficulty remaining seated
  3. Runs about or climbs excessively (in adults may be limited to subjective feelings of restlessness)
  4. Has difficulty engaging in activities quietly
  5. Often acts as if "driven by a motor"
  6. Talks excessively
  7. Blurts out answers before questions have been completed
  8. Difficulty waiting in taking turns
  9. Interrupts or intrudes upon others
- *Combined type:* The individual meets both the inattentive and the hyperactive/impulsive criteria.
- *Not otherwise specified:* The individual demonstrates some characteristics of the disorder, but the number of symptoms is insufficient to reach a full diagnosis. These symptoms, however, disrupt everyday life.

impairment of family relationships, and of course can block success at school.

Prevalence ●   In addition to the 3 to 5 percent of the school-aged population who have the full ADHD syndrome, without symptoms of other disorders, another 5 percent to 10 percent have a partial ADHD syndrome or one that includes other problems, such as anxiety and depression.

Another 15 to 20 percent of the school-aged population may show transient symptoms that resemble ADHD, but ADHD is not diagnosed if these behaviors produce no impairment at home and school or are clearly identified as symptoms of other disorders.

Gender and age affect the ways in which people with ADHD express their symptoms. Boys are about three times more likely than girls to have symptoms of ADHD. Symptoms of ADHD decrease with age, but symptoms of associated features and related disorders increase with age. Between 30 and 50 percent of ADHD children still manifest symptoms into adulthood.

A significant percentage of children who have ADHD also have a learning disability, such as dyslexia. It can be difficult to sort out which of their learning difficulties stem from processing deficits for specific learning tasks, such as letter identification or phonemic awareness, and which are due to distractibility and attention problems. As a teacher, you must approach each child's learning profile individually, because you will find variations in strengths and weaknesses among all children, regardless of whether they carry the same diagnosis.

ISSUES OF IDENTIFICATION AND TREATMENT

Use and abuse of medication

One of the most pressing issues facing parents and teachers of students with emotional and behavioral disorders is the use of medications to help control behavior. You have probably heard of children who take Ritalin, a drug often used to treat ADHD. According to a study published in the *Journal of the American Medical Association,* Ritalin prescriptions to children of ages two to four have increased dramatically in recent years (Zito et al., 2000). In 1996, the United Nations released a report stating that 10 to 12 percent of all male school children in the United States take Ritalin, a rate far surpassing that in any other country in the world (International Narcotics Control Board, 1996). The concern is that such medications may be overprescribed and that they may not have long-term effectiveness.

In light of this concern, what position should a teacher take? If a child consistently "acts out" in your classroom, should you assume that some kind of

The Ritalin Controversy: State Legislatures Respond

The use of behavior-modifying medications for students with any condition has always been a central issue in the minds of parents and teachers. In addition to concerns about side effects, many feel a natural desire to help children learn ways to manage their own behaviors.

Lately, Ritalin, a drug prescribed to many children with ADHD, has been a source of particular concern. In response to complaints of overprescription of Ritalin and similar medications used in the treatment of ADHD, some states have either passed or initiated legislation to limit or eliminate recommendations to parents that they seek drug treatment for their children. For example:

- In July 2001, Minnesota prohibited schools and child protection agencies from insisting that parents use drug treatments for disorders such as ADHD.
- In October 2001, a Connecticut law went into effect requiring that school personnel not discuss drug treatment with parents and that such discussions take place with physicians.
- Legislative action like that of Minnesota and Connecticut has been initiated in Arizona, New Jersey, New York, Utah, and Wisconsin.

Reporting these legislative actions, the *New York Times* noted an increase in the amount of direct advertising to consumers by pharmaceutical companies that make drugs similar to Ritalin. According to a Drug Enforcement Administration official interviewed by the *Times,* such advertising, while not illegal, breaches agreements made in a 1971 international treaty not to market controlled substances directly to consumers (Zernike & Petersen, 2001).

On September 30, 2001, the American Academy of Pediatrics published for the first time its guidelines for the treatment of ADHD. The guidelines state that greater evidence indicates the effectiveness of medication—that is, stimulants like Ritalin—in ADHD treatment than for behavioral therapy. However, the guidelines recommend using behavioral techniques in combination with medication, as well as monitoring medication for side effects and appropriate dosage (American Academy of Pediatrics, 2001).

As we consider ways to make the most of advances in technology, particularly in the area of medicine, we must consider the total impact on each child and make our decisions accordingly. As a teacher who may work with medical doctors, keep in mind that our greatest promise should be to "do no harm."

medication is necessary? If you see that one child who is taking a medication like Ritalin shows improved behavior, should you suggest that another child could benefit from the same treatment? The fact is that diagnosis of ADHD and other behavioral disorders requires careful assessment and ongoing evaluation. Although you may believe that something is definitely "different" about a particular student's behavior, you must consider carefully before labeling that student or coming to your own conclusions about the sort of treatment that would work best.

In addition to medications, treatment options include psychotherapy (particularly of the cognitive or behavioral management type) and social skills training. Even if it is determined that a child needs medication, behaviorally based treatment is often important as well.

Families of children with emotional disturbances may also need help in understanding their child's condition and in learning how to work effectively with the child. In fact, recognition is growing that many families, as well as their children, need support, respite care, intensive case management services, and a multi-agency treatment plan. More and more communities are working toward providing these "wrap-around services," and a growing number of agencies and organizations are actively involved in establishing support services in the community. Parent support groups are also important, and organizations such as the Federation of Families for Children's Mental Health and the National Alliance for the Mentally Ill (NAMI) have parent representatives and groups in every state.

Support for the family

TEACHING CHILDREN WITH EMOTIONAL AND BEHAVIORAL DISORDERS

Children who have had neuropsychological or psycho-educational testing have a distinct advantage in planning an optimal educational program. Skilled evaluators will include a list of detailed recommendations for teaching strategies and remedial activities for the child. As a teacher, you may want to consult with the evaluator or with the school psychologist regarding those specific recommendations. The child's IEP may include psychotherapy or counseling as a related service. Speech and language therapists and occupational therapists can also make significant contributions. The more data that converge to support conclusions and recommendations for a specific child, the more certain you can be that your educational program will target that child's needs and tap his or her abilities.

Children with EBD may receive treatment in the regular education classroom or in a residential treatment center. Chapter 2 describes the series of steps a teacher must take before deciding on the treatment environment. These decisions are made with the input and relevant evaluations of the entire IEP team.

Educational programs for students with EBD must include attention to mastering academics, developing social skills, and increasing self-awareness, self-esteem, and self-control. Career education (both academic and vocational) is also a major part of secondary education and should be a part of the transition plan in every adolescent's IEP.

Among the successful school-based techniques are these:

Effective techniques

- Life Space Crisis Intervention (Fescer and Long, 1998) is a program in which teachers and other caregivers learn to identify and defuse classroom crises by being supportive of students' emotions and understanding the cycle of a crisis. This program has proved successful with nondisabled students as well as those with emotional and behavioral disorders. The program identifies specific strategies that can help teachers and students work through problems.

- The Conflict Resolution Program (Crawford and Bodine, 1996) is designed to help students work through conflicts by creating safe classrooms and focusing the curriculum on principles of problem solving. The program helps schools select students and adults to act as mediators, focuses on peer-to-peer conflict resolution, and builds on the support of the greater community. Research on conflict resolution and mediation programs show that they can be effective in reducing violence in schools and helping students feel more confident about solving problems (Carpenter, 1993, 1994; Smith, 1996).

It is difficult to be knowledgeable about every intervention being promoted for use with EBD students. Many teachers and school administrators lack the time required for intensive review of research. Furthermore, they often lack easy access to sources that publish research supporting or refuting intervention effectiveness. The field of EBD is not immune to what Achenbach (1996) calls "Bad Information." In his essay on the pervasiveness and types of misleading, incomplete, and just plain wrong information in our society, Achenbach argues that it is becoming increasingly difficult to distinguish bad information from good. One reason is that bad information looks a lot like good information. Another is that bad information can be widely disseminated and endorsed by apparently reputable professionals.

Green (1996) offers a set of guidelines to help families determine the soundness of a given intervention for children with autism. These suggestions are also helpful for teachers and school administrators who determine interventions for students with EBD:

Guidelines for evaluating an intervention

- If it sounds too good to be true, it probably is. Professionals need a healthy skepticism about new interventions, particularly those offering dramatic results. As Achenbach (1996) says, "It takes an extremely practiced eye, a kind of controlled skepticism that never quite slides into abject nihilism, to spear Good Information from the thick bog of Bad."

- Be cautious when the only evidence given is testimonials, particularly when those promoting the intervention stand to gain financially from sales of the program.
- Ask to see published research supporting the intervention.
- Ask someone skilled in reading and interpreting research for help in understanding the research.
- Ask many questions, such as these:
  How do you know this works?
  What is the basis for your claim?
  Who has conducted the research?
  Where is the research published? Are these peer-reviewed, scientific journals?
  How many children with EBD have been included in the studies? How many improved? What specifically were the improvements?

The most basic criterion is this: Avoid interventions that pose a risk of harm to the student, either directly by use of the procedure or indirectly as a result of nonuse of other procedures (Freeman, 1993; Kauffman, 1996). Hippocrates, referring to the treatment of diseases, said, "Make a habit of two things—to help, or at least, to do no harm" (cited in Bartlett, 1992). Educators should adhere to these words of wisdom when selecting interventions for students with disabilities.

On a more basic level, you can take steps to make your classroom suitable for children with EBD. Establish clear rules and a regular routine, for instance. Offer many hands-on, creative activities to provide outlets for the children's energy. The accompanying feature, "Focal Points for Teaching Students with

T ECHNIQUES FOR YOUR CLASSROOM

Focal Points for Teaching Students with EBD

- Focus on structure and routine.
- Create clear rules and consequences.
- Use rewards for good behavior.
- Ignore bad behavior when possible.
- Be consistent.
- Offer lots of praise and encouragement and create a supportive environment.

- Use plenty of hands-on activities.
- Use art activities to provide an enjoyable outlet for emotions.
- Utilize extracurricular activities—they help channel energy.
- Give all students responsibility in the classroom.
- Involve families and friends.

EBD in Your Classroom," offers some additional guidelines. Think about which of these techniques you can put into practice in your own teaching.

ACADEMIC AND SOCIAL PROBLEMS: A VICIOUS CYCLE

Behavioral and emotional difficulties can lead to academic failure, just as academic frustration can lead to behavioral and emotional problems. Sometimes students fall into a vicious cycle: frustration and failure trigger maladaptive behavior that further obstructs learning and increases the likelihood of failure.

Finding where the cycle began

When you teach a student identified as having an emotional or behavioral disorder, you may puzzle about where the cycle began. Take a look at the times of day that the child acts out or is unruly; is it always during math period or during PE? Perhaps the behavior is the result of frustration with algebra. Maybe it stems from a poor physical self-concept. Context and timing can provide clues to improve your understanding of the problem.

The interaction between student and teacher can also affect a child's behavior: does he or she do better or worse with a specific teacher? You can ask yourself whether you have feelings or responses toward this child that differ in a distinct way from your feelings and responses toward other children. Does he or she make you feel more concerned, frustrated, nurturant, or angry than most of your students? Do you change your way of relating when it comes to this student? Answering these questions can lead you to positive change.

Typically, programs that focus on children with behavioral disorders attend first to the child's behavior problems, and academics run a distant second. In residential treatment, for example, the focus of "school" is on getting along in a group setting, not necessarily on the curriculum. An additional problem for students with behavioral and emotional disorders is that this area of special education has the greatest number of teachers with emergency or alternative certification, rather than specialized training and certification in the field of emotional and behavioral disorders. This is unfortunate, especially because these are the children who stand to benefit most from quality academic education.

These intensive programs work to help children function in everyday life, and many achieve that goal. Nevertheless, children with behavioral disorders can and do benefit from quality academic instruction. In programs where classroom conditions are inadequate, children not only suffer from diminished academic content and opportunity, but they often learn negative behaviors in response to problems in the classroom environment.

Technology Applications for Students with Emotional and Behavioral Disorders

Computer use can help students with emotional and behavioral disorders simply because the child receives instruction at his or her own pace. Researchers have found that any instruction that is appropriately paced and matched to the student's skill level not only produces academic success, but leads to less of the unwanted behavior (Lambert, 1988; Keilitz and Dunivant, 1986; Catalano, Loeber, & McKinney, 1999; Sugai and Horner, 1999). Because the computer can be a multimedia, individualized, personalized, and private instructional tool, some students with emotional and behavioral disorders benefit greatly from using it. The following sections look at ways of using computer software in several areas of the curriculum.

Benefits of self-paced instruction

● Mathematics and Science

Across all areas of disability, mathematics instruction receives less time than any other subject—even though, for most children, mathematics takes the longest to learn. In the case of children with behavioral disorders, time is the most significant factor in academic skill building. These students need increased time and exposure to all areas of mathematics, from basic mathematical drills to advanced applications.

Like mathematics, science is often left out of the curriculum for children with emotional and behavioral disorders. However, as any scientist will tell you, science can be an engaging opportunity for interdisciplinary study. A focus on science allows all children to apply what they learn and make connections to the "real world." Recall what chapter 3 said about how students with learning disabilities benefit from project-based learning, which involves using a project or problem as the focus of a series of lessons. Students with EBD often find project-based learning an excellent approach in science and math. For instance, students can explore a local riverbed or use a telescope in an astronomy lesson, giving them the opportunity to focus attention beyond the classroom, find new areas of meaningful interest, and use talents that may not flourish in a formal classroom setting.

Project-based learning for math and science

Because children with behavioral disorders often have learning disabilities, you may want to begin your search for math and science instructional tools by looking at the applications suggested in chapters 3 and 4, on learning disabilities and developmental delays. These programs may be equally successful with the EBD child, depending upon the child's difficulties.

● Reading and Language Arts

Students with behavioral disorders are more likely to have difficulty in reading and language than other students (Gable, Quinn, Rutherford, and Howell, 1998). These limited language skills may in fact add to frustration and aggression at school. Helping students strengthen language skills may give them alternative ways to communicate about how they are feeling. They may decide that schoolwork is something they are capable of—and perhaps actually good at!

Software applications can provide individualized and remedial instruction to improve language skills. These are some notable examples:

*Software for improving
language skills*

- Earobics (Cognitive Concepts) can increase phonemic awareness, such as the ability to identify common sounds, and it builds up to recognition of phonemic blends (for example, "cl" and "sh"). The software has variations designed for young children through adults.

- Away We Go! (Scientific Learning), an alternative to Fast ForWord (also made by Scientific Learning and discussed in other chapters), can be used at home as well as in school. This program helps develop phonemic awareness, sound discrimination, and rhyming.

- Phonics Alive! (Advanced Software) is based on prescriptive teaching and drills on sounds and letters. It progresses to teach grammar and upper-level language skills.

- That's a Fact, Jack! Read (Tom Snyder Productions) focuses on literature with a game-show format that can be motivating for students.

- Reading for Meaning (Tom Snyder Productions) is a reading comprehension program that uses the Internet. Students log in for personalized lessons.

- Text-to-speech technologies such as the Kurzweil 3000 (see chapter 3) can scan text and read aloud to the student who is having problems in decoding.

Web addresses for the publishers of these software packages and other programs mentioned in this chapter are listed in the Resources for Further Investigation at the end of the chapter.

● Problem Solving and Organization

Software that allows a student to organize material and use it creatively, such as SimCity and SimTown by Maxis, can help develop problem-solving skills and organization. The Encarta Researcher, included with the Encarta Encyclopedia (Microsoft), helps students organize research notes and keep track of citations while they are on the Internet.

Using Spreadsheets for Monitoring Behavior

A spreadsheet program can help students with emotional and behavioral disorders keep track of their behavior. The simple process of having students use the spreadsheet graphing functions to chart their behavior can help them identify how often and when they engage in disruptive behaviors or depressive thoughts. This process can give the children a greater sense of control and improve their ability to make adaptive behavioral choices. In therapeutic settings, the data children themselves gather can give the child and his or her therapist a shared understanding of the child's experience and a structure for setting treatment goals.

● Social Skills

In light of all the emphasis on specific knowledge and skills instruction, it is interesting to note that technology also has worked well to present knowledge and skills associated with social interactions in many settings. For instance, Blaiwes and Weller (1978) reported a successful six-year effort to improve the leadership and management practices of Navy recruit company commanders using computer-based instruction. In the later multimedia realm, Schroeder, Hall, and Morey (1985) found that interactive videodisc presentations were effective in teaching interpersonal skills for leading small groups.

Video-based CD-ROMs for learning social skills

Two programs by the Attainment Company are designed to help improve social skills. Working It Out Together is a video-based CD-ROM designed to teach peer mediation. Students view an actual conflict played out by real students and analyze the resolution that took place. The Community Success CD-ROM is designed to help students prepare for community outings by learning appropriate interactions and understanding public instructions and information.

● The Internet and Students with EBD

The Internet offers many opportunities for students with emotional and behavioral disorders to communicate with others, to learn, and even to receive therapy. But all of these Internet uses require thought and planning.

Communication and Therapy ● Some researchers and teachers have suggested that the Internet can be an excellent medium for communication

Elizabeth Atkins

Elizabeth works on a poetry assignment for her writing course.

Elizabeth Atkins is a thirteen-year-old girl with depression and an eating disorder. She currently lives in a residential treatment center, away from her home and school. She was placed in the center about six months ago after attempting suicide. The main purpose of this placement is to provide a twenty-four-hour-a-day setting where she can be supervised and where her health can be carefully monitored.

Prior to this move, Elizabeth was in the gifted and talented program at her junior high. Some research indicates that highly gifted girls are more likely to be depressed than other groups. Elizabeth has always excelled in math and science, is known to be a creative writer, and was active in drama and theater at her school. According to her mother, Elizabeth has always been surrounded by many friends and until recently has seemed to be a normal, well-adjusted young person.

About a year and a half before she attempted suicide, Elizabeth began losing weight and became overly conscious of her appearance, so much so that her mother and father discussed having her see a family therapist. But Elizabeth convinced her parents that she was doing just fine and promised to keep her weight up. She hid the fact that she continued to lose weight; she became more and more depressed about her appearance and more worried about her prospects for the future. Over the winter holidays she attempted suicide by taking her mother's prescription migraine medication. Elizabeth now sees a psychologist three times a week, and she is taking antidepressant medication.

PROFILE CONTINUED

Since she came to the treatment center, Elizabeth has found technology an extremely valuable tool. She has enrolled in an online course in creative writing through a local university, giving her the opportunity to earn college credits. Her instructor in the online course knows that she is young but has no idea that she is in a treatment center. She submits creative writing papers to her instructor and peers in the class and helps others in the class with editing and suggestions. She likes the fact that she can be "normal" in this course; "no one judges me for how I look," she says. She has expressed an interest in becoming a part-time writer and college writing teacher. Overall, she seems more interested now in becoming healthy and returning to school.

opportunities and even for private therapy for children with EBD. These children may be more willing to "open up" online, feeling they are in a safe and protected environment. This is true for some children, but caution requires that the types of communication children engage in be carefully chosen and monitored. In particular, online "therapists" must be checked out; they may be preying on those who seem susceptible.

Web safety rules

Children need some "web smarts." Always advise students of web safety rules such as "Don't give out information about yourself, your parents, or your family." Many children are willing to exchange private information for a reward or toy. According to a report by the Annenberg Public Policy Center (Turow & Nir, 2000), older children (ages thirteen to seventeen) are more likely than younger ones (ages ten to twelve) to give out personal information, and boys are more likely than girls to say it is all right to supply sensitive family information in exchange for a gift.

Online Academic Studies ● The accompanying profile describes Elizabeth Atkins, a student with EBD who is using an online course to learn, to express herself, and to build her self-confidence. The DO-IT program, sponsored by the University of Washington (**http://www.washington.edu/doit/**), brings similar opportunities to many students with disabilities.

DO-IT Scholars are high school students with disabilities who have an interest in and aptitude for science, engineering, or math and a desire to go to college. The program supports them in their interests in the following ways:

Facets of the DO-IT program

- *Internetworking.* DO-IT Scholars receive loaned computers, modems, software, and adaptive technology for use in their homes. They learn how to use powerful computer systems and the Internet to access information and to communicate with vast numbers of people in the expanding global electronic community.

- *Mentoring.* DO-IT Scholars gain valuable academic, career, and personal insights by communicating electronically with mentors. Mentors are students, faculty, and practicing scientists, engineers, and mathematicians, many of whom have disabilities themselves.

- *Summer study.* DO-IT Scholars attend summer study programs at the University of Washington. They experience college life by participating in science, engineering, and mathematics lectures and labs, living in university residence halls, and practicing skills that will help them be more independent and successful in a college setting.

USING TECHNOLOGY TO ASSESS EMOTIONAL AND BEHAVIORAL DISORDERS

Software to aid assessment

The 1997 amendments to the Individuals with Disabilities Education Act (Public Law 105-17) require that a **functional behavioral assessment** (FBA) be conducted for children who exhibit behavior that interferes with the educational process. This means that school personnel must conduct preintervention assessments of the functional relationships between a child's behavior and the suspected causes of that behavior. Subsequently, school personnel must develop intervention plans based on the information this assessment provides. The law did not, however, define the actual FBA process. As a result, educators and researchers must themselves establish the procedures for functional behavioral assessment. Some recent software products are proving useful in this respect.

The Student Adjustment Inventory (SAI) from MetriTech (**http://www.metritech.com/Metritech/Products/sai.htm**) assesses common affective-social problem areas for upper elementary, junior high, senior high, and beginning college students. The inventory assesses seven problem areas: self-esteem, group interaction and social processes, self-discipline, communication, energy/effort, learning/studying, and attitude toward the learning environment. In the words of its developers, "The Student Adjustment Inventory is designed to help students understand their own attitudes and feelings regarding these problem areas."

Charles Greenwood, a researcher at the University of Kansas, has successfully applied technology to the assessment of student behavior by developing the EcoBehavioral Assessment Systems Software (EBASS), a highly sophisticated computer program (**http://www.lsi.ukans.edu/jg/ebass.htm**). Educators use EBASS to document student behavior, teacher behavior, and the instructional features of the classroom environment. A trained observer uses a laptop computer to record classroom events such as the student reading aloud, the teacher at the front of the room teaching, or the subject of the lesson. EBASS then analyzes the information and isolates the impact of individual variables on student learning. The program also graphically portrays the effect of individual variables on behavior over time. Teachers use the EBASS data to analyze how effective different behavior modification techniques are in changing behavior. Researchers Woolsey, Gardner, and Harrison (2001) found this system effective in helping teachers identify strategies that increased positive behavior. Khang and Iwata (2000) found that a system like this can be an affordable and effective way to assess and treat problem behaviors.

SUMMARY

Emotional and behavioral disorders, also known as serious emotional disturbance, can involve any of a wide range of behaviors, from depression, extreme anxiety, and social withdrawal to aggressive outbursts such as fighting and tantrums. Children with EBD often struggle to maintain appropriate relationships with their peers and teachers. Many have learning disabilities as well. The most extreme cases involve psychoses such as schizophrenia.

Attention-deficit/hyperactivity disorder (ADHD), sometimes referred to as attention deficit disorder, is an especially controversial condition because of its prevalence and the use of medications to control students' behavior. Children with ADHD exhibit symptoms such as inattention, distractibility, restlessness, hyperactivity, and impulsive behavior.

Appropriate treatments for emotional and behavioral disorders are often the subjects of fierce debate. More and more children are being medicated (with Ritalin for ADHD, for example), but the drugs' effects and suitability are being questioned. Psychotherapy or behavioral therapy may be better alternatives for many children with EBD. Any decisions about medication or therapy should be based on a thorough evaluation by a health professional so that the treatment program will suit the child's individual needs.

You will find that evaluations and testing by professional evaluators will give you a good starting point for teaching a child with EBD. You may also secure help from other professionals, such as the school psychologist, speech and language therapists, and occupational therapists. Although certain programs claim to assist teachers in crisis intervention and conflict resolution, you must remain cautious and skeptical about inflated claims. You can always use basic classroom techniques such as setting clear rules, giving rewards for good behavior, offering plenty of encouragement, providing hands-on and creative activities, and giving all students a chance to exercise responsibility in the classroom.

Many programs for children with EBD pay great attention to behavioral problems while neglecting the child's academic progress. This is not a wise approach. Children with EBD can learn, given the right opportunities; in fact, their academic frustrations may trigger their behavioral and emotional problems.

Computer technology offers individualized, personalized instruction at the child's own pace. In math, students can develop skills with the same types of software described in chapters 3 and 4 on learning disabilities and developmental delays. In reading and language arts, computer programs can assist with skills ranging from phonemic awareness to reading comprehension. Software like SimCity helps develop problem-solving skills and organization. Spreadsheet programs enable students to monitor their own behavior and begin to understand their own emotional crises. Other programs improve social skills by teaching students how to interact with others and handle disputes. Internet use can provide extra opportunities for learning and the chance for students to "open up" in a new environment. Through the Internet, students can also receive mentoring and, in some cases, online therapy.

Technology plays an additional role in assessing students with emotional and behavioral disorders—both in the functional behavioral assessment that, by law, must precede intervention and in the analysis of how classroom activities affect students' behavior and learning.

KEY TERMS

emotional and behavioral disorders (p. 106)
serious emotional disturbance (p. 106)
attention-deficit/hyperactivity disorder (ADHD) (p. 109)
attention deficit disorder (ADD) (p. 109)
functional behavioral assessment (p. 122)

RESOURCES FOR FURTHER INVESTIGATION

Online Resources

American Academy of Child and Adolescent Psychiatry.
http://www.aacap.org/
    The academy's site offers fact sheets, answers to common questions, a glossary of mental illnesses and their symptoms, and more.

American Psychological Association.
http://www.apa.org/
> The APA website contains a large amount of research and information about EBD and about human behavior and development in general.

Computers and ADD.
http://www.ncpamd.com/ComputersAndADD.htm
> Here you will find an article by Carol Watkins, MD, from the Northern County Psychiatric Associates in Baltimore, Maryland, on how technology can help students with ADHD. The site contains a great deal of information about emotional and behavioral disorders from the perspective of medical caregivers.

Council for Children with Behavior Disorders.
http://www.ccbd.net/
> CCBD, a division of the Council for Exceptional Children, is a professional organization for teachers who work with children with EBD. The site has information for parents and students, as well as advocacy information and research.

Federation of Families for Children's Mental Health.
http://www.ffcmh.org/
> The Federation of Families is a parent-run organization to help parents and students understand, treat, and overcome behavioral and emotional disorders. The site includes position statements and links to other sites for more information.

Focus Adolescent Services.
http://www.focusas.com/BehavioralDisorders.html
> This site discusses a range of behavioral disorders and treatments.

National Alliance for the Mentally Ill (NAMI).
http://www.nami.org/
> NAMI is an advocacy group for people with all types of mental illnesses and emotional disorders. The site has a large database of conditions with information about treatments and support groups.

National Attention Deficit Disorder Association.
http://www.add.org/
> This site has many articles relevant to teachers and parents of children with ADHD.

Product Resources

Attainment Company. Verona, WI.
http://www.attainmentcompany.com/
    Publishers of Working It Out Together and Community Success.

Away We Go! Oakland, CA: Scientific Learning.
http://www.ScientificLearning.com/ or http://www.scilearn.com/

Earobics. Evanston, IL: Cognitive Concepts.
http://www.earobics.com/

Encarta Researcher (part of Encarta Encyclopedia). Redmond, WA:
Microsoft.
http://www.microsoft.com/

Kurzweil 3000. Burlington, MA: Kurzweil Educational Systems.
http://www.kurzweiledu.com/

Maxis. Walnut Creek, CA.
http://thesims.ea.com/us/
    Publishers of SimCity and SimTown.

Phonics Alive! Mona Vale, NSW, Australia: Advanced Software.
http://www.phonicsalive.com/

Tom Snyder Productions. Watertown, MA.
http://www.tomsnyder.com/
    Publishers of That's a Fact, Jack! Read and Reading for Meaning.

Print Resources

Adamec, C. (1996). *How to live with a mentally ill person: A handbook of day-to-day strategies.* New York: Wiley.

Barkley, R. A. (1990). *Attention deficit hyperactivity disorder: A handbook for diagnosis and treatment.* New York: Guilford Press.

DuPaul, G., & Stoner, G. (1994). *ADHD in the schools: Assessment and intervention strategies.* New York: Guilford Press.

Goldstein, S. (1997). *Managing attention and learning disorders in late adolescence and adulthood: A guide for practitioners.* New York: Wiley Interscience.

Jordan, D. (1996). *A guidebook for parents of children with emotional or behavior disorders.* Minneapolis: PACER Center.

TECHNOLOGY FOR STUDENTS WITH COMMUNICATION DISORDERS

FOCUS QUESTIONS

As you read this chapter, think about the following:

- What is involved in communication?

- What are communication disorders?

- What instructional needs does a student with a communication disorder have?

- How can technology be incorporated into the instruction of a student with a communication difficulty?

Technology provides many useful helps to students who have communication disorders. These students generally work with related services specialists, such as speech-language therapists rather than a special education teacher.

As a regular classroom teacher, you will need to learn and use the techniques these specialists use. You'll use them in your classroom on a regular basis—and help your students and their parents use the same techniques at home and elsewhere. Thankfully, technologies available today enable students with communication disorders to communicate and participate within the regular classroom environment. In this chapter we describe software and adaptive tools that can encourage success in the classroom and in society for students who have a variety of difficulties in communication.

WHAT ARE COMMUNICATION DISORDERS?

Communication disorders include disorders of speech and language. To many people, the terms *communication, speech,* and *language* mean essentially the same thing, but to special educators and speech-language therapists these are significantly different concepts that require different approaches to instruction:

Distinguishing three terms

- *Communication,* the broadest of the three terms, includes both speech and language. Communication also includes cues such as intonation, pace of speech, and stress (emphasis), as well as nonverbal information such as gestures, facial expressions, and eye contact.
- *Language* can be defined as a socially shared code or system of conventions that represents and expresses ideas through symbols and rules. All language is communication, but not all communication involves language. Language can be spoken, written, or signed.
- *Speech* is a particular type of language. Speech refers to language that involves the coordination of oral-neuromuscular movement to produce sounds.

Figure 6.1 illustrates the relationships among communication, language, and speech. As you can see from the figure, communication is the broadest of the three terms, speech the narrowest.

An interesting illustration of the differences among language, speech, and communication can be seen in children with normal hearing who are born to deaf parents. A child born to parents with hearing impairments may have difficulty with speech but not with language if she starts using sign language at a young age. Infants who learn sign language can begin to communicate their needs as early as six months. Speech, however, may be delayed or different because the child has little experience with the spoken word.

Although some students have difficulty with both speech and language, the majority of students can be identified as having either speech or language disorders. According to the U.S. Department of Education (2000), 10 percent

● FIGURE 6.1

The relationships among communication, language, and speech

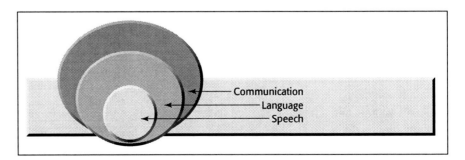

of school students have some sort of communication disorder. The majority of these students are not in special education; 87 percent study in the regular classroom and work with a speech/language therapist.

Many children with other exceptionalities also have communication disorders. For example, children with autism or pervasive developmental disorder are likely to have language delays (see the profile later in this chapter). The special education teacher, regular education teacher, and language therapist must work together to design teaching and learning techniques for these children.

● Speech Disorders

Disordered speech is significantly different from the usual speech of others, and it detracts from the communicative abilities of the speaker. It is important to point out that differences in speech such as dialects or accents are not disorders. Only when a child's speech is significantly different from normal speech in his or her developmental context should the child be sent for a speech and language evaluation.

There are three types of **speech disorders:**

Types of speech disorders

1 **Articulation disorders** account for the majority of speech disorders. The child is unable to produce sounds appropriate for his or her age. Articulation disorders also include substitution or omission of sounds: for instance, saying "th" for "s," or leaving out the "l" sound in words like *clue* (saying "coo" instead).

2 **Fluency disorders** are interruptions in the flow of speech. These can include difficulties with the rate, rhythm, or repetition of sounds, syllables, words, or phrases. Examples of fluency disorders include stuttering and "cluttering," in which the forward pace of speech is confused or full of extra sounds.

3 **Voice disorders** are impairment of the voice itself, and they affect the quality, pitch, or intensity of the person's speech. For example, students with voice disorders may sound hoarse all the time or speak too loudly.

● Language Disorders

The term *language disorder* indicates a difficulty in understanding and using speech, the written word, or another symbol system. According to the American Speech-Language-Hearing Association (ASHA), a language disorder is "the impairment or deviant development of comprehension and/or use of a

P RINCIPLES AND PRACTICE   Language Disorder or Language Delay?

One issue in the field of communication disorders is the current understanding of the terms *language disorder* and *language delay*. These terms are not interchangeable.

A *language delay* means that the student has the ability, but fails to use or understand language in an age-appropriate way. The child is progressing normally, but slowly. A child with a *language disorder* is missing one or more pieces of the language skills puzzle, and the result is different language.

This important distinction allows the speech-language therapist to decide which techniques are appropriate for the child. The child with a language delay would need interventions to help him or her move along the normal developmental path for language. The child with a language disorder may need special techniques and alternative strategies to overcome particular deficits in language skill.

spoken, written, and/or other symbol system" (Bernthal and Bankson, 1993). The disorder may involve any of the following elements of language:

Potential elements in a language disorder

1 Form
   - **Phonology:** the sound system of a language and the rules that cover sound combinations: in English, for instance, a short *a* sounds like "ahhh"; an *x* usually sounds like "ks"; a *ph* sounds like "f."
   - **Morphology:** the structural system for words and word construction in a language. For example, the verb *run* can become the participle *running*. One way to remember the meaning of *morphology* is to think about how words "morph" into other words when the meaning changes.
   - **Syntax:** the system in a given language for combining words to form sentences. English sentences typically put the subject first, then the verb, then the direct object, and so on.

2 Content
   - **Semantics:** the meaning of words and sentences in a language. Skill in semantics includes the ability to visualize or interpret what someone has said or what you have read and to understand it.

3 Function
   - **Pragmatics:** the ability to combine form and content to communicate functionally and in socially acceptable ways—for example, knowing when to say what to whom.

A student with a language disorder may be unable to understand spoken language or to produce sentences and share ideas in an age-appropriate way. The roots of these comprehension and production difficulties may reside in any of the areas of language just named.

● Auditory Processing Disorders

General deficit in processing information from the ears

Some communication problems cannot be categorized strictly as speech or language disorders. Rather, they are broadly classified as *auditory processing disorders*. This term describes a general deficit in processing sensory information from the ears. A child with a learning disability who has such a disorder may take longer to "process" a question or direction and can appear to be ignoring you, not attending to the class activity, or acting disobedient. Because auditory information processing takes longer for such a child, the information may never reach short- or long-term memory. A child with an auditory processing disorder needs specific techniques to attend to the important parts of language and speech.

Meeting Needs of Students with Communication Disorders

Your role as the teacher

Most children with communication disorders work in the regular classroom and receive special instruction in speech and language, usually with a speech-language therapist. As the classroom teacher, you can help identify the child with a communication disorder by listening to how the child speaks and what he or she says. The key is to look for consistent differences in language use, articulation, and comprehension. When a child consistently misspeaks (saying "th" for "s," for example), you should recommend to the parents that the child be evaluated for speech-language therapy. You must have parental permission before you have a student tested or evaluated in any way.

When you invite a speech-language therapist (or any other specialist) into your classroom, it is important to prepare your students for the visit. Letting the students know that a visitor will be observing the class can reduce their fears and curiosity. Talk with the student you are concerned about, and let him or her know that you've asked someone to come help you understand what is going on in the classroom. Try to make the student comfortable. Avoid giving a special lesson on that day or treating the student differently than you normally would. Allowing the specialist to observe the normal

● FIGURE 6.2

A classroom speaking
checklist

Uses correct grammar and sentence structure	Always	Sometimes	Never
Formulates sentences correctly	❏	❏	❏
Uses verbs correctly	❏	❏	❏
Forms plurals correctly	❏	❏	❏
Asks grammatically correct questions	❏	❏	❏
Uses pronouns correctly	❏	❏	❏
Meaning	**Always**	**Sometimes**	**Never**
Uses age-appropriate vocabulary	❏	❏	❏
Uses concepts of location, time, and quantity	❏	❏	❏
Uses humor, sarcasm, and figures of speech appropriately	❏	❏	❏
Produces complex sentences	❏	❏	❏

Source: Adapted from J. B. Tomblin, H. L. Morris, and D. C. Spriestersbach. (2000). *Diagnosis in speech-language pathology*, 2nd ed. San Diego, CA: Singular.

classroom routine will ensure that both you and your students receive the help you've asked for.

Prior to the classroom observation the specialist may ask you to fill out a checklist like the one shown in Figure 6.2. This checklist can help you organize your concerns and focus your own observation of the child. Again, it is absolutely necessary that you obtain parental permission before you have a student tested or observed.

Once a child has been identified as having a communication disorder, he or she will receive special instruction, most likely outside the regular classroom. This instruction will include techniques to help the child with specific needs: for instance, practice in understanding language rules or exercises to teach the child how to position his tongue while he says a sound. The child will spend only a small portion of total school time in speech-language therapy, so it is important to ask the specialist for techniques you can use in the classroom to reinforce what the child is learning. Be sure to share with the parents what the speech therapist is doing so they can complement this work at home.

Here are some recommendations to keep in mind with regard to language and speech development for any child (with or without an identified communication disorder):

Guidelines for promoting speech and language development

- *Modeling.* When a child mispronounces a word or is not clear, restate what the child has said. That is, instead of saying "What?" or "I don't understand you," say, "Did you just ask me to _____?" Think of a one-year-old child you know. When he or she says, "Baa," you might say "Ball" or "Bottle," but you would never say "What?" to a child so young. Help the child by modeling what you think she is trying to say. It is frustrating for her to repeat herself with no feedback about what you did or did not understand.

- *Making speech clear and easy to understand.* Organize your classroom and student seating so that all students can easily see and hear you. Reduce background noises as much as possible, and eliminate distractions like an open door into a noisy hallway. Make sure a student knows that you are addressing him or her before you start speaking. Be sure to speak loudly enough for your students to hear, and if you know you tend to be a fast talker, slow down!

- *Promoting language exchange.* Show students you are interested in them by listening. This may sound simple, but in a typical classroom of twenty-five students we all ignore what someone is saying from time to time. Let your students know you are interested by making time every day to talk to each of them—when they arrive at school in the morning, at lunch, recess, or during a small-group activity. Be sure to encourage students to talk to you and each other and elaborate on their comments and responses. By creating an environment where all students regularly talk, you will encourage language development in all children.

- *Read to your students.* At every level, students can increase their language skills by hearing text read aloud. Read a news story to your high school students, make time after lunch to read to your first graders, or read a student's paper to the class. Although some students will be reluctant to read aloud during a lesson, all students appreciate a good story, and reading to them is a great way to model interacting with text. It also helps by differentiating between conversational speech and reading, increasing vocabulary, and providing a quiet break for everyone in the classroom.

TECHNOLOGY APPLICATIONS FOR STUDENTS WITH COMMUNICATION DISORDERS

Children with communication disorders benefit from many types of technological applications and tools. Some popular off-the-shelf programs can help students develop basic skills in speech and communication. Specialized software programs and hardware, such as augmentative and alternative communication devices, find use in clinical settings.

TECHNIQUES FOR YOUR CLASSROOM

Tips for Using Instructional Software for Remediation

When you use instructional software for remediation purposes, research suggests that you follow these guidelines (Fitzgerald & Koury, 1996):

1 Control the size of the instructional set. For example, break down concepts into smaller pieces. Instead of asking students to understand all of the aspects of estimation in one lesson, focus on vocabulary in the first lesson, then on procedures in another. Don't try to push too much information at one time.

2 Use time delay and controlled response times to build fluency (speed of reading). This means that lessons should give students "wait time" to think about what they've read and opportunities to break reading texts down into smaller sections.

3 Maintain learning and build successful rates of responding by interspersing mastered items with new items.

4 Provide immediate and meaningful feedback.

5 Limit the use of extraneous graphics and arcade-game formats in skill-and-drill materials.

6 Provide opportunities for the learner to use hypermedia enhancements and speech synthesizers to support understanding.

These recommendations are particularly important to the child with a communication disorder. When you have children with communication difficulties in your classroom, carefully evaluate the software applications you are using to be sure they meet these standards.

The process of choosing technology appropriate to the student with a communication disorder includes assessing needs, defining goals, identifying characteristics or features that best meet the individual's communication needs, and matching these features to the most suitable system. In addition, this assessment can provide information on funding sources and lead to recommendations for training and follow-up services, particularly if the child needs the equipment at all times. This section provides an overview of technologies for use with children with communication disorders.

● Speech Skills

Earobics (Cognitive Concepts) software series teaches language skills through a process called phonemic awareness. The idea behind this process is that students learn to read and use language through the ability to recognize and manipulate speech sounds (Torgesen & Mathes, 1998). Earobics Step 1 provides activities and games to practice elements of phonemic awareness such as auditory attention and letter-sound correspondence. Earobics Step 2 helps students with skills such as auditory memory and segmenting. This program can provide helpful instruction on these specific language skills to students with communication and language disorders. Earobics CD is for older students who are working on the skills presented in Step 1; here the games are more mature, though the instructional method remains the same. Many teachers find Earobics a useful tool in their classrooms for students with a wide range of language and reading skills, including students for whom English is a second language. Make sure, though, that you have headphones for your computer before you start using Earobics; the amount of sound that it uses can be distracting to other students.

Software to aid speech assessment and instruction

Video Voice (Micro Video Corporation) software is used in both speech-language assessment and instruction. Speech-language therapists can use the program to assess students by forming a visual picture of the child's speech and comparing it to "normal" speech in terms of pitch, frequency, and articulation. The system offers reports helpful not only in analyzing a child's speech during an initial assessment session, but also in providing updated information and reports as the child works with the program. During instruction, the student uses games and activities to practice speech. For example, Pitch Painting allows the student to paint with different colors depending on the pitch he or she is using. The package also includes games that can help students with rhythm, articulation, and amplitude. You can download a demonstration version of this software from the company's website (**http://www.videovoice.com/**).

A program called Tiger's Tale (Laureate Learning Systems) can help younger children work on producing voice sounds. The idea behind this program is that the child is helping a little tiger that has lost his voice, and the child must "speak" for the tiger to help the story move on. By recording and replaying the child's voice, the program can help children who are working on making speech sounds or having trouble with articulation. Laureate Learning Systems also publishes software programs designed to help with syntax and grammar. For example, the Words and Concepts Series helps students build language skills by teaching a core vocabulary and related adjectives. Swim, Swam, Swum helps students with irregular verbs through a series of games and practice activities.

LocuTour Multimedia, another company that specializes in software for students with communication disorders, offers a series of software applications that help students with articulation by providing direct instruction in speech sounds and pronunciation. In the Articulation I: Consonant Phonemes program, students look at photographs depicting words, listen to how each word is pronounced, and then practice saying the word. In the Phonology program, the student practices auditory discrimination skills and recognizing speech patterns. LocuTour also has a series of music CD-ROMs;

many children with stuttering or articulation difficulties seem able to sing with fewer problems.

Students use Visual Voice Tools (Edmark) to practice various speech skills, from making speech sounds to loudness and pitch control. The program contains seven different activities in which the student uses his or her voice to control the action on the screen. The program provides visual and auditory feedback to the user while focusing on pitch, loudness, and fluency. Visual Voice Tools is sold separately and is also included in SpeechViewer III (IBM), which was discussed in chapter 3. SpeechViewer III includes additional features that provide in-depth information about speech skills and offer a wide array of practice opportunities in pitch and loudness.

● Reading and Writing

Computer applications that provide productive practice in reading or prereading skills address three areas crucial for meeting the instructional needs of children with varying communication difficulties (Lyon, 1995; Wise and Olson, 1994):

1 Development of phonological awareness as a prereading skill

2 High-quality, context-free practice in specific word identification skills

3 Practice in reading as an element of comprehension

The best approach, research suggests, is to use teacher-directed instruction for initial skills acquisition, followed by computer-assisted instruction to decrease response time and gain mastery of skills (Fitzgerald & Koury, 1996).

Useful applications include programs that focus on reading readiness, sight vocabulary, phonics, comprehension, and whole language activities. Even simple software programs can assist students with reading readiness by helping them understand that words are made up of sounds represented by letters. Programs that teach beginning reading skills often use graphics and synthesized speech to introduce new sounds, words, or word segments. Here are a few examples:

Applications to teach reading skills

- In JumpStart Kindergarten (Knowledge Adventure), children hear a sound from the computer and click on the letter that corresponds to that sound.

- Simon Spells (Don Johnston Incorporated) and other spelling software programs use several formats to present spelling practice words: flashed words, scrambled words, missing-letter exercises, and activities in which students must identify the correctly spelled word or segment.

- That's a Fact, Jack! Read (Tom Snyder Productions), uses a gameshow motif to help students review books they have read. This software can develop vocabulary as well as improve understanding and reading fluency.

Applications to teach writing skills

Tools such as Co:Writer and Write:OutLoud, both produced by Don Johnston Incorporated (see chapter 3), help children who have communication disorders. Like students with learning disabilities, these students use the programs to produce written documents and stories and to gain a sense of accomplishment. Another useful writing help program is WriteAway (Information Services), which works like the two Don Johnston programs by providing word-prediction and text-to-speech interaction. Programs of this type encourage the development of literacy skills important to children with communication disorders.

Proportional Reading is a specialized program designed to teach children with speech and language disorders. In this program, words are presented one at a time on the screen. The longer the word, the longer it stays on screen. When sentences are displayed, they are separated by intervals with no textual display. The software uses three basic steps:

Steps in using Proportional Reading

1 The user enters text into a computer. Text can be typed in, scanned, or copied from a CD-ROM, a diskette or hard disk drive, or the Internet.
2 The student chooses one of fourteen different speeds for reading the material. The student can change speeds instantly, or reread the current sentence or paragraph at a different pace.
3 Pausing the program, the student can take voice-activated audio notes or typewritten notes, look up a word, hear it pronounced and defined, or move to another part of the text.

The student can personalize the program to some extent by choosing font color and size and background color. Notes, five-level outlines, and two-sided flash cards can be created from the text. The computer presentation can be recorded on standard videotapes and loaned out for home use. A teacher can program any book or text to be read aloud in a real human voice (fluent speech) while the text is displayed on the screen, either one word at a time or one sentence at a time. More information, including research studies conducted by the creator of this program, is found at **http://www.proportionalreading.com/**. Proportional Reading has other features as well. A "Talking Dictionary" may prove useful for students with different types of exceptionalities, such as learning disabilities or mental retardation. It should be noted, though, that the software currently costs three hundred dollars and is available for the Macintosh operating system only.

Phonics-based software

Lexia Learning Systems produces two phonics-based interactive reading programs that help students gain decoding skills and lay the foundation for developing more advanced comprehension, fluency, and critical analysis skills. Phonics Based Reading (Figure 6.3) teaches fundamental reading skills to younger children. The program starts with short vowels and single-syllable words and moves gradually to more advanced material using engaging exercises and simple animation to maintain students' interest. Automatic branching provides supplemental material for students who are having difficulties. The program also loops back to provide extra work for students who advance initially by using their sight vocabulary but find that they cannot read more difficult words later on. Lexia's Reading SOS teaches basic reading skills to older students (grades four and up). Starting with short vowels and single-syllable words, this program moves—as quickly as the student is able—into silent *e,* hard and soft *c* and *g,* multisyllabic words, and reading in context. These two programs provide the skill-and-drill practice that students with communication disorders find helpful. Because the programs are phonics-based, they both focus on providing basic rules for decoding and sounding out.

Temporally modified speech

Many speech-language pathologists use Fast ForWord (Scientific Learning), which differs from phonics-based programs. Fast ForWord uses an instructional element known as **temporally modified speech,** or speech that is modified in terms of time. Theoretically, children with a language-based disability have difficulty discriminating between speech syllables such as *ba* and

● FIGURE 6.3

A screen from Phonics Based Reading, Version 2.2

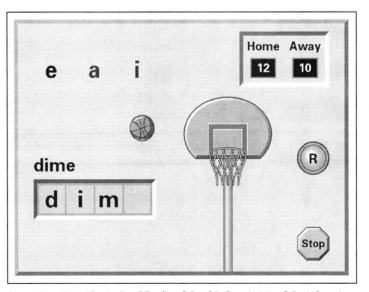

Source: From Lexia Phonics Based Reading ® Level 2, *Score* Activity, © Lexia Learning Systems, Inc. Reprinted with permission.

da that are characterized by rapid frequency changes occurring during the initial few tens of milliseconds. Therefore, in the initial lessons of Fast ForWord, the child hears sounds drawn out to allow the brain time to process and understand them. Over time, the sounds are speeded up, but they go no faster than the child can learn. If the child reaches a difficult point and begins to make errors, the computer automatically slows down until the child begins to process without errors. Some researchers believe that the intense repetition used with this technique strengthens the neural connections involved in the fast processing of sounds (Walton, Frisina, & O'Neill, 1998). Training with temporally modified speech has been demonstrated to improve both speech perception and language comprehension (Tallal, Miller, Bedi, & Byma, 1995).

Other synthesized voice applications like DECtalk (Force Computers) and the Kurzweil text-to-speech system (described in chapter 3) can provide an auditory clarification of words or word parts. Such programs show text on the screen and allow the student to select words for the computer to pronounce. Children with communication difficulties can receive feedback on words they find difficult, and instruction speed and level can be adjusted. Studies with such programs suggest that children with reading disabilities can make substantial gains in their reading skills with as little as six to eight hours of exposure (Blischak, 1999; Torgesen & Barker, 1995).

● Hypermedia

Software such as HyperStudio (Roger Wagner Publishing), an authoring tool discussed in chapter 3, has considerable potential for students with communication disorders. HyperStudio can combine and integrate various types of media—such as sound, text, graphics, video, and synthesized or digital voice—to create a finished product. Using sounds and pictures to tell a story, in addition to text, can help the student with a communication disorder express his or her ideas more easily. In the authoring process, students use peripherals such as scanners to import content, either visual images or text, and need not create all new pictures to help tell the story. HyperStudio includes text-to-speech capability, so that the words on the screen can be read aloud in the final product. The final product can be loaded onto the school's network or onto the Internet, or presented to other students in the class instead of an oral report.

Authoring tools:
HyperStudio

Researchers have found that using tools such as HyperStudio can benefit students with a range of reading and communication problems. For example, Boone and Higgins (1993) found that when students with learning and communication disabilities used a hypermedia reading program, reading scores improved. The hypermedia reading selections used in this study added

Chris Castellon

Chris takes a break from speech therapy to explore the playground.

Chris is four years old and has been diagnosed with a communication disorder. He and his twin brother, Michael, go to a prekindergarten program at his local elementary school in the morning five days a week, and every afternoon he attends a university center for speech, language, and hearing.

Chris was diagnosed with a language disorder when he was three. His speech and language are both delayed. His brother Michael, though not diagnosed with a language disorder, also has a language delay. Although communication disorders are not inherited, when one fraternal twin has a language or speech problem it is common for the other twin to also have communication difficulties. The boys have an older sister who has no language delays and was early in reaching each developmental milestone.

When the boys were infants, their mother believed that they were slow because of their low birth weight and prematurity. But Chris's increasing bizarre behavior and lack of any type of communication persuaded her and her pediatrician to take both boys to the local university for a thorough evaluation. Chris screamed if anyone tried to hold him or hug him, and he would stand against a wall, banging his head on it. He rarely made eye contact, and when he did, it seemed to Mrs. Castellon that he was "looking through me." The diagnosis relieved both Mr. and Mrs. Castellon in some ways, but they were concerned about how to ensure for their children the special treatments and therapies they needed.

At the local university they found a wonderful resource. The graduate program that trains speech-language pathologists has an on-campus treatment center, where both boys receive one-on-one instruction from trained therapists, participate in small-group learning activities and playtime, and work on several computer programs. Both boys use Fast ForWord for approximately

PROFILE CONTINUED one hour every afternoon, and the results of their work are sent via the Internet to the program's publisher, Scientific Learning, which then provides updated lessons. The boys also use a typing tutor, Reading Blaster (Knowledge Adventure), and JumpStart Kindergarten, both at home and at the center, gaining practice with basic keyboarding, spelling, and word usage.

The key to using these software applications is the level of consistency that both boys receive. They use the programs at the same time each weekday, and they have become comfortable with each program's interface (the look of the computer screen when the program is in use). Mrs. Castellon has seen some obvious signs of improved vocabulary and sentence length in Michael, and Chris is now more comfortable talking and expressing his wants and feelings.

computerized pictures, animated graphic sequences, definitions, synonyms, and digitized speech, and used links to words and pictures from the original basal text. The text was enhanced with three types of assistance: students selecting a key word from the text (those that were underlined and in boldface type) could see a graphic illustrating the meaning of the word, hear the word pronounced, or see a structural analysis of the word. During the second and third year, instructional enhancements were added for understanding syntactic and semantic structures in the text and using comprehension strategies. The lessons were integrated into the normal activity pattern of the students as they moved from teacher-directed reading groups to more independent activities. The project accumulated longitudinal information on five separate subgroups, with particular attention to the reading progress of low-achieving students in regular education classrooms. Hypermedia programs such as these—built into the curriculum and integrated into the school day—have proven more effective than drill-and-practice programs for students with reading and communication disabilities (Nelson and Masterson, 1999).

● Augmentative and Alternative Communication Tools

To assist children with communication disorders, teachers and parents may turn to a specific type of adaptive and assistive technology known as **augmentative and alternative communication (AAC)** tools. These can be defined as any technique or aid that supplements, replaces, or enhances conventional communication methods such as speech or writing. When a person cannot communicate effectively with traditional methods, these tools enhance (augment) or completely replace (serve as an alternative for) the customary modes of communication.

Although they sound specialized, AAC tools may include some types of tools mentioned in other sections of this book, such as communication boards, special keyboards, and text-to-speech software. In fact, most of us incorporate AAC methods into our communication when we use facial expressions, head nods, or hand gestures. Telephones, fax machines, typewriters, and computers can all serve as AAC devices. Other well-known technologies with AAC potential include teletypewriters (TTY) and telecommunication devices for the deaf (TDD), which are discussed in the chapter on hearing disabilities.

Many forms of AAC have been developed specifically for people with severe communication difficulties. These forms typically fall into two categories: *aided techniques,* such as communication boards and electronic devices, and *unaided techniques,* such as sign language and gestures. As with all methods of integrating technology into an exceptional student's program, an interdisciplinary team conducts an assessment to determine the most effective AAC intervention for an individual. The team traditionally includes a speech-language therapist, an occupational therapist, the student, his or her family members, and you, the classroom teacher.

Categories of AAC

Low-Tech AAC Devices ●
Communication boards are typical low-tech devices, relatively inexpensive and easy to create. The "board" is just a flat surface on which language choices are displayed using pictures, photographs, textured materials, letters of the alphabet, words, symbols, or any combination of these. The illustrations can involve everyday objects—for instance, a soda can, a cup, a toy, or a candy bar. The child uses a finger, headwand, light pointer, or eye-gaze to point out needs and ideas.

Manual communication boards

Typically, manual communication boards are an introduction to AAC, although they do not always precede use of high-tech devices. They have proven beneficial as a communication aid for individuals who are just beginning to recognize abstract concepts through pictorial representations; as a tool for emergent literacy; and for individuals who have difficulty responding to auditory feedback. They are also an important component for high-tech users, both as a complement to an electronic device and as a backup system.

High-Tech AAC Devices ●
High-tech AAC systems typically fall into two broad categories: dedicated communication systems and computer-based communication systems. Dedicated devices are stand-alone systems designed for communication. They incorporate voice and can include printers and other features. Computer-based systems are typically laptop computers outfitted with communication software and, commonly, a speech synthesizer. Such configurations can be used for applications other than communication.

Electronic devices that "speak"

The majority of high-tech AAC devices generate language through pictures, symbols, traditional writing, or a combination of these. Pictures or symbols may represent a word, phrase, sentence, or concept. Two or more pictures sequenced together create a phrase or sentence. The language is then "spoken," using synthesized speech, digitized speech, or a combination. *Synthesized speech* uses a computer chip to generate spoken words from written text, based on phonetics. *Digitized speech,* an actual recording of an individual's voice, requires more memory than synthesized speech. If digitized speech is the sole output method, it eliminates the ability to communicate spontaneously, because every word, phrase, and sentence must be thought out beforehand and recorded in the device.

Many devices allow language creation on different levels. For example, the first level may be used to represent communication concerning activities at home, the second level for school activities, and the third level for community-related activities. Other systems have a single level but allow students to generate unique messages by combining or sequencing pictures in different ways.

Systems that rely on traditional orthography require users to spell out messages. Techniques such as word prediction and automatic expansion of abbreviations can enhance the user's speed. Obviously this kind of system puts higher cognitive and sensory/perceptual demands on the user than a system based on pictures.

The SpeakEasy Communication Aid (AbleNet) and the DigiCom communication board (Great Talking Box Company; see Figure 6.4) are two examples of high-tech communication devices. Both students and teachers can use them to identify symbols and to hold prerecorded messages.

DIFFERENT TECHNOLOGIES FOR DIFFERENT STUDENTS

When you teach a child with a communication disorder, you will likely work in concert with speech-language therapists and other specialists. You as classroom teacher should make sure that all the technologies employed by the various people involved complement one another, and that all work to meet the unique needs of each child. You must look at the whole picture.

Multiuse applications

As you have noticed, many technologies suggested in this chapter are mentioned earlier in the book—for instance, Co:Writer, Fast ForWord, and Jump-Start Kindergarten. Remember Principle 3 from the opening chapter: applications can be used in different ways with different students. Having access to these off-the-shelf programs can help children with even the most severe communication disorders gain language skills and improve self-esteem. Conversely, some of the more specialized programs mentioned in this chapter

● FIGURE 6.4

The DigiCom communication device

Source: Photo courtesy of The Great Talking Box Company, creator of the Digicom Communication Device. Picture communication symbols (PCS) are copyrighted © 1981–2002 Mayer-Johnson, Inc., and are used with permission.

can help children with mild communication problems, even if they have not been diagnosed as having a communication disorder.

SUMMARY

Communication disorders can include a wide variety of difficulties: speech disorders (involving articulation, fluency, or voice); language disorders (involving phonology, morphology, syntax, semantics, or pragmatics); and auditory processing disorders (general difficulties in processing auditory information). Most children with these disorders learn in a regular classroom, though they receive some services from specialists such as speech-language therapists. In the classroom you should be sure to use techniques that coordinate with and reinforce the instruction that children receive from specialists. You can also accomplish a great deal with simple techniques such as modeling what you think a child is saying, reading to your students, and making time to talk with each student individually every day.

Technology for students with communication disorders is as diverse as the disorders themselves. It includes off-the-shelf software to aid speech, reading, and writing; specialized computer programs designed expressly for children with speech and language disorders; hypermedia applications; and augmentative and alternative communication devices ranging from low-tech communication boards to high-tech synthesized speech systems. As the classroom teacher, it is your responsibility to make sure that all the technology choices add up to a sensible program that meets each child's particular needs.

KEY TERMS

communication disorder (p. 128)
speech disorder (p. 129)
articulation disorder (p. 129)
fluency disorder (p. 129)
voice disorder (p. 129)
language disorder (p. 129)
phonology (p. 130)
morphology (p. 130)
syntax (p. 130)
semantics (p. 130)
pragmatics (p. 130)
temporally modified speech (p. 138)
augmentative and alternative communication (AAC) (p. 141)

RESOURCES FOR FURTHER INVESTIGATION

Online Resources

American Speech-Language-Hearing Association.
http://www.asha.org/
   The American Speech-Language-Hearing Association is the main professional organization for speech and language pathologists. The organization holds a national conference every year as well as local chapter meetings. The ASHA website includes factual information about speech, language, and hearing disabilities, links to research, and information about contacting a communication specialist in your area.

Communication Disorders.NET.
http://www.communicationdisorders.net/
   This useful website has links to information about different communication disorders and information about using technology.

International Society for Augmentative and Alternative Communication.
http://www.isaac-online.org/

> This society publishes the journal *Augmentative and Alternative Communication* and offers a variety of online resources.

National Institute on Deafness and Other Communication Disorders.
http://www.nidcd.nih.gov/

> Part of the National Institutes of Health, the NIDCD website has a great section for kids and teachers. If you click on "Kids and Teachers," you'll find information on hearing (such as "How Loud Is Too Loud?") and about communication disorders. The "Parents" section has a nice section on speech and language milestones.

Product Resources

Assistive Technology, Inc. Newton, MA.
http://www.assistivetech.com/

> Dealer for Gemini communication devices and other products for people with communication disorders.

Earobics. Evanston, IL: Cognitive Concepts.
http://www.earobics.com/

> Software for building phonemic awareness.

The Great Talking Box Company. San Jose, CA.
http://www.greattalkingbox.com/

> Manufacturer of the DigiCom and other communication devices.

Information Services, Inc. St. John's, Newfoundland, Canada.
http://www.is-inc.com/

> Publisher of WriteAway software.

Laureate Learning Systems. Winooski, VT.
http://www.laureatelearning.com/

> Publisher of Tiger's Tale, the Words and Concepts Series, and other software useful for children with communication disorders.

Lexia Learning Systems. Lincoln, MA.
http://www.lexialearning.com/

> Publisher of Phonics Based Reading and Reading SOS.

LocuTour Multimedia. San Luis Obispo, CA.
http://www.learningfundamentals.com/
    A company that offers a variety of software for students with communication disorders, including Phonology and Articulation I: Consonant Phonemes.

Proportional Reading. Beverly, MA.
http://www.proportionalreading.com/
    Publisher of the Proportional Reading software.

Video Voice. Ann Arbor, MI: Micro Video Corporation.
http://www.videovoice.com/
    Software for both assessment and instruction in speech and language.

Visual Voice Tools. Redmond, WA: Edmark.
http://www.edmark.com/prod/vvt/
    A program with seven activities for practicing speech skills.

TECHNOLOGY FOR STUDENTS WITH HEARING DISABILITIES

FOCUS QUESTIONS

As you read this chapter, think about the following:

- What are the types of hearing disabilities?

- Why is terminology important to families and children with hearing disabilities?

- What sorts of educational needs does a child with hearing problems have?

- How do I integrate the child with a hearing disability into my class?

- How do people with hearing problems use technology, and what technological aids might I use in my classroom?

As a teacher in a typical school, sooner or later you will most likely have a student with a hearing disability in your classroom. Students with hearing disabilities bring a variety of strengths, weaknesses, and needs to the learning process. They will require your special attention to participate in hearing-based activities. However, new and emerging technologies allow these students to enter more fully into regular education than ever before. Through tools that encourage communication, the child with hearing disabilities can be "just another kid." This chapter discusses issues that arise in teaching students with hearing disabilities and presents technologies that both offer these students greater accessibility to learning and improve their communication opportunities.

WHAT ARE HEARING DISABILITIES?

Hearing loss affects a student's ability to speak and to understand spoken language. A person with deafness cannot process any linguistic information, and a person who is "hard of hearing" can process some linguistic information. The Individuals with Disabilities Education Act (IDEA) offers the following definitions:

IDEA definitions of hearing disabilities

- A **hearing impairment** is an impairment in hearing, whether permanent or not, that affects a child's educational performance. This definition includes children who have the capacity to receive some auditory stimuli, including speech and language; this capacity is known as *residual hearing,* which can be supported by the use of a hearing aid.

- **Deafness** is a severe hearing impairment that impedes the child's processing of linguistic information through hearing, with or without amplification. A student with this condition cannot receive sound in all or most of its forms.

In other words, the student with a hearing impairment or hearing disability can respond to certain auditory stimuli, whereas the student who is deaf cannot process any information through hearing. Students anywhere along the hearing continuum will, of course, require appropriate accommodations. During the 1998–1999 school year, about 1.3 percent of the students who

TECHNIQUES FOR YOUR CLASSROOM

What's the Right Term?

Although IDEA uses the term *hearing impairment,* many people dislike this wording, preferring to be called either "deaf" or "hard of hearing." For example, the National Association of the Deaf (NAD), which takes a clear and strong position on terminology related to deafness, states that people in the deaf community greatly resent the label *hearing impaired.* According to NAD, *hearing impaired,* although well-meaning and often considered politically correct, focuses on what people can't do and implies that a "hearing" standard is the only proper standard (National Association of the Deaf, 2001).

The words people use to describe themselves have importance and should be respected. Chances are, not every student you meet who is deaf or hard of hearing will be insulted by the term *hearing impaired,* but you should notice how the student describes him- or herself. Be sure to follow the student's lead. We use the term *hearing disability* in this chapter in an effort to be impartial in the terminology debate and respectful toward all people, be they hearing or not.

received special education services (and 0.1 percent of the overall school-age population) were classified as either hearing impaired or deaf (U.S. Department of Education, 2000).

● Degrees of Hearing Loss

Hearing losses can be more precisely described in terms of the degree to which hearing (the ability to receive sound) is impaired. Sound is measured in two ways:

- Intensity (loudness) of the sound, measured in decibels (dB)
- Frequency (pitch) of the sound, measured in hertz (Hz)

A hearing disability can occur in one or both areas and may affect one or both ears (NICHCY, 2001a).

Figure 7.1 shows two audiograms (graphs of hearing ability) that compare a person who has normal hearing to a person with a typical hearing loss. The individual represented in audiogram B cannot hear high-frequency sounds without a hearing aid. This person has difficulty understanding what others say, because much speech information, particularly for consonants, is inaccessible.

We typically classify degrees of hearing disabilities as follows:

Categories of hearing loss

1 Slight: 15–25 dB of hearing loss
2 Mild: 20–40 dB of loss
3 Moderate: 40–65 dB of loss
4 Severe: 65–95 dB of loss
5 Profound: more than 95 dB of loss

A child who cannot hear sounds at less than 90 decibels is considered deaf for the purposes of educational placement.

● Types of Hearing Loss

Hearing loss is further categorized into four types:

Four kinds of hearing loss

- **Conductive hearing loss** is caused by disease or obstruction in the outer or middle ear. An individual with this condition can usually use a hearing aid.
- **Sensorineural hearing loss** is the result of damage to the delicate sensory hair cells of the inner ear.

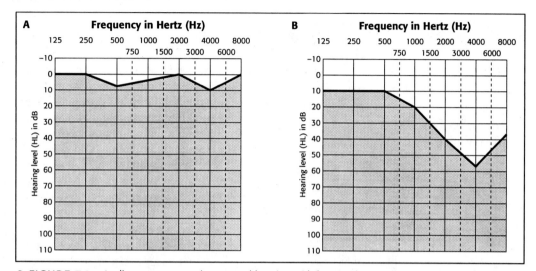

● **FIGURE 7.1** Audiograms comparing normal hearing with hearing loss. (A) Typical audiogram for a person with normal hearing. The shaded areas represent all sounds the person would hear. White areas indicate sounds the person would not hear. (B) Audiogram for a person with a moderate hearing loss.
Source: Adapted from Audiology Awareness Campaign, "Normal Hearing Audiogram" and "Sensorineural Hearing Loss Audiogram," http://www.audiologyawareness.com/hhelp/.

- **Mixed hearing loss** combines both conductive and sensorineural losses, meaning that a problem exists in the outer or middle ear as well as in the inner ear.
- **Central hearing loss** results from damage to the central nervous system, either in the nerves that occupy the pathways to the brain or in the brain itself.

In planning instruction for a student with a hearing disability, you may benefit from knowing which type of loss is involved, so that you can determine what technological aids are in place and which might further your student's educational goals. Technologies have developed to assist individuals with specific types of structural damage to the ear. For example, some types of hearing aids can help students with conductive hearing loss. Cochlear implants can assist persons with sensorineural damage.

● Effects of Hearing Loss on Language Development

Hearing loss can be either *prelinguistic*—that is, it precedes a child's language development—or *postlinguistic,* occurring after a child has acquired some degree of speech and language skill. Hearing disabilities can also be described as

P RINCIPLES AND PRACTICE | Hearing Tests

Hearing tests take many forms, but they often begin with the familiar hearing examination you might remember from your school days. In this test, called the *tone test,* you raise your hand when you hear a sound in one ear or the other. This classic test gives a rough estimate of hearing, but more specialized tests can identify minor hearing problems and isolate specific types of noises that the student finds challenging. These tests include the following:

• *Pure-tone audiometry.* The student puts on a pair of headphones and listens to tones at different pitch and decibel levels. Whenever the student hears a

tone in his left ear, he raises his left hand; for a tone in the right ear, he raises his right hand.

• *Speech audiometry.* Sounds are played through one earphone at a time. The sounds can range from whispers through normal speech and can include specific sounds such as a ticking clock. This test measures not only the decibel level, but also the ability to understand different elements of speech.

• *Specialized tests.* Specialized tests evaluate infants or people with more severe hearing loss to determine the degree of residual hearing. For example, with infants, the child usually sits on a parent's lap and sounds are played from behind the child. If the child turns to look for the sound, the tester determines that he or she heard it.

---

congenital or adventitious. *Congenital* means that the hearing loss is genetic or occurred at birth, and *adventitious* means that it occurred because of an accident or illness after birth.

Students who have lost their hearing postlinguistically or adventitiously may continue to use speech as a method of communication. Or they may use speech together with sign language or speech reading (lip reading). Students who lose their hearing before developing speech may not use speech at all, communicating solely with sign language. However, as with all other types of disability, no two students are alike. Trying to fit a student into a preconceived category will likely lead to embarrassment or frustration for you, the student, and the parents.

How age of occurrence affects hearing loss

The long-term educational effects of a hearing loss can depend to a great extent on the age at which the loss occurred. Children with hearing and those with hearing losses (of normal or above average intelligence) follow the same pattern of cognitive development, including initial phases of language development such as babbling and the production of other sounds. Further development may, however, proceed at a different rate in children with hearing loss. Between the ages of one and three, the average child's vocabulary jumps from 200 words to 900 words. This is when both hearing and nonhearing children make the greatest gains in language acquisition. A child who has not begun to build a vocabulary or to figure out the rules of grammar by age three can find these tasks extremely difficult later on. That is why early interven-

---

P RINCIPLES AND PRACTICE | Early Intervention Programs

Students with hearing disabilities have greater difficulty learning vocabulary, grammar, and other aspects of language. Early intervention can help to avoid delays in the development of language and improve a child's ability to communicate in the classroom. An early intervention program might employ the following methods:

- *Oral communication.* Programs based on **oral communication** teach students to speak and to use speech reading as well as to use their residual hearing with the assistance of a hearing aid. **Speech reading** is a more accurate term for what is commonly known as lip reading—that is, understanding speech by interpreting the movements of the speaker's lips and facial muscles.
- *Manual communication.* In **manual communication** programs students learn to use sign language and finger-spelling (the spelling-out of words using various finger positions for letters of the alphabet). Most manual communication programs in the United

States use **American Sign Language (ASL)** as the language of preference. ASL relies on its own syntax, grammar, and semantics. Some programs use a different method called **Signed Exact English (SEE)**, in which the signs are similar to those of ASL but the word order follows that of American English. Some specialists believe that SEE is easier to use in integrated classrooms, because it helps the student with a hearing disability to follow the speech of hearing students more easily. In addition, some experts believe that SEE makes learning to read easier, but this has not been proven. Children who learn ASL from an early age show no significantly different problems with learning to read written English than those who learn SEE.

- *Total communication.* A program of **total communication** teaches both oral and manual communication. Most programs do use a combination of the two to some extent.
- *Speech therapy.* Speech therapists can help students "voice" their words by using visual images, symbols, and visual and tactile feedback.

---

tion programs for students with hearing disabilities are extremely important. (See Principles and Practice: Early Intervention Programs.) It is critical, according to some experts (Solit, Taylor, & Bednarczyk, 1992), for children to experience rich language environments whether they can hear or not.

● Placement Decisions

Educators who must decide whether to include a child with a hearing problem in the regular classroom follow the same general process as they do when evaluating inclusion for other exceptionalities. In order to provide the best learning environment for a child, teachers, parents, and related services specialists review the child's particular needs before making any placement decision.

In the case of a child with a hearing problem, communication issues are the first addressed. A student who has learned speech reading and sign language in an early intervention program and is comfortable around hearing persons might be best placed in a regular classroom where he can focus on age-appropriate academic material. A student who is not comfortable with speech reading and lacks good communication skills might learn best in a self-contained classroom.

Although some students with hearing disabilities find inclusion easy, others struggle with loneliness in inclusive classrooms. They have difficulty communicating with peers and with hearing teachers and parents; often they feel "different." As a teacher, be prepared to help the hearing-disabled student in your classroom who does experience feelings of isolation.

Variations in response to inclusive classrooms

Many students succeed in the regular classroom once they have mastered communication techniques. However, some parents of children with hearing disabilities prefer that their child be placed with children who have similar issues and experiences. Many in the deaf community assert that deaf people have their own culture, with distinct folkways and a separate language (American Sign Language). These convictions should not be ignored. As is the case with all the laws relating to students with exceptionalities, parents have the final say in where their child will be placed.

Some children with hearing disabilities may attend a residential program. For example, the Arizona State School for the Deaf and Blind in Tucson offers both day school and residential programs. Because Arizona is a fairly large state with many rural areas, a residential program—rather than a long daily commute—might be the most logical choice for a child who is learning sign language or mobility skills. In fact, many families of children who are deaf or hard of hearing want their children to have a school experience with other students like them, rather than be included in a regular school where they might be the lone student with a hearing disability.

In addition to school-year programs, students with hearing disabilities may participate in summer-school programs. The Texas School for the Deaf has summer sports camps, driver-education programs, communication skills workshops, and high school retreats.

Meeting the Needs of Students with Hearing Disabilities

Teachers who have students with hearing disabilities in a regular classroom find a challenge in achieving effective communication that assures the child complete access to an education. The challenge implies both a classroom environment and instructional techniques that have a strong visual orientation. Here are some suggestions to keep in mind:

Tips for teaching

• The teacher should refrain from speaking with his or her back to the students. This is of particular importance when a child is using speech reading.

- The student with a hearing disability should be able to see the teacher and peers from his or her vantage point in the classroom. During discussions, too, the student should be able to see the faces of all the other students (a circle can work nicely).

- If a sign-language interpreter is present, the lesson pace should allow the interpreter enough time to convey the information before the instructor moves on to the next point.

- The student should receive visual aids to reinforce the instructor's verbal delivery of lessons. Copies of overhead transparency lecture notes, writing on the board, and written handouts of instructions can all reinforce learning. As a side note, giving *all* your students copies of a presentation outline can be helpful, especially for any student who has trouble taking notes or focusing on the important elements of a lecture or presentation.

The Techniques for Your Classroom on this page lists additional ideas for organizing your classroom.

Ⓣ ECHNIQUES FOR YOUR CLASSROOM

Integrating Students with Hearing Disabilities into the Regular Classroom

- Arrange the class so that the student who is deaf or hearing disabled can see all the other students' faces.
- Seat the child at or near the front of the class, or on an aisle so that his or her view cannot be blocked.
- Eliminate all obstacles and hindrances to the student's view, including excessive sunlight or glare.
- Repeat questions (and answers) from other students. Have them raise their hands so it is clear who is speaking.
- When using an overhead, computer projection, or slide show, make sure to keep your face illuminated so that you can be seen at all times (especially if the student is speech-reading).
- Keep directions, main points, and verbal instructions short and to the point (a good recommendation in general).

- Avoid moving around the room and turning your back to students.
- Use bullets to highlight important points of a lesson on the blackboard or overhead or in a computer presentation. Point to the bullet as you discuss each point.
- Supplement verbal instructions and presentations with written handouts or notes on the board.
- Learn ASL yourself.
- Teach ASL to other students in the classroom.
- Avoid using videotapes that lack subtitles.
- Have the student, or a guest speaker, talk about some of the concerns and needs of a student with a hearing disability.
- Discuss the student's needs frequently with the special education teacher.

● Facilitating Interaction with Other Students

Successful classroom discussions and socialization rely on helping your hearing students to understand how to communicate effectively and respectfully with a student who has a hearing disability. Be sensitive in planning discreet opportunities to convey this information to keep the student with special needs from feeling separated from the rest of the class. A few modifications to your basic classroom procedures can give the student with a hearing impairment an opportunity to be included more fully with his or her peers.

Discussions and study buddies

To make communication easier for the student with a hearing impairment, have students arranged in a circle or semicircle and remind them to speak one at a time. A simple strategy is to point to the person who will speak next and wait for the hearing-disabled student to locate the speaker. You might also pair each student with a partner or study buddy. Each person can count on her partner's help to fill any gaps in class notes, clarify directions or assignments, or assist with class work. The buddy would *not* be responsible for taking care of the student with a hearing disability, but could provide support and act as a special contact in the classroom. Using a buddy system can also give the student with hearing loss an opportunity to share responsibilities and to feel that he or she can contribute to the learning of another.

As mentioned earlier, loneliness or lack of social interaction with the hearing world may be the most significant challenge a hearing-disabled student faces. As a teacher, you should make every effort to plan classroom activities that include the student to the greatest extent possible. For the most part, this student should be treated no differently than others; focus on the student's challenges only when hearing is an integral part of your lesson. In those instances, your role is to provide assistance, restructuring, or other interventions necessary to help the student participate in the learning activity.

● Working with Specialists

Your school may have a sign-language interpreter available to assist students with hearing disabilities. Some schools and school districts assign an interpreter to each student with a hearing disability. Others place several students with hearing difficulties in a classroom where the interpreter is working. A sign-language interpreter translates the spoken communication of the classroom into signs for the hearing-disabled student, and also voices (speaks aloud) the signs that the student is making.

Keep in mind these two points if you have a sign-language interpreter in your classroom:

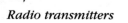

Tips for working with a sign-language interpreter

1 The interpreter's job is to facilitate communication between the student with hearing problems and you and the other students, *not* to teach. Do not expect the interpreter to act as a teacher's assistant or classroom aide.

2 You and your students should be sure to address the student, not the interpreter, when talking or asking questions. Don't ask the interpreter, "What did he just say (sign)?" Instead, tug on the interpreter's sleeve and then turn to the student and ask, "What did you say?"

Don't be afraid of using words like *say* or *hear* when addressing a student with a hearing disability. These words are regular parts of our vocabulary, and the student knows what you mean.

Close communication with the school speech-language specialist can also furnish you with practical suggestions for modifications in the curriculum or its presentation. The speech-language specialist may also work individually with a particular student and have tips to share about past successes with that student.

TECHNOLOGY APPLICATIONS FOR STUDENTS WITH HEARING DISABILITIES

Increasing advances in technology mean that deaf or hard-of-hearing people no longer need be isolated. Useful technology applications range from hearing aids to telecommunications devices and speech recognition software.

● Common Forms of Assistive Technology

Hearing aids

The most popular and affordable assistive technology device for those with hearing disabilities is the hearing aid. Over the years, as transistors and other parts have become smaller and lighter, the hearing aid has become more portable and more sophisticated. The hearing aid does not "correct" or "undistort" sound; it only amplifies. It has no benefit for the deaf student. Moreover, as a child grows, hearing aids must be replaced.

Radio transmitters

Radio transmitters, another type of assistive device, look like microphone systems. Typically the teacher wears the microphone, and the student wears a headset or earpiece with a receiver that amplifies the teacher's speech. This device allows a student with a mild or moderate hearing disability to hear the teacher even when he or she is far away or looking in the other direction. Of course, a student must have some residual hearing to use this system. If you use a radio transmitter in your classroom, keep in mind that you have the microphone on. Too many teachers and students can tell great stories about when the teacher whispered something not meant for student ears or kept the microphone on in the teachers' lounge!

Cochlear implants

A **cochlear implant** is a medical device that transmits sounds by electrically stimulating the nerve fibers in the cochlea (a fluid-filled tube in the inner ear). It is designed to replace the function of damaged sensory nerve cells in persons with sensorineural hearing loss. Cochlear implants are perhaps the most debated technology in the deaf and hard-of-hearing community today. (See Principles and Practice: The Controversy About Cochlear Implants.)

Lights as signals

Around the house, assistive technologies include flashing lights and other inaudible cues for doorbells, telephones, alarm clocks, and other devices that usually rely on auditory stimuli. Instead of a regular alarm clock, someone with a hearing disability might have a clock equipped with a bed-shaking feature or flashing lights. At school, the fire alarm might be supplemented with attention-grabbing lights. Lights and vibrating alarms could also signal the time to change activities or classes or to signal the student when the teacher is far away.

P RINCIPLES AND PRACTICE   The Controversy About Cochlear Implants

A cochlear implant is an electronic device designed to provide sound information for adults and children who have a profound sensorineural hearing loss ("nerve deafness") in both ears and show no ability to hear speech through hearing aids. The first research on cochlear implants was conducted in France thirty years ago. Early cochlear implants used a single electrode as a channel for transmitting sounds. Contemporary systems transmit greater amounts of sound information using multiple electrodes.

Cochlear implants are controversial in the deaf and hearing-disabled community. Some members of this community strongly believe that the dominant "hearing" culture fails to recognize or value deafness as a distinct culture with its own language. Some see implants as an attempt to force the hearing disabled into an identity defined by the hearing world. In this view, deafness is a difference, not a deficit or disability, and it should not be treated as a condition that must be remedied. Other deaf or hearing-disabled individuals, however, see cochlear implants as a useful option and do not believe such "hearing" behaviors devalue deaf culture. Either way, cochlear implants carry significant educational implications. Children with no experience with auditory information suddenly can hear, and this may have great significance for language development. Researchers are just now beginning to plumb the implications of implants.

The complex issues and feelings on both sides can be extremely powerful. As a teacher, you should familiarize yourself with the differing points of view so that you can better understand the feelings of your students and their families.

● Telecommunications Devices

Section 255 of the Telecommunications Act of 1996 requires that persons with disabilities have access to and use of telecommunications equipment and customer premises equipment. This law and the Americans with Disabilities Act have helped make telephone-related devices widely available for the deaf to communicate with each other and with hearing people.

Text telephones

The primary tool of people with hearing disabilities and deafness is the **text telephone,** a generic name for a device that allows two-way conversations over a telephone network using typed text instead of spoken words. Common varieties include the **teletypewriter (TTY)** or **telecommunication device for the deaf (TDD),** terms we use interchangeably. Figure 7.2 shows a typical text telephone. As you can see, it looks like a small keyboard with a text screen across the top. The user types into the telephone, and the information is transmitted to another such device, where it is displayed on the screen.

TTY communication is similar in some ways to instant messaging. People typically use short phrases and abbreviations as well as personalized greetings. Modern TTYs can be programmed to send a message with the push of just one key. For example, you can program a special key on the keyboard to say, "I know the answer" or "I think it's my turn."

If you don't have a TTY but want to talk to someone who is deaf or hard of hearing, you can use a relay service. The **telecommunications relay service (TRS),** mandated by the Americans with Disabilities Act, allows for conversations between hearing individuals and those with hearing disabilities through

● FIGURE 7.2

The Q90, a portable TTY produced by Ameriphone

Source: Ameriphone, www.ameriphoneinc.com.

Conversation via a relay service

the assistance of a third party. When the nondisabled user speaks, the relay operator types the message to the hearing-disabled person via TTY. That person responds via TTY, and the operator reads the response aloud to the first person. Relay service is available in the United States and throughout Europe. If you ever have occasion to use a relay service, keep in mind that you are talking to the person with the hearing disability, *not* to the operator. Moreover, the operator will type everything you say to the person on the other end of the line, including every "hmmm" and "uh-huh." Relay service is provided at no cost to the user on either end of the line.

Other widely used primarily visual telecommunications devices that accommodate people with deafness or hearing disabilities include the following:

- *Email.* The abundance of computers and email ensures that more people can communicate directly with others than ever before. As a teacher, you may use email to communicate on a more regular basis with parents who are deaf or hard of hearing. You can also consult experts and specialists more readily via email. A student with a hearing disability can use email to communicate with other students in a group project, to submit homework, or to ask a question of the teacher.

- *Fax machines.* Like email, a fax is more private than a relay service, and more homes and businesses have fax machines than have TTY machines. The fax machine can also allow you to send forms, hand-drawn pictures or artwork, or other paper-based information that you might not be able to import into your computer. The student who is deaf or hard of hearing can use a fax machine to submit homework, interact with other students, and send forms to the school office.

- *Instant messaging and chatting.* Instant messaging is a "real-time" alternative to email or fax. A messaging program such as AOL's Instant Messenger (**http://www.aol.com/aim/**) or an Internet chat program such as ICQ (**http://web.icq.com/**) allow you to instantly communicate with another user who is online at the same time. Both Instant Messenger and ICQ allow you to keep a "buddy list" and check who is online at any time. ICQ allows character-by-character (a letter or symbol at a time) chatting, which is more like TTY, rather than line-by-line chatting as Instant Messenger does. Instant messaging and ICQ are popular in schools today, with students who can and cannot hear. Students use a Palm or other handheld computer to send short messages to one another without disrupting the classroom (and without the teacher's knowing, in some cases). A student with a hearing impairment may relish the greater independence and convenience of responding to the teacher or to another student with instant messaging rather than through an interpreter or other traditional communication method.

- *Alphanumeric paging.* A simple, lightweight pager can be a nice option for classroom and mobile use. A pager with a text screen can send a message while the student is away from home or a computer. In school, hearing disabled students can exchange short messages with other students. Wireless phones (both digital and analog) can be hooked up to a TTY, but this can be a lot of equipment to carry around.

Conversation via video

Another alternative to a TTY is a videophone or videoconferencing system. **Videophones** use high-speed phone lines to allow two people to see each other and then use sign language to communicate. **Videoconferencing** uses two computers, each with a small camera connected to it so that users can see each other as they communicate; Figure 7.3 diagrams two possible videoconferencing arrangements. Two issues affect videophoning and videoconferencing for people at home or school. First of all, these systems require high-speed phone lines or Internet connections, which may not be available everywhere. Second, the equipment can be quite expensive. However, these technologies promise future benefits as tools for students who use sign language.

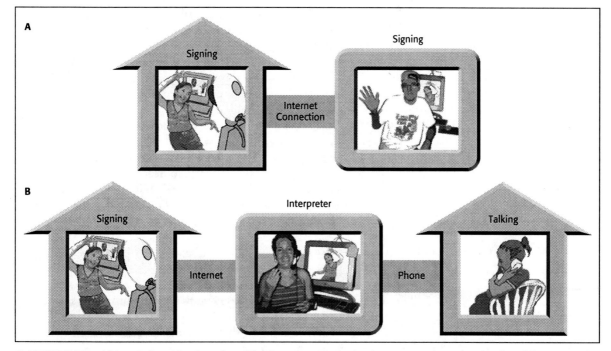

● **FIGURE 7.3** Videoconferencing in action. (A) Direct communication between two people who sign. (B) Communication between a hearing person and a nonhearing person with an interpreter as intermediary.

Maria Zamora

Maria and friends plant a garden as part of a science lesson on the environment.

Maria is ten years old. She was born two months premature, and this most likely caused her to lose much of her hearing. Maria attends a regular public school in Washington, DC, where almost all of the other students are hearing.

Maria spends part of the day in a special fifth-grade class that is just for hearing-disabled children. She works on reading, speaking, spelling, and writing with her special teacher. Then she joins the hearing fifth-grade students for math, science, music, art, and gym.

Maria wears two small, behind-the-ear hearing aids at home, but at school she uses a special hearing aid that involves a radio transmitter. Her teachers talk through a special microphone, which sends the sound directly to Maria's hearing aid. This device allows Maria to hear the teacher even when the classroom is noisy. Some hearing-disabled children at Maria's school use another communication tool called *cued speech,* with which the children learn to recognize certain hand signals that help them understand spoken words.

The software that Maria uses includes Accelerated Reader by Renaissance Learning. This program allows Maria to log into the Renaissance Learning website (**http://www.renlearn.com/**) and take quizzes on books she has read. She also uses several computer-based math learning programs such as Math Blaster (Knowledge Adventure). At home, she uses email and AOL's Instant Messenger to stay in touch with her friends, and she frequently uses the Web to research for school projects.

Deaf or hard-of-hearing television viewers now have open and closed captions for just about every television program and on just about every television set (in fact, they are required for sets of nineteen inches and larger). *Closed captions* can be seen only with a special decoding device, but *open captions* are already decoded. They appear on the television screen like subtitles in a movie. Make sure that any video you use in class contains either closed or open captions and that your school televisions can display that information.

● Computer Software Applications

Many advances in computer technology, including the Web and email, have allowed students with hearing disabilities to reduce their isolation and increase their communication with others who have similar hearing difficulties. The Internet has broken down some barriers to knowledge, information, and integration into society faced by people who are deaf or hard of hearing. Generally, computers provide visual aids in writing down important notes, projecting notes onto a screen, and saving and sharing spoken information.

Students with hearing disabilities can use common varieties of educational software, because most are visually oriented and text-based. A program such as The Logical Journey of the Zoombinis (The Learning Company) is great for introducing problem solving in mathematics. As you select any software application, follow the guidelines set out in chapter 2, "Selecting Technology for the Classroom." Specifically, be sure that important elements of the program's lesson do not rely on auditory information and feedback. Gallaudet University's Laurent Clerc National Deaf Education Center offers the following guidelines for evaluating software that includes sound:

Criteria for evaluating software

> If deaf or hard of hearing evaluators/users cannot understand what the software is about [without the ability to hear the sound accompanying the program], then the importance [of sound in its use] would be MAJOR. If some portion of the product can be understood despite the fact that the audio information cannot be heard, then its importance is MODERATE. If the sound is not critical to using the product successfully, then it is MINOR. If you are a hearing reviewer, please be sure to evaluate the product with the speakers turned off. (Laurent Clerc National Deaf Education Center, 1999)

Among more specialized software applications, **automatic speech recognition (ASR)** software is especially beneficial for the student with hearing disabilities or deafness. ASR allows for the conversion of speech to text and vice versa. Originally intended for dictation, this type of software allows the

Low-cost ASR software

student to type in a message and have it converted to speech, which the hearing person receives through headphones. Students can also use the software to record the speech of a presenter or teacher and convert that speech to text to be read at a later time. Two low-cost, portable products, Dragon NaturallySpeaking (Scansoft) and ViaVoice (IBM), are widely available.

Other software program adaptations specifically assist students with hearing disabilities. For example, Aesop in ASL, a CD-ROM produced by Gerald Pollard at the Texas School for the Deaf, takes the text from four of Aesop's fables and adds ASL movies, animation, and a speech component. The fables are "The Milkmaid and Her Pail," "The Tortoise and the Hare," "The Fox and the Grapes," and "The Lion and the Mouse." At the end of each story, the user engages in five activities that practice skills involving pronouns, sequencing, reading comprehension, synonyms, and vocabulary. Teachers from the Texas School for the Deaf have used similar techniques in redesigning other software applications to make them more useful to students with hearing disabilities. The CDs can be ordered from Harris Communications at **http://www.harriscomm.com/**.

Software that assists students with speech and language problems may also help students with hearing disabilities. For example, SpeechViewer III (IBM), which gives visual feedback about auditory stimuli, can help a student who is learning to voice (speak out loud) recognize how to pronounce letters, letter-combinations, sounds, and words.

SUMMARY

A hearing disability can range from a slight hearing loss, correctable with a hearing aid, to total deafness. Losses stem from a variety of reasons. Conductive hearing loss is caused by disease or obstruction in the outer or middle ear; sensorineural hearing loss, by damage to the hair cells of the inner ear; mixed hearing loss, by a combination of conductive and sensorineural problems; and central hearing loss, by damage to the central nervous system.

A child whose hearing loss occurs at a postlinguistic stage (after the child has begun to acquire language) may continue to use speech as an important means of communication, perhaps in combination with sign language and speech reading. If the hearing loss is prelinguistic, though, the child may not use speech at all. The situation varies for each child, as does the best choice of educational placement: regular class, special class, or residential program. Some deaf and hard-of-hearing children thrive in inclusive classrooms; others feel lonely and isolated in a class of hearing students. The family's attitude toward deaf culture is also critical in the placement decision.

When your class includes a child with a hearing disability, certain instructional techniques will reduce obstacles for the child and maximize his or her ability to participate in the class. For instance, always face your students when you speak. Remove obstructions so that the child with a hearing disability can see you clearly. Arrange discussions so that the student can see the other students' faces. Use visual aids as much as possible. Study buddies can be useful for all students, including ones with hearing disabilities. If you are working with a sign-language interpreter, be sure to address your questions and responses to the student, not to the interpreter.

Hearing aids are the most common form of assistive technology for students with hearing disabilities. In some cases, teachers wear microphones that use radio transmission to send the sound to the student's earpiece. Cochlear implants can make up for damage to nerve cells in the inner ear, but their use is controversial among proponents of deaf culture.

People with hearing disabilities often use text telephones (TTYs or TTDs). Email, instant messaging, paging, and fax technologies are also important, as are closed and open captions for videos. Videoconferencing will probably become more widely available as the technology develops further.

Because most educational software packages stress text and graphics, they can prove effective for students with hearing abilities. You should evaluate each program beforehand, however, to make sure it does not rely on sound. Automatic speech recognition (ASR) software is especially valuable, and low-cost varieties are now available. Hearing-disabled students who use speech to communicate find that software can provide visual feedback to help them improve their pronunciation.

KEY TERMS

hearing impairment (p. 149)
deafness (p. 149)
conductive hearing loss (p. 150)
sensorineural hearing loss (p. 150)
mixed hearing loss (p. 151)
central hearing loss (p. 151)
oral communication (p. 153)
speech reading (p. 153)
manual communication (p. 153)
American Sign Language (ASL) (p. 153)
Signed Exact English (SEE) (p. 153)
total communication (p. 153)
cochlear implant (p. 158)

text telephone (p. 159)
teletypewriter (TTY) (p. 159)
telecommunication device for the deaf (TDD) (p. 159)
telecommunications relay service (TRS) (p. 159)
videophone (p. 161)
videoconferencing (p. 161)
automatic speech recognition (ASR) (p. 163)

RESOURCES FOR FURTHER INVESTIGATION

Online Resources

Alexander Graham Bell Association for the Deaf and Hard of Hearing.
http://www.agbell.org/
> An excellent resource for learning about deaf culture, how to integrate a
> student with a hearing problem into your classroom, and social implica-
> tions for the deaf child.

American Society for Deaf Children.
http://www.deafchildren.org/
> Provides excellent resources for parents and teachers, as well as activities
> and materials for kids. Lots of links, resources, and suggestions.

Council on the Education of the Deaf.
http://www.deafed.net/
> Curriculum information on math, reading, language, history, and science
> as well as resources for teaching and suggestions for instructional materials
> are available here. You might enjoy the "Dizzy Bees" learning center, an
> auditory training center for children who have already developed word
> recognition skills.

Deaf Resource Library.
http://www.deaflibrary.org/
> An online collection of reference material and links intended to educate
> and inform people about deaf cultures in Japan and the United States.
> Also addresses topics related to people who are hard of hearing.

Gallaudet University Technology Access Program.
http://tap.gallaudet.edu/
> This site, sponsored by a research group at Gallaudet University, provides
> up-to-date, comprehensive information on the latest trends in technology
> for people with hearing disabilities.

The Listen-Up Web!
http://www.listen-up.org/
> A great website for educators and parents of children who are deaf or hard of hearing. The site provides information for parents about fun places to visit and a list of useful books and publishers. Also available are many tips on everything from early intervention to support groups for parents, as well as the latest information on national legal issues.

National Association of the Deaf.
http://www.nad.org/
> Lots of vibrant colors, video clips, and visual stimulation introduce you to this site with a focus on policy issues, advocacy, conferences for parents and professionals, and employment resources.

Software to Go.
http://clerccenter2.gallaudet.edu/stg/index.html
> Sponsored by the Laurent Clerc National Deaf Education Center, this website is a clearinghouse for software evaluation information. It has a searchable index that you can use to look for material by grade level, subject area, and instructional mode.

Print Resources

Chaplin, S. (1986). *I can sign my ABC's*. Washington, DC: Gallaudet University Press. (Grades preschool–1.) Shows the hand shape for the sign for each letter of the American manual alphabet.

Flodin, M. (1991). *Signing for kids: The fun way for anyone to learn American Sign Language*. New York: Putnam. (Grades 3–9.) Introduces signs in categories, such as pets and animals, snacks and food, family, friends, travel and holidays, time, days, seasons, and weather. Introductory materials include tips to make signing easier and some facts about deafness. The American manual alphabet and finger-spelling activities appear in chapter 1.

Greene, L., & Dicker, E. B. (1988). *Sign language talk*. New York: Franklin Watts. (Grades 5 and higher.) Introduces American Sign Language, the visual/gestural language used by most deaf people in the United States and Canada. Provides background information on the language and examines some of its grammatical structures. Includes some exercises and games for beginning signers and information about the role of poetry and music in the deaf community.

Moores, Donald F. (2001). *Educating the deaf: Psychology, principles, and practices,* 5th ed. Boston, MA: Houghton Mifflin. A good general introduction to deaf education.

Sesame Street Staff & Hayward, Linda. (1980). *Sesame Street sign language fun with Linda Bove, featuring Jim Henson's Sesame Street Muppets.* New York: Random House/Children's Television Workshop. (Grades preschool–3.) Presents signs for words commonly used by young children. Linda Bove, a deaf actress, works with *Sesame Street* characters to demonstrate the signs in categories such as "In the Morning," "School Days," "Action Words," and "People in the Neighborhood."

TECHNOLOGY FOR STUDENTS WITH VISUAL IMPAIRMENTS

FOCUS QUESTIONS

As you read this chapter, think about the following:

■ What conditions does the term *visual impairments* include?

■ What sort of educational modifications do I make when I have a child with a visual impairment in my classroom?

■ Who will provide this student with specialized training in mobility or how to read Braille?

■ What sorts of resources exist to support students, teachers, and parents of sight-impaired children?

Some of the most exciting advances in technology have great potential for students with visual impairments. Tools such as screen readers with computerized voices, voice-activated software, Braille notetakers, and optical character recognition software allow students with visual impairments complete participation in classroom activities. This chapter presents ways in which these new technologies can be used in the classroom.

WHAT ARE VISUAL IMPAIRMENTS?

The term *visual impairments* describes a wide variety of conditions that affect vision abilities. We use the term to denote mild to most severe vision loss, rather than to defects in the eye itself. According to the Individuals with Disabilities Education Act (IDEA) of 1997, a visual impairment refers to "an impairment in vision that, even with correction, adversely affects a child's educational performance. The term includes both partial sight and blindness."

Sight impairment terminology can sometimes be confusing. Most people classified as "blind" have a visual sense of lightness or darkness, as well as an ability to see some shapes and images. To avoid confusion, you should know the following terms commonly used to designate degrees of visual impairment:

Common terms for visual impairments

- **Totally blind.** This term usually implies little or no visual sensitivity to light at any level. This condition is rare, and people who are totally blind typically have severe physical damage to the eyes themselves or to the visual nerves.

- **Legally blind.** A person who is legally blind has a visual acuity of 20/200 or less in the better eye, after correction. This means that what an individual with normal (20/20) vision sees at two hundred feet, the legally blind person cannot see until he or she is within twenty feet. In addition, a person can be classified as legally blind if she has a field of vision no greater than twenty degrees at the widest diameter. (A normal field of vision is close to 180 degrees.) Only about 20 percent of legally blind people are totally blind. Legally blind individuals typically use Braille and visual aids.

- **Low vision.** People with low vision can read with the help of large-print reading materials and magnifying objects. They may also use Braille.

- **Partially sighted.** Partially sighted individuals have less severe loss of vision than people in the other three categories. A person with partial sight may be able to see objects up close or far away and with corrective lenses may be able to function at normal levels.

A student with a visual disorder can succeed in school if given the right support and accommodations. If you have a student with a visual disorder in your class, remember this: *An inability to see does not create an inability to learn.*

To emphasize that the legal or medical classification may be less relevant than what a student can do in the classroom, educators often describe students with visual impairments in terms of classroom functioning. Typical educational classifications are moderate, severe, and profound visual impairment. These classifications refer to the extent to which the student needs special

*Educational categories
of visual impairment*

education adaptations to learn. A child with **moderate visual impairment** (a corrected visual acuity between 20/70 and 20/160) works well with visual aids, perhaps even to the point of eliminating the impairment's effect. A student with **severe visual impairment** (a corrected visual acuity of 20/200 to 20/400) will have difficulty even with visual aids, but can use vision to some degree in the learning process. Students with **profound visual impairment** or **total vision impairment** (corrected visual acuity of 20/500 or worse) cannot use vision as an educational tool and must rely predominately on their remaining sensory functions.

● Prevalence of Visual Impairments

Although many students have some type of visual problem, the great majority of cases resolve the difficulty, usually with eyeglasses or contact lenses. These students need no special education services. Among students who do receive services under IDEA, only about 0.5 percent have visual impairments (U.S. Department of Education, 2000). Severe visual impairments are even less common. According to the National Information Center for Children and Youth with Disabilities (NICHCY, 2001b), severe visual impairments occur in only .06 of every 1,000 individuals.

However small their numbers may be, students with visual impairments must have a free and appropriate public education like all other students. As a teacher, therefore, you should understand the implications of visual impairments for learning and the modifications and accommodations that are essential for the student's success.

TECHNIQUES FOR YOUR CLASSROOM

Recognizing Degenerative Eye Disorders

Degenerative eye disorders deteriorate the eye and degrade visual ability. Such disorders include diabetic retinopathy, glaucoma, retinal degeneration, and cataracts. Diabetic retinopathy, for example, affects approximately half of the population with both type 1 and type 2 diabetes. In this disease, damaged blood vessels in the eye can leak fluid into the retina and cloud a person's vision.

Early treatment of this disorder, as well as other eye diseases, may prevent unnecessary damage to the eye.

If you notice that one of your students seems to have progressive problems with sight, make sure that he or she visits an ophthalmologist as soon as possible. Regular eye examinations can help determine if changes in the eye are taking place.

● Educational and Social Development

Children with visual impairments and children with unimpaired sight both go through a series of stages in their language development. Infants alter the quality of their cries to express different needs, move on to babbling, then to using one-word sentences, and eventually to constructing increasingly complex sentences as they refine their linguistic abilities and respond to input from adults. A child who is visually impaired lacks the advantage of reinforcing and expanding his or her vocabulary through visual input. This child misses most types of body language and facial expressions, although tactile experiences provide an important alternative.

Early vocabulary based on direct experiences

As a result, most of the visually impaired child's early language is based on his or her direct personal experiences. For example, Joey will quickly learn that Mom is the person with a certain voice, whose hands hold him a certain way, and who cares for him. He is less likely to grasp the meaning of an abstract word, such as *mothering* or *motherhood.* Such nuances would have to be explained to him.

Activity limitations have the greatest impact on the social domain of visually impaired individuals. Young children with visual impairments need a great deal of orientation and support to be as mobile and independent as sighted

P RINCIPLES AND PRACTICE   How Do People with Visual Impairments Experience the World?

Blind and visually impaired people use other senses to experience life fully. Though their sight is inhibited, they use hearing, touch, and smell in order to "see" the world. When you are traveling, for example, you rely mostly on your vision to read directions and find your way around. A person with a visual impairment uses his or her sense of touch to operate a cane or other mobility tool and to read Braille signs. He or she may have location markers just as you do. You know to turn left when you see the Taco Bell; the person with a visual impairment may know to turn left at that certain Taco Bell smell. When chatting with a friend, you watch for visual cues of interest or agreement; a person with a visual impairment is alert for changes in a listener's voice and touch.

A sight-impaired person's other senses are no better than yours, but he or she is more accustomed to using them. If you close your eyes and listen to the sounds around you, you will become more and more confident that you could experience life in this way. In fact, some people with visual impairments believe that sighted people miss out on a great deal in life. That is, we let our vision allow us to ignore what people are saying or how they are saying it. We don't appreciate the smells, sounds, movements, and feelings always in play in the world.

Effect on social interactions

children. Even when support is available, such children are often restricted from certain activities, and this can significantly curtail the amount and quality of their interaction with peers. For example, soccer is a popular sport for most young children, boys and girls alike. A child with a visual impairment *can* play soccer, with support and training. A "beeping" ball can allow the child to know where the soccer ball is. A coach on the sidelines shouting clear instructions (instead of just shouting, as some coaches do) can help all players. A raised edge around the field can help all the young players notice when the ball goes out of bounds. Most important, the experience of playing soccer with his or her peers can help the child with a visual impairment socialize, compete, use language, and gain physical agility as well as confidence.

Parents and teachers who push students with visual impairments to have as normal an experience as possible not only help them gain skills and develop self-reliance, but also help other students understand how to work with people who are different. For more information about including children with visual impairments in physical education programs, visit **http:// www.midlandschool.org/art1.htm** to read an article by Kathy Letcher on adapted physical education for the blind and visually impaired. Sports and physical activities are obviously not the only way to increase the verbal, social, and mobility skills of children with visual impairments. Being active in music, clubs (such as the Girl Scouts), and after-school programs can help the child strengthen language skills and understand social situations.

● Placement Decisions

A central issue in placing a student with a visual impairment is whether the necessary specialized training is best delivered in the regular school setting or in a special school. Students with visual impairments often need to learn special skills such as how to use a walking cane and how to use special computer applications. Special schools for the visually impaired provide this training, but these skills can also be taught by an itinerant specialist at the student's home school.

Special schools offer students a place to interact with other students with visual impairments. Such schools can give students a solid grounding in skills and techniques they will use throughout their lives, and with which they can succeed more easily in further education and at home. Because of the low prevalence of severe visual impairments, however, the school may be some distance from a child's home and may require that the student live on campus, away from his or her family.

Resource programs

Many school districts offer resource programs for children with all degrees of blindness, in which the students attend a special program for part of the school day and then return to their home classrooms. For example, a student might spend the morning learning mobility skills or how to use specific technology tools, and then in the afternoon return to "regular" high school. Classes such as mathematics and science, in which much of the information is written on the board, might require the student to have special tutoring.

The pros and cons of deciding where to place a student with a visual impairment are significant and can have a major impact on the child's long-term success. As the teacher, you can offer information, support, and insights to parents as they try to make this important decision.

ADAPTING INSTRUCTION FOR STUDENTS WITH VISUAL IMPAIRMENTS

Just as visual impairments fall along a continuum, so do students' abilities to see and use learning materials. Someone with low vision or moderate visual impairment can read with magnification aids, which might range from a simple magnifying glass to a computer technology like ZoomText Xtra (Ai Squared), which provides magnification and screen-reading capabilities. Students with profound visual impairment might use Window-Eyes (GW Micro) or JAWS (Henter-Joyce), two screen readers that use a voice synthesizer to read the contents of the computer screen aloud via the computer's speakers.

Classroom teachers can make many other modifications for the visually impaired student, too. Books on tape can replace textbooks. Tape recorders can capture lectures or assist in composition. Computers can help compose papers, while voice synthesizers can read each page back to the student. Partners assigned within the classroom can provide specific assistance such as help with gathering materials and organizing for work.

Young students find certain toys helpful and adaptive. The Explorer Globe (LeapFrog Enterprises) is an interactive globe that introduces the names, elevation, and other information about different geographical locations. Another LeapFrog toy, The Fun & Learn Phonics Bus, promotes language use by coordinating alphabet letters with phonetic sounds and words.

Before putting any toys, tools, or modifications in place, however, you must discover which skills or tasks present a challenge to an individual student, and how specific modifications will help overcome these challenges. Students with visual impairments can often explain exactly which experiences are the most useful to them; all you have to do is ask. The next section presents some guiding principles that can assist you in adapting instruction for a student with a visual impairment.

● Guiding Principles for Instructional Adaptations

Three principles are especially important when you consider how to modify your instructional practices to meet the needs of a student with a visual impairment:

Offer tactile experiences

1 *Concreteness.* Students with visual impairments need opportunities to observe their environment through tactile means. Therefore, when discussing abstract concepts in your classroom, allow children to manipulate the object or some representation of it. For example, when teaching about human biology, you might want to borrow a skeleton so that the student can feel how the "shinbone is connected to the knee bone." Characteristics like texture, weight, fragility, size, and shape make for a richer set of elements with which to create mental associations.

Provide synthesis and context

2 *Unifying experiences.* Because students with visual impairments cannot automatically distinguish the part from the whole, you must provide this information. For example, at different points during the semester, the class may discuss trees and leaves, seasons, and the earth's rotation. For a student with a profound visual impairment, who doesn't see the leaves falling from the trees or the sun setting earlier in the evening, it may be necessary to provide a synthesis and context for those discussions, to explain the interconnectedness among topics.

Engage students in hands-on activities

3 *Learning by doing.* Students with visual impairments need hands-on experiences. We know that everyone learns best by active involvement with ideas, and the same is true for students with visual impairments. Give students as many opportunities as possible to participate in a hands-on activity through which they can truly learn the day's lesson. For example, if you and your students are studying ancient Egypt, you can have the students build a replica of a pyramid or make bricks using sand and water. This way, all your students will get a feel for the amazing architecture of the time.

● Responding to the Uniqueness of Each Student

Teachers should acknowledge the student with a visual impairment as a unique individual. One way to discover exactly what works best for a student is to ask him or her to describe what you (and the other students) can do to be helpful. Interviewing the student guides the educator to hidden talents that can aid learning. Hardships in learning can be counterbalanced by the

Ask the student how to help

student's interests. Interviewing can also let you know which tasks and aspects of learning a student prefers to pursue independently.

When you have a child with a visual impairment in your classroom, you must be organized. For instance, you'll want to prepare materials ahead of time so that they can be scanned into a Braille printer or recorded onto tape. Even more important, you must think especially clearly about your class learning objectives. Integrating each piece of the lesson plan into the whole will ensure that the student with a visual impairment gains the academic strengths to develop new skills and complete new material.

Technology Applications for Students with Visual Impairments

Like children with other types of disabilities, students with visual impairments can benefit from a great variety of technological aids. Some students may need special adaptive technologies. Others may profit from the same

---

PRINCIPLES AND PRACTICE   Following a Universal Design for Learning

As we examine ways to adapt your instructional techniques to meet the needs of students with visual impairments, we should again visit the idea of a Universal Design for Learning, introduced in chapter 1. As explained by David Edyburn at the University of Wisconsin (Edyburn, 1999), Universal Design for Learning means that *all* instruction is designed to meet the diverse learning needs of students in the classroom. As a teacher, you know in theory that no two students are alike. When you follow a Universal Design for Learning, you put this theory into direct and immediate practice.

For example, if you are presenting an activity on adding fractions, you think about how students with a range of learning styles will best comprehend this material. Some students will understand the concept when you describe the rules for finding common denominators; other students need

to see you use blocks; still others might need to have a picture drawn on the board. The concept of alternative modes of presentation can extend to the way you prepare support materials. You can give certain students a printed outline of your plan; other students will do well taking their own notes. In this context, a student with a visual impairment fits right in. Yes, he or she has particular learning needs—but so do all your other students. As you plan any lesson, think about how any student who learns primarily through visual, tactile, or auditory channels might best learn the information you are presenting.

For more information about the concept of a Universal Design for Learning, see the website of the Center for Applied Special Technology, **http://www.cast.org/udl/**. Here you can read detailed documentation concerning implementation of the idea for students with a range of exceptionalities.

types of educational software mentioned in earlier chapters. The following sections review the most widely used options.

● Recorded Books

The most basic technology tool available to students with visual impairments is recorded books and readings on tape, CD, and other media. A main source of many prerecorded books is the National Library Service for the Blind and Physically Handicapped (NLS), through the Library of Congress. Public libraries also stock many recordings, although the time required to record new books can sometimes be up to one year. Through the support of IDEA, which states that the individual with a disability has the legal and civil right to materials necessary to receiving an education, recorded books are becoming more and more available. Your local library will know which materials are currently available.

Recorded books available in libraries

Recording for the Blind and Dyslexic, a nationwide organization that brings in volunteers to record books, often offers support to schools and universities. New books may not be as readily available, but many classics and textbooks are. You can find out about your local chapter at **http://www.rfbd.org/**. In addition, many texts can be downloaded off the Internet in audio format, allowing for quicker access to modern works.

● Braille Technologies

Braille is a system of raised dots that represent letters and punctuation. Louis Braille created this system of six dots while he was a student in Paris during the early 1800s. Although speech-to-text software and screen readers are gaining in popularity, Braille remains the most popular text system among people with visual impairments. Nevertheless, the National Federation of the Blind estimates that only 10 percent of people without sight in the United States can decode Braille (Schroeder, 1999).

Computer support for Braille

Many people with visual impairments consider Braille *the* written text of the blind and believe that its use should continue. Learning Braille differs significantly from learning to use the computer to read and write (Cranmer, 2000). However, computer technologies can support Braille use. For example, Braille displays, such as the ALVA Delphi Braille Display (ALVA Access Group), allow a user to input information and "feel" it printed back with raised Braille dots. This piece of equipment connects to a computer, so the student can type in notes on a laptop or read information from the computer screen (such as website text). This tool also includes speech output and activation.

Keith Thomas

Keith's use of technology ranges from the use of a Braille watch to a voice-activated computer system.

Keith Thomas was born in Washington, DC, in 1978 with Leber's congenital amaurosis (LCA). This condition results in lack of vision, roving eye movements, and deep-set eyes. Although he cannot see, Keith is sensitive to light and wears sunglasses inside and out.

His parents always pushed Keith to do everything his brothers and sisters could do, and they were determined to rear him in as "normal" an environment as possible. Before he started school, Keith took gymnastics and swimming lessons and he began to learn Braille with the help of an occupational therapist. He attended public schools throughout his education, from kindergarten to college. Keith also studied in a "vision program" in which he learned mobility skills, Braille reading and writing, and skills for using technologies such as the screen reader JAWS and the Kurzweil reader.

Keith currently works for the city of Washington as a consultant in providing public and educational services for people with visual impairments. He does most of his work from home, but he has a Braille pager that sends email, his main mode of communication, to him via a Braille keyboard. Keith uses email to keep on top of all types of projects and to prepare information for others that is organized and "looks" nice. He uses the Internet and a screen reader to gather information, and he has even created a few web pages on his own.

Though he sometimes uses the public transportation system, Keith has learned that he can't always depend on it to deliver him to his destination on time. More often, he catches a ride with a friend. For walking around the city, he uses a cane that he can collapse and store in his briefcase.

PROFILE CONTINUED

Around the house, Keith likes to cook. He uses various assistive devices, such as a talking microwave oven and a device called a Say When, which hangs over the side of a container and beeps when the liquid fills near the top. He has also installed Braille or embossed knobs on cabinets. He has a Braille watch and Braille alarm clock (which has a nice loud ring and allows him to "see" the time by touching it).

For the most part, Keith uses technologies little different from ones you might use. His main recommendation to any person with a visual impairment is to stay organized and to persuade others around him or her to realize that organization is important!

Braille printers emboss the Braille system of type onto paper. Just as with a traditional printer, any information on the computer screen can be printed out. Another useful tool is an electronic Braille notetaker, a portable device with a small keyboard for information input. The notetaker can output typed information in Braille or in speech. The Braille 'n' Speak (Blazie) electronic notetaker includes a calculator, calendar, and stopwatch and operates like a personal digital assistant. Users can connect a Braille notetaker to a computer to upload notes or to back up information.

● Screen Readers, Speech Recognition, and OCR

A **screen reader** is a software application that reads aloud what appears on the screen. The best ones can be used with any word-processing program, web browser, email application, drop-down menu, or desktop item—practically any "text object" that appears on the user's monitor. Examples of this type of program include:

Sample screen readers

- JAWS (Job Access with Speech) from Henter-Joyce
- Window-Eyes (GW Micro)
- WinVision (Artic Technologies)
- ASAP (Automatic Screen Access Program) for Windows from MicroTalk Software
- Window Bridge (Syntha-voice Computers)
- The Reading Edge (Telesensory)
- outSPOKEN (ALVA Access Group)

P RINCIPLES AND PRACTICE Accessible Web Design

The World Wide Web can be an excellent tool for people with visual impairments, but only if website creators follow the principles of **accessible web design.** Website designers must keep in mind that some site visitors cannot see the visuals and frames that make up a web page.

For example, if you visit a website while using a screen reader such as JAWS, you can read only the text that is typed on that page. You cannot interpret the images and other visual devices. Next time you visit a site, look at how much the web page relies on visual information in the form of pictures or pull-down menus to help you navigate the site. If you couldn't see those pictures, but could only read text written on the page, would navigation be difficult, or even impossible?

Likewise, an entire website composed of frames provides little or no information to the person with a visual impairment. The solution to this problem is simple: create a "text-only" version of the website. This option is typically built into advanced web-design tools, such as Dreamweaver (Macromedia).

Learning to use these programs requires that students exercise a good deal of computer aptitude and patience. Formal training in the use of such programs can help. Advanced screen readers are essential for students who use the Internet or prepare word-processed essays.

The counterpart to a screen reader is speech recognition software that allows a computer to accept voice commands. Tools such as Dragon NaturallySpeaking (Scansoft) offer advanced speech recognition software. These packages have dictionaries of more than 120,000 words for recognizing voice commands.

Scanning with OCR software

Optical character recognition (OCR) devices are another complementary tool. The Versatile Image Processor (JBliss Imaging Systems) and the Kurzweil 3000 (Kurzweil Educational Systems) use a scanner with OCR software to convert printed documents into text files. After scanning a document as text, the user can enlarge it, improve its contrast, and choose from among various display options. The document can be saved and retrieved, word processed, and printed. If a sound card is installed on the computer, the Versatile Image Processor can provide speech output as well as magnification. Another popular program, OPENBook (Henter-Joyce), uses OCR to translate the words on a page into spoken text, heard through the computer speakers.

Another technology that helps people with visual impairments access text is the Road Runner (Ostrich Software). This lightweight, easy to use handheld tool holds up to two thousand pages of text. After scanning book text into a computer, the user downloads the text files to the Road Runner and uses headphones to listen to the book. Similarly, the user can listen to email or to any other text downloaded to the Road Runner. Instead of sitting in front of the computer, Road Runner gives the student mobility and access to written material when Braille is not available.

● Adaptive Technologies

Traditional adaptive devices for people with visual impairments include the widely used walking canes and guide dogs. Today, adaptive and assistive computer applications include, for example, software programs such as MAGic (Henter-Joyce), which magnifies the computer screen for use by a person with some level of measurable sight.

Electronic adaptive devices

Other adaptive devices go a long way toward increasing the options available to those with visual impairments. For example, the AudioCalc-Talking Scientific Calculator (Blazie) voices the number entered, calculation performed, and answer received. Talking calculators are also available in Spanish and for financial functions. Similarly, the Franklin Language Master (Blazie) allows students to look up and hear definitions, pronunciations, and spellings. The Reading Pen (Wizcom Technologies), mentioned in the chapter on learning disabilities, allows the user to scan in text from a page and then have it read aloud, look up the dictionary definition for a word, or find the word's derivation.

Adaptive keyboards are also useful in many cases. For example, Maltron makes a one-handed keyboard with a microphone attached to the computer. Visually impaired students can type and speak into the computer at the same time.

Closed-circuit television (CCTV) assists people with some sight because images can be magnified on the television screen. This system requires a television camera and a monitor and can be used across networks so that the person can use the device at a distance from the information provider. Descriptive Video Service (DVS) uses the "second audio program" (SAP) option available on most newer television sets to provide narrated descriptions of what is happening on screen without interrupting the dialog. DVS is available on most PBS programs and on many popular VHS videotapes.

SUMMARY

The term *visual impairments* covers a wide range of conditions. In order of increasing severity of vision loss, the common categories are partially sighted, low vision, legally blind, and totally blind. Many educators, however, prefer to use categories related more directly to classroom functioning, such as moderate, severe, and profound visual impairment. As a teacher, you should watch for signs of visual trouble that may indicate a degenerative disorder such as diabetic retinopathy or glaucoma.

Children with visual impairments may have particular difficulty in learning the meanings of abstract words, and their socialization opportunities may be reduced by their mobility restrictions. Schools for the visually impaired can provide the specialized training such children need, as well as opportunities to interact with other similar students; but they often have the disadvantage of removing the child from his or her family. Placement decisions have to be made carefully, and your role as a teacher is to offer as much guidance and support as possible.

In adapting instruction for students with visual impairments, keep in mind three general principles: (1) Instruction should be as concrete as possible, allowing students to manipulate actual objects. (2) Students need unifying experiences—that is, discussions and activities that synthesize the diverse parts of the curriculum and tie them explicitly together. (3) Students with visual impairments need frequent opportunities for hands-on activities related to the lesson's subject matter. Often the best way to find out what a student needs is simply to ask.

Recorded books are the most basic technological tool for students with visual impairments. Braille continues to be the most popular form of presenting text, and recent Braille products include special displays, notetakers, and printers. A variety of screen readers are also available to read aloud the text on a computer screen. OCR tools help scan text or images into the computer, and speech recognition software allows users to control the computer with voice commands.

Adaptive technologies range from screen magnifiers to audio calculators and talking dictionaries. Special keyboards help visually impaired students with input, and closed circuit television can be helpful because of its magnification capabilities.

KEY TERMS

visual impairments (p. 170)
totally blind (p. 170)
legally blind (p. 170)
low vision (p. 170)
partially sighted (p. 170)
moderate visual impairment (p. 171)
severe visual impairment (p. 171)
profound visual impairment (p. 171)
total vision impairment (p. 171)
Braille (p. 177)
screen reader (p. 179)
accessible web design (p. 180)

RESOURCES FOR FURTHER INVESTIGATION

Online Resources

American Council of the Blind.
http://acb.org/
> A simple website with links to various resources. The articles are specially formatted for printing in Braille.

American Foundation for the Blind.
http://www.afb.org/
> Great resources in simple-to-read, large text, including books for children and parents as well as the periodical *Access World: Technology for Consumers with Visual Impairments.*

The American Printing House for the Blind.
http://www.aph.org/
> One web page at this site is dedicated solely to the demonstration of software and associated product information. The organization also offers an enormous array of computer software, as well as materials such as bold lined paper, raised lined paper, tape recorders, and Braille-like equipment.

Association for Education and Rehabilitation of the Blind and Visually Impaired (AERBVI).
http://www.aerbvi.org/
> This organization's resources include instructional suggestions, recorded books, and tips for accommodating a blind or visually impaired child in your class. The group also offers a support network for parents and for the individual with visual impairments.

A Blind Net.
http://www.blind.net/
> This site provides general information for the blind. It lists companies and organizations that sell equipment and educational products, as well as libraries, rehabilitation agencies, and other services for the visually impaired.

Guide to Toys for Children Who Are Blind or Visually Impaired.
http://www.toy-tma.org/industry/publications/blindcurrent/cover.html
> Sponsored by the Toy Industry Association, this site includes a page devoted to educational toys.

The National Federation of the Blind.
http://www.nfb.org/
Provides information on services, products, and technology aids, as well as general information.

The New York Institute for Special Education.
http://www.nyise.org/
A private, nonprofit, nonsectarian educational facility with quality programs for children who are blind, visually disabled, or emotionally and learning disabled, and for preschoolers who are developmentally delayed. In the Blindness Resource Center, you can find information about organizations, university programs, technology, publications, as well as educational and fun computer software for children.

Product Resources

ALVA Access Group. Oakland, CA.
http://www.aagi.com/
Maker of outSPOKEN and the ALVA Delphi Braille Display.

ASAP. Louisville, KY: MicroTalk Software.
http://www.microtalk.com/

Blazie. Stuart, FL.
http://www.blazie.com/
Maker of the AudioCalc-Talking Scientific Calculator, Braille 'n' Speak, and the Franklin Language Master.

Dragon NaturallySpeaking. Peabody, MA: Scansoft.
http://www.lhsl.com/naturallyspeaking/

Henter-Joyce. St. Petersburg, FL.
http://www.hj.com/
Maker of JAWS, MAGic, and OPENBook.

Kurzweil 3000. Burlington, MA: Kurzweil Educational Systems.
http://www.kurzweiledu.com/

LeapFrog Enterprises. Emeryville, CA.
http://www.leapfrog.com/
Manufacturer of the Explorer Globe and The Fun & Learn Phonics Bus.

Maltron adaptive keyboards. East Molesey, Surrey, England: PCD Maltron Ltd.
http://www.maltron.com/

Reading Pen. Acton, MA: Wizcom Technologies.
http://www.wizcomtech.com/products/readingpenII.html/

Road Runner. Danville, CA: Ostrich Software.
http://www.ostrichsoftware.com/

The Reading Edge. Sunnyvale, CA: Telesensory Corporation.
http://www.telesensory.com/

Versatile Image Processor. San Jose, CA: JBliss Imaging Systems.
http://www.jbliss.com/

Window Bridge. Stoney Creek, Ontario: Syntha-voice Computers.
http://www.synthavoice.com/

Window-Eyes. Fort Wayne, IN: GW Micro.
http://www.gwmicro.com/

WinVision. Troy, MI: Artic Technologies.
http://www.artictech.com/

ZoomText Xtra. Manchester Center, VT: Ai Squared.
http://www.aisquared.com/

TECHNOLOGY FOR STUDENTS WITH PHYSICAL DISABILITIES

9

FOCUS QUESTIONS

Many technologies, both familiar and cutting edge, help students with physical disabilities participate more easily in everyday life. Wheelchairs, hands-free telephone systems, and an array of other assistive and adaptive technologies make classroom activities and daily life more accessible and a little simpler. This chapter presents the ways in which these tools—and new tools on the horizon—can assist the student with a physical disability to become as independent as possible.

As you read this chapter, think about the following:

- How would you define a "physical disability"?

- What sorts of educational needs does a student with a physical disability have?

- How does a teacher modify a classroom to support this student?

- What sorts of technologies are available to help children with physical impairments?

- What resources help others learn more about physical and health impairments?

WHAT ARE PHYSICAL DISABILITIES?

The term *physical disabilities* is broad and covers a range of disabilities and health issues, including both congenital and acquired disabilities. Within that range are physical disabilities or impairments that interfere with a child's ability to attain the same developmental milestones as his or her age-mates. The number of students with physical disabilities is expected to grow as medical advances continue to reduce mortality rates for infants and children.

IDEA definition

According to the Individuals with Disabilities Education Act (IDEA), a person with an orthopedic impairment, brain injury, or other health impairment who, by reason of that impairment, needs special education and related services is considered to have a **physical disability.** The condition must interfere with or substantially limit the child's ability to take part in routine school activities. A physical disability or health condition need not limit activity; instead, it may involve other restrictions, such as a special diet or the student's need to use medical equipment.

The U.S. Department of Education estimates that 0.6 percent of the school-aged population has physical or health disabilities. This figure may be misleading in some ways, because it includes only those students who are eligible for special services. If medication or other assistance controls a condition, the child is ineligible.

● Types of Physical Disabilities

Physical disabilities and health conditions are classified as either congenital or acquired. Students with *congenital* conditions either are born with physical difficulties or develop them soon after birth. *Acquired* disabilities are those developed through injury or disease while the child is developing normally. The age at which a condition develops often determines its impact on the child.

Table 9.1 lists some commonly occurring physical and health impairments. Others not shown in the table include Tourette's syndrome, hydrocephalus, cleft palate, asthma, and AIDS. Because no such list includes all the conditions that may afflict children in your classroom, you must gather specific information about each child in your classroom and their conditions.

Conditions involving spinal cord damage

You may hear the phrase *physical and motor disabilities* used in reference to injuries that inhibit movement. Such injuries typically pertain to physical disabilities involving the spine. When spinal nerves are damaged, the individual loses both movement and feeling.

A **quadriplegic,** for example, has suffered damage to the nerves that manage the arms and legs, resulting in paralysis and loss of sensation. These nerves

Condition	Description	Prevalence in the United States
Traumatic brain injury (TBI)	TBI refers to any injury to the head and brain. It is the leading cause of death and physical disability to children in the United States. Boys are twice as likely as girls to sustain a brain or spinal cord injury.	95 per 100,000
Spinal-cord injury	An acquired neurological disorder in which the spinal cord has been damaged	40 per 1,000,000
Cerebral palsy	A disorder of movement caused by damage to the motor-control areas of the brain, affecting muscle tone and voluntary movements. Damage occurs from injury before or after birth that leads to oxygen deprivation or head injury.	500,000; approximately 5,000 new cases each year
Epilepsy	A seizure disorder in which the brain cells do not work properly in one or both sides of brain, causing a range of seizures from tonic-clonic (momentary loss of consciousness, with muscle twitching) to my-oclonic (abrupt jerking of muscles) and atonic (sud-den loss of muscle tone and loss of consciousness)	2.3 million
Neural tube defects	Included in these disorders are spina bifida, en-cephalocele, and anencephaly. Spina bifida exhibits a small gap or defect in the backbone and the spinal cord itself or the spinal column is exposed. En-cephalocele is an opening in the brain, and anen-cephaly is a major malformation of the brain that causes death of the fetus or infant in most cases.	Spina bifida affects approximately 1 of every 1,000 children.
Muscular dystrophy (MD)	A progressive disease of the musculoskeletal system (the muscles and the skeleton) that affects all mus-cles and eventually the heart and diaphragm, leading to death.	50,000–250,000 diagnosed annually
Juvenile rheumatoid arthritis (JRA)	Arthritis is a group of disorders that affect the joints. JRA causes stiff and swollen joints and pain.	Approximately 300,000 children
Cystic fibrosis	A genetic cardiopulmonary disorder that results in severe respiratory and digestive problems.	Approximately 30,000

● **TABLE 9.1**   Commonly occurring physical and health impairments

Sources: National Center for Injury Prevention and Control (http://www.cdc.gov/ncipc/), Centers for Disease Control and Prevention (http://www.cdc.gov/), Spinal Cord Injury Information Network (http://www.spinalcord.uab.edu/), United Cerebral Palsy Association (http://www.ucpa.org/), Spina Bifida Association of America (http://www.sbaa.org/), Muscular Dystrophy Family Foundation (http://www.mdff.org/), Arthritis Foundation (http://www.arthritis.org/), Cystic Fibrosis Foundation (http://www.cff.org/).

lie within the cervical vertebrae, and damage to them causes an inability to transfer messages to the brain. A **paraplegic** has lost the use of the trunk, legs, or pelvic organs; this condition results from trauma to the thoracic, lumbar, or sacral spinal nerves. In both conditions, the spinal cord remains in place but is incapable of transferring neurological information.

Figure 9.1 shows the placement of various types of nerves within the spine. The severity of an injury to the spinal cord depends in part on the location of

● FIGURE 9.1

The spinal cord and related functions

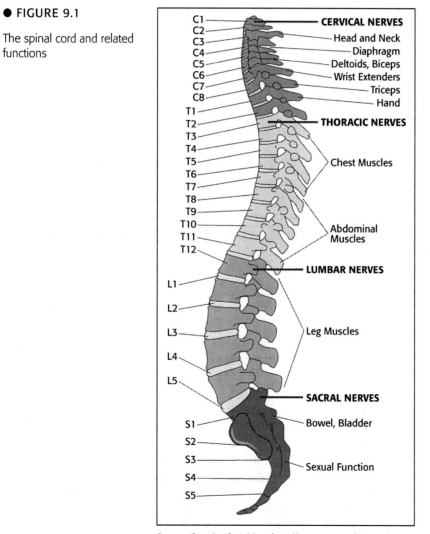

Source: Cure Paralysis Now, http://www.cureparalysis.org/.

the damage. Generally speaking, the higher the location of the injury, the more serious the paralysis will be. For example, in his book *Still Me,* Christopher Reeve (the actor who starred in *Superman*) explains that his injury from his horseback riding accident was between the C1 and C2 cervical vertebrae. The injury requires him to use a respirator and prevents movement from the neck down.

The effects of spinal damage are further divided into levels of injury. *Complete* injury refers to the inability to move and to be aware of movement and sensation; the cervical nerves have lost all their ability to connect with the brain. An individual with an *incomplete* injury retains some degree of mobility and at least a partial capacity to acknowledge sensation and voluntary movement.

INSTRUCTIONAL ADAPTATIONS FOR STUDENTS WITH PHYSICAL IMPAIRMENTS

A physical disability may or may not affect a child's academic performance. Therefore, although you might not need to make curriculum adaptations for such a student, you may need to modify performance requirements or implement adaptations to allow the student access to instructional materials. Children who often miss school because of their medical conditions may require adjustments to the pace of instruction or to the amount of information they must learn.

Students with physical disabilities often need special professional services outside the classroom. Orientation and mobility specialists can assist the student in using a wheelchair. Occupational therapists can teach daily living activities such as dressing, and physical therapists can help with walking or keyboarding skills. Doctors and nurses may be involved in this student's life to help with mediation and pain management.

Importance of keeping informed

Most of all, as a classroom teacher of a student with a physical impairment, you must stay informed on three points: (1) warning signs that the student needs help or is having a problem, (2) the student's limitations and their influence on defining reasonable expectations, and (3) how to handle an emergency brought on by the student's condition. Take the time to learn as much as you can about the child's condition while keeping in mind that the student is an individual, not a health condition. You shouldn't be afraid to talk to the student about what works or doesn't work for him or her, but seek first an understanding of the student as a person. Involved medical and therapeutic specialists can give you some insight into classroom modifications that will ensure the greatest opportunity for success.

Accessibility in the Classroom and Elsewhere

Accommodating a student with a physical disability requires you to carefully examine your classroom in order to make everything accessible. This might mean lowering the pencil sharpener or arranging furniture to make aisles easy to navigate in a wheelchair. This is another opportunity to think about the Universal Design for Learning, a concept mentioned in earlier chapters. In this case, if you consider all your students in terms of their range of motor skills, you'll begin to think beyond the group labeled "physically disabled." You will see students with a range of, say, physical coordination or artistic skill, and you will design lessons that offer alternatives to kinesthetic learning or to demonstrations of learning that require fine motor skills.

Consider all learning situations

One of your greatest challenges will be to ensure that the student with a physical disability is comfortable in all the learning situations to which your class is exposed. For example, when planning a field trip, you need to confirm that the location is wheelchair accessible, that it has parking nearby, and that the entire class can participate in the activities. Most museums and sites of interest are accessible to students with physical limitations, but always confirm access. It can be distressing to everyone, including you, to discover on the spot that a location or activity is inaccessible.

Classroom Strategies

Some strategies to help incorporate the student with a physical disability into your classroom include the following:

Ideas for an inclusive classroom

- Set up a buddy system so that another student can take notes for the student with a physical disability and assist him or her with other in-class requirements.
- Arrange the room so that everyone can move around easily.
- Have students with difficulty speaking (as is the case with cerebral palsy) use an alternative presentation format in place of oral reporting.
- Make sure all activities include all students.
- Be flexible and accept suggestions.
- Talk to the student about what he or she likes to do and can do.
- Identify a student's areas of expertise. Out of necessity, for instance, the student may have become extremely proficient with the computer, and perhaps he or she can share that knowledge with the class.

Jacqueline Montgomery

Screens from Jacqueline's HyperStudio project on the "Turkey Chase" 5k Race—a project to demonstrate how authoring tools can be used.

On Thanksgiving morning, instead of sleeping or cooking dinner, I ran in a race, called the Bethesda Turkey Chase. Both runners and wheelchair racers were competing. I was so nervous!

S T A R T

me

I could see the Finish line. Was I excited!!! I pushed my wheelchair faster and faster until the race was over. I was so surprised to find out that I was in first place for the wheelchair racers. I was so happy. What a great day!

F I N I S H

J acqueline Montgomery is a classroom teacher. She happens to be in a wheelchair. The author first met Jackie some years ago, when she was a student in an "Introduction to Special Education" course. She later took the author's "Uses of Technology in Education" course, in which she created the accompanying illustrations as a sample of what she would have her students do with software like HyperStudio. After graduating with a B.A. in elementary education in 1997, Jackie began teaching first grade in New Jersey. By all reports she's a great teacher and wheelchair athlete, and her students do well.

In her early teens Jackie was quite active in sports; in fact, she was a soccer star. Between her sophomore and junior years in high school, Jackie was in a car accident that caused severe damage to her spinal cord. The accident damaged her spine at the L4 level and caused paralysis from the waist down. After many years of rehabilitation, she re-entered the sports world, and is an extraordinary wheelchair athlete.

Motivating her students is sometimes the greatest challenge for Jackie, as it might be for you. Another challenge she has is that parents are sometimes concerned about how Jackie might do in an emergency situation. She frequently must deal with people who are poorly informed about people with disabilities.

PROFILE CONTINUED Jackie's technological aids mainly focus on mobility—the wheelchair, most obviously. Her wheelchair has no handles on the back of the seat. Jackie has had too many experiences with people, trying to be helpful, who push her places she doesn't want to go or offer help when she doesn't need it. Jackie's sport utility vehicle has hand controls so that she can drive it. Because her school is on one level, she needs no ramp to her classroom. In her apartment she has a shower with a seat so that she can transfer from her wheelchair. Eventually, when she buys a house, she'll install lower cabinets and countertops in the kitchen and bathroom.

Aside from these personal adaptations, Jackie's primary concern with technology is the same as yours—she is always trying to find ways to incorporate it into her classroom. Recently she noted that her first-graders like to use computers. She looks for software that helps her emergent readers, and she seeks ways to help the kids be creative when they are using the computer.

ADAPTIVE AND ASSISTIVE TECHNOLOGY

The phrase "technology in special education" often brings to mind the adaptive and assistive devices designed for persons with physical limitations. As you know from earlier chapters, technology can include any tool that we use to improve learning conditions, including such simple devices as pencil grips, lowered tables, and ramps, or more sophisticated tools such as computers and software. Handheld computers (such as the Palm Handheld and the Handspring Visor) help many people, including some with physical impairments, organize and manage their lives. Voice-activated computers, touch screens, and text-to-speech software can help with a variety of physical and health impairments. All of these constitute technologies that may assist the person with a physical disability. Optimally, the parents, child, special education teacher, and other specialists will have researched the student's needs and the environment of the school before the student is placed in your classroom. Table 9.2 offers a quick summary of useful technologies, and the sections that follow describe a number of them in more detail.

● Toys and Games

One key goal for a child with a physical or health impairment is to make life as accessible and enjoyable as possible. Toys and games that are easily adaptable or that have large buttons can help the child continue to develop

● TABLE 9.2

Technologies useful for students with physical disabilities

Area of Adaptation	Examples
Architectural access	Automatic doors with pressure plates
	Wide hallways
	Handrails in bathrooms
	Lower drinking fountains, with push lever rather than buttons
	Ramps
	Lowered and/or adapted switches for lights and other devices
	Robotic tools for hard-to-reach places
Mobility	Wheelchairs
	Walkers
	Canes
Communication	Augmentative and alternative communication devices
	Book holders
	Telephone adaptations
	Text-to-speech devices
	Screen readers
Computer access	Joysticks
	Handheld computers
	Specialized keyboards and keypads
	Keyguards
	Touch-screen monitors
	Mouth- or foot-controlled switches
	Voice-activated systems
	Accessible websites
Developmental activities	Toys with large buttons or other adaptations

both physically and intellectually. Dragonfly Toy Company sells specially designed toys and games, as well as "traditional" toys that can provide a child with a physical or health impairment with an opportunity for fun and development.

● Augmentative and Alternative Communication

The field of augmentative and alternative communication, discussed in detail in chapter 6, focuses on providing technology support to people who have

The DynaMyte keyboard

difficulty communicating through speech, writing, or sign. These low-tech or high-tech tools can assist students with cerebral palsy, traumatic brain injury, stroke, amyotrophic lateral sclerosis (ALS), and any other students who need help in expressing their ideas or wishes. For example, the DynaMyte keyboard (Figure 9.2) from DynaVox Systems translates a student's typed words into speech. It can be programmed to use different voices, depending on age, gender, and situation (for example, one voice might be suitable for travel, another for class discussions). This communication device has large touch-screen buttons. Depending on the cognitive development of the child, larger picture-only buttons or smaller words-only buttons can be used.

● Computer Access

Using a computer—including entering information into the computer (input) and receiving information from the computer (output)—can be challenging to a person with a physical or health impairment. In today's world, easy assess to the computer and to the Internet is especially important, given the ease of communication and the plethora of information on the Web.

● FIGURE 9.2

The DynaMyte 3100 from
DynaVox Systems

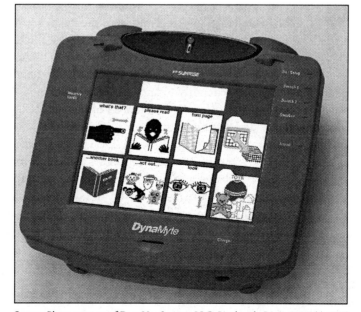

Source: Photo courtesy of DynaVox Systems LLC, Pittsburgh, PA (1-800-344-1778).

Fortunately, a person with limited movement has many ways to use the computer. Specialized keyboards and keyboard adaptations are available, and keyboard emulators can make the computer "think" that its own keyboard is being used. Examples of such devices are

Adaptive devices for computer use

- Alternative keypads (such as a sketch pad or graphic pad)
- Fist/foot keyboard (a keyboard designed with the foot or fist in mind as the input technique)
- Joystick (used instead of a mouse)
- Keyboard emulators, such as HandsOFF! (Sensory Software International), that allow a person using a switch or mouth control to press on-screen "keys"
- Keyguard (a raised overlay placed over the keyboard to guide the placement of fingers and to avoid mistaken striking of keys)
- Touch-screen monitors that allow the person to make selections by touching the screen itself rather than by using a pointing device
- Mouth- or foot-controlled switches, which allow the user to guide the mouse or pointer with his or her mouth or foot

● Environmental Adaptations

Environmental controls and manipulators can modify the operation of a device to compensate for a student's disability. For example, a person with paralysis can have a voice-activated telephone connected to her wheelchair. Wide hallways and greater space in the classroom can allow a child to move around more independently. Again, the idea of universal design is important. In fact, the main principles of the Universal Design for Learning are grounded in universal design architecture.

The Center for Universal Design at North Carolina State University (**http://www.design.ncsu.edu/cud/**) lays out some principles for universal design in building and engineering. These principles state that buildings (including classrooms) should be designed so that all users can have easier mobility. For example, automatic doorways are a nice way to enter a store for all people, whether or not they use wheelchairs. Some examples of environmental controls and manipulators designed specifically for people with physical impairments are

Technology for environmental design

- Adapted timers, light switches, telephone/radio amplifiers, headphones, buzzers that are easier to manipulate

- Pressure plates to control automatic doors or elevators
- Robotics: for example, in a large library a robotic arm could reach the higher shelves

SUMMARY

A physical disability can involve any physical or health impairment, congenital or acquired, that affects a student's ability to take part in school activities. Motor disabilities, such as those experienced by people who are quadriplegics or paraplegics, typically involve damage to the spinal nerves. Other physical disabilities include conditions such as cerebral palsy, epilepsy, and muscular dystrophy.

A physical disability does not necessarily impair a child's academic performance. However, many children with physical disabilities need some degree of instructional adaptation, at least for accessibility to classroom spaces and tools. Some also require the services of therapists and other specialists. Buddy systems can help you make sure that a student with a physical disability is not left out of classroom activities. Adaptive and assistive technology can range from low-tech devices such as pencil grips and ramps to sophisticated software and hardware. Specially designed toys and games can keep a child developing both intellectually and physically. Alternative keyboards and keypads can aid communication and computer access, as can joysticks, touch-screen monitors, and special switches.

Remember that every student with a physical disability is an individual, not a condition; become acquainted with the student and take advantage of his or her areas of expertise. The Universal Design for Learning concept is also an excellent guide to developing instructional techniques. In planning an activity, if you think of your students in terms of their full range of physical capabilities as a group—instead of focusing just on those who are physically "disabled"—you'll be able to develop lessons that involve everyone and capitalize on your students' many abilities and learning styles.

KEY TERMS

physical disability (p. 187)
quadriplegic (p. 187)
paraplegic (p. 189)

RESOURCES FOR FURTHER INVESTIGATION

Online Resources

Arthritis Foundation.
http://www.arthritis.org/
> In addition to offering information about treatment and therapies for all types of arthritic conditions, this site includes a section on juvenile arthritis, with pertinent information for parents and teachers.

Cystic Fibrosis Foundation.
http://www.cff.org/
> This foundation's website includes facts about the disorder, links to organizations and support groups, and information about research on the disease.

Epilepsy Foundation.
http://www.efa.org/
> The Epilepsy Foundation offers a great deal of information about working with people who have epilepsy—information that is particularly useful for teachers and schools. The website also provides links to local organizations and research groups.

Muscular Dystrophy Association.
http://www.mdausa.org/
> This organization, which supports research on preventing and healing MD, offers links to experts as well as to local organizations that support children with the disease.

National Center for Injury Prevention and Control.
http://www.cdc.gov/ncipc/
> This unit of the Centers for Disease Control and Prevention provides information about a range of different injuries and accidents, including traumatic brain injury and spinal cord injury. It also offers helpful guidance concerning safety and education.

Spina Bifida Association of America.
http://www.sbaa.org/
> The association's website includes information about the condition as well as related neural tube defects. It also offers various publications and links to local chapters.

Spinal Cord Injury Information Network.
http://www.spinalcord.uab.edu/
> This website provides information about spinal cord injuries, and it has an excellent listing of organizations to support people with such injuries.

Sports 'n' Spokes.
http://www.sportsnspokes.com/
> Published by the Paralyzed Veterans of America, this magazine is dedicated to providing information about wheelchair athletics and recreational activities for people in wheelchairs.

Tech Connections.
http://www.techconnections.org/
> Sponsored by the Center for Rehabilitation Technology, this site offers information on assistive technology designed to create accommodations for people with disabilities in the workplace and in everyday life activities.

United Cerebral Palsy Association.
http://www.ucpa.org/
> This association is an advocacy group for people with CP. It also provides information and support for teachers and parents, and sponsors research into prevention of the disease.

Product Resources

Dragonfly Toy Company. Winnipeg, MB, Canada.
http://www.dftoys.com/
> Maker of toys and games for children with physical disabilities.

DynaMyte keyboard. Pittsburgh, PA: DynaVox Systems.
http://www.dynavoxsys.com/

HandsOFF! Great Malvern, UK: Sensory Software International.
http://www.zygo-usa.com/handsoff.html

Organizations

Administration on Developmental Disabilities
Administration for Children and Families
U.S. Department of Health and Human Services
Mail Stop: HHH 300-F
370 L'Enfant Promenade, S.W.
Washington, DC 20447
(202) 690-6590
http://www.acf.dhhs.gov/programs/add/

Easter Seals
230 W. Monroe Street, Suite 1800
Chicago, IL 60606
(312) 726-6200
(800) 221-6827
http://www.easter-seals.org/

National Institute of Neurological Disorders and Stroke (NINDS)
National Institutes of Health
P.O. Box 5801
Bethesda, MD 20824
(800) 352-9424
http://www.ninds.nih.gov/

10

TECHNOLOGY FOR STUDENTS WITH OTHER DISABILITIES

FOCUS QUESTIONS

As you read this chapter, think about the following:

- What is autism? What sorts of students are labeled as having autism or autistic-related disorders?

- What sorts of instructional methods benefit a child with autism?

- How will technology play a role in the life of a child with autism?

- What does the term *deaf-blind* mean?

- What sorts of needs might a deaf-blind student have?

- In what ways can technology help a student who is deaf-blind?

- What do we mean by the term *multiple disabilities*?

- How do we determine appropriate interventions for a child with multiple disabilities?

- How can technology assist a student with multiple disabilities?

This chapter offers a brief overview of disabling conditions other than those discussed in earlier chapters. A look into technology that helps students with autism, deaf-blindness, and multiple disabilities provides a model for selecting tools to meet the diverse needs of children in your classroom. You will need to stay informed about the developmental and physical health of your students and to communicate with parents when a child in your care has any condition requiring your understanding and attention.

AUTISM AND RELATED CONDITIONS

Although we have mentioned autism in previous chapters, this section describes the condition in greater detail, as well as related disorders such as Asperger's syndrome and pervasive developmental disorders. Generally, autism can be described as a range of behaviors and conditions that present from mild to severe. According to the Individuals with Disabilities Education Act (IDEA), **autism** is

Autism defined

> a developmental disability significantly affecting verbal and nonverbal communication and social interaction, usually evident before age 3, that adversely affects a child's educational performance. Other characteristics often associated with autism are engagement in repetitive activities and stereotyped movements, resistance to environmental change or change in daily routines, and unusual responses to sensory experiences.

Autism was first used as a clinical diagnosis in 1943, when Dr. Leo Kanner described eleven children who possessed a cluster of characteristics, most strikingly a social separateness on the part of the child (Kanner, 1943). At about the same time, Hans Asperger's dissertation work outlined qualities shared by a group of "disturbed" children and adults whose traits and tendencies were remarkably similar to those of Kanner's autistic children, but who had better language skills (Frith, 1999). These two descriptions now form the basis for the definitions of autism and Asperger's syndrome found in the *Diagnostic and Statistical Manual of Mental Disorders,* known as the DSM (American Psychiatric Association, 2000).

The DSM includes autism and Asperger's syndrome in the more general category of **pervasive developmental disorders** (PDD), a category that also includes *Rett's disorder, childhood disintegrative disorder,* and *pervasive developmental disorder not otherwise specified (PDD-NOS).* The pervasive developmental disorders all include, to some degree, the following triad of clinical findings:

Characteristics of pervasive developmental disorders

- Qualitative impairments in social interaction
- Qualitative impairments in communication
- Restricted, repetitive, and stereotyped patterns of behavior, interest, and activities

Children with various types of PDD have other important features in common. First, in physical terms, these children typically have a normal and attractive appearance. Second, the disorder always manifests itself in several different areas of development at once, usually between 1.5 and 3 years of age. Third, the child has not only developmental delays but also developmental deviations or distortions that are qualitatively abnormal at any stage of development. What might such "distortions" include? Dr. Kanner noted a set of distinguishing aspects of cognition and behavior that set these children apart from others:

1 Exceptional inability to relate to others
2 Mutism or atypical language
3 Insistence on maintaining sameness in the environment
4 Rigidly stereotyped play with small objects
5 Lack of imagination and playfulness
6 Certain isolated areas of ability (such as good rote memory, fine motor skills, or spatial perception)

Other noticeable traits in children with autism include these:

- Short attention span and impulsivity
- Self-injurious behaviors
- Odd responses to sensory input
- Abnormalities of mood
- An uneven profile of skill development (some skills develop much more successfully than others)
- Abnormalities in eating, drinking, or sleeping
- Unusual fears or anxieties
- A strong need for routines: if an autistic child's routines are imposed upon, he may scream, throw a tantrum, or engage in self-stimulatory behaviors such as hand flapping

Most autistic children show some degree of mental retardation, as identified by intelligence tests. However, because the children are often noncommunicative and introverted, these tests are difficult to conduct, and their reliability and validity are therefore suspect. A relationship appears to exist between intelligence test scores and behavior. That is, the degree of retardation has a positive correlation with self-injurious and self-stimulatory behavior. Nevertheless, rather than emphasizing mental retardation, it is more useful to focus on the way the student functions in ordinary home and school situations. (See Principles and Practice: Autism as a Continuum of Behaviors.)

P RINCIPLES AND PRACTICE   Autism as a Continuum of Behaviors

Autism and related disorders occur on a continuum from low to high functioning. For example, a low-functioning person with autism may be severely nonverbal and noncommunicative. Usually she engages in repetitive behaviors, such as rocking, self-abuse (for instance, harmful head banging or serious self-scratching), spinning, or hand flapping. Many low-functioning individuals, if they employ language at all, use it in a way that authorities characterize as "echolalic" and without any "true meaning." *Echolalic* speech often involves echoing or repeating words or stock phrases over and over, or saying them immediately after another person has used them. For example, the child may say "no problemo" in response to every query, or she might just repeat the question back to the speaker. The child may also repeat phrases or dialogue from a television show or a prior situation in seemingly inappropriate contexts, without showing any grasp of their meaning.

Autistic people at a higher level of functioning can use some language but have serious language-processing difficulties or social impediments, such as a consistent preference for being alone. Their interactions with other people tend to be utilitarian; they may need others to perform functions such as opening a door and pouring juice.

Some people with autism show "splinter skills" or savant behavior. A *splinter skill* is one area of function in which the person excels, usually in sharp contrast to the individual's general level of performance. The most frequently used illustration of a splinter skill is the character played by Dustin Hoffman in the movie *Rain Man*. This character, a fairly good example of a high-functioning person, expresses his wants and needs and has a complicated set of splinter skills that enable him to count quickly. Overall, however, the movie *Rain Man* is not particularly representative of most people with autism.

Asperger's syndrome, which was first identified as a separate disorder in the 1994 DSM, now sometimes provides a label for people with less severe forms of autism, such as social interaction impairments or difficulty comprehending verbal and nonverbal language, especially nonliteral language such as idioms and sarcasm.

Autism exists in four or five of every ten thousand children. Boys are much more at risk than girls. It may be accompanied by other handicapping conditions, such as a seizure disorder or significant cognitive delays. It is important to note, though, that the symptoms displayed by an individual with autism can change as he or she matures or receives treatment.

● Instructional Methods for Autistic Children

Autistic children receive educational support in a variety of settings from the regular classroom to residential treatment centers. The decision on where to place a child with autism, Asperger's syndrome, or any other type of PDD obviously depends on the degree to which the child can function in normal situations. Often, because the child with autism needs strict adherence to routines and schedules and may engage in distracting, self-stimulating behaviors, it is hard for him or her to function in a regular classroom. However, some children with autism, through behavior modification techniques, medications, or other supports, can function well in mainstream environments. As with any exceptional student, placement decisions must be individual and reviewed regularly.

Educational programs for children with autism often include some element of behavior modification. **Behavior modification** can be described as any system of directly instructing the child to manage his or her own behavior and reactions to the environment. The following sections describe three common approaches to behavior modification.

Behavior modification: child learns to manage own behavior

Applied Behavior Analysis ●

One technique of behavior modification that works well with children with autism is *applied behavior analysis* (ABA). ABA helps a child replace negative behaviors (such as hand flapping) with more positive behaviors (such as sitting still or focusing on a task).

ABA: rewards for specific behaviors

When teacher and therapists decide to use ABA, they start with specific behaviors designed to replace other behaviors. For example, teachers and parents may decide to help a child learn to assemble his own writing supplies. The first step is to break down the task of collecting supplies using task analysis (described in the chapter on learning disabilities). One element might involve having the child organize materials on his desk. Each time the child puts his paper in the center of his desk, he may receive a checkmark, treat, or sticker. The child must see the reward as worthwhile. Some children are happy just to receive "points" with no other apparent value; other children may need the motivation of cashing in a page of checkmarks or stickers for free time, time to work on puzzles or mazes, or computer time.

Another important element of ABA is *fading*—that is, reducing the reinforcement or reward until the child completes the task without any outside checks. In the example of a student who is learning to collect his writing supplies, the teacher may slowly move away from rewarding the student when he has his paper ready. The goal is for the student eventually to understand when "writing time" takes place and to begin work on his own.

The most successful uses of ABA, for students with and without autism, occur when the student has some degree of control over the reinforcement, including self-monitoring of behavior, and when the task is most specific. The teacher, parent, or therapist must find and reinforce specific, measurable behaviors that replace other distracting or troubling behaviors.

Lovaas Treatment ●

Another behavior modification technique, grounded in applied behavior analysis, is known as *Lovaas treatment* after its developer, Ivor Lovaas. The Lovaas program focuses on teaching children skills such as attention, receptive and expressive language, and self-help. The Lovaas method uses an ABC (*antecedent, behavior, consequence*) model to look at why behaviors occur. Its premise is this: Each behavior has an *antecedent,* the request or action that requires the child to act. Following the antecedent, the *behavior* itself takes place, followed by the *consequences* of the behavior. Therefore, if you want to know why a child with autism reacted in a certain way, you investigate the antecedents and consequences of the behavior. Then you can begin to design a way to modify the behavior. The Lovaas method requires one-on-one therapy and makes use of reinforcements to help shape the child's behavior. This method has been effective for many children (American Society for Autism, 2001).

Lovaas method: analyzing antecedents and consequences

TEACCH ● A third technique that helps autistic children is the *TEACCH method.* TEACCH, a loose acronym for Treatment and Education of Autistic and related Communication Handicapped Children, was designed in 1968 by a group of teachers and therapists. The TEACCH method uses an individually designed instructional program both at home and at school to build general autonomy. The program focuses on visual learning, and it uses structure and predictability to support spontaneous communication. Although this approach has been considered appropriate only for autistic children, its techniques may actually help students with other developmental and behavioral disorders.

TEACCH: individualized program of visual learning

The TEACCH program has been criticized for requiring extensive training by teachers and caregivers and for the difficulty in implementing it across various settings (Marcus & Schopler, 1994; Mesibov, 1995). You can read more about this method at the Autism Society of America website (**http://www. autism-society.org/**).

In your own teaching, you may work with a child who is participating in TEACCH, Lovaas, ABA, or some other behavior modification method. Whatever the treatment modality, a few simple techniques can help you attain success with the child. For guidelines, see the feature Techniques for Your Classroom: Tips for Working with a Student with Autism.

● Technology for Autistic Children

One main area in which technology can benefit autistic children is communication. A popular educational technique, known as the *Picture Exchange Communication System* (PECS), makes use of pictorial representations to help the child express ideas and develop communication skills. PECS is popular in programs for children with autism, and it easily incorporates the use of technology.

TECHNIQUES FOR YOUR CLASSROOM

Tips for Working with a Student with Autism

When you teach a student with autism, remember these important points:

- Have high expectations.
- Tasks should be complete. That is, students should have a sense of the beginning and end of any task and its relation to themselves. Students should also be expected to complete any given task.
- Like other students, the child with autism should clean up after himself or herself.
- Set ground rules and be consistent in enforcing them.
- Apply the rule of consistency to handling tantrums.
- Praise the student (and all other students) for good behavior as a way of eliminating negative behavior.
- Ignore negative behavior whenever possible.
- Avoid unnecessary routines; don't ask the child to engage in an activity that has no purpose. For example, don't have the student with autism follow a complex procedure for getting ready to go to recess. Set clear guidelines for the student, but don't create special tasks that have no value or alternative use.

- Seat the student close to you but in a social setting.
- Expose the student to new social and physical situations.
- Avoid physical struggles. If a child needs physical restraint, do *not* attempt to do this yourself without proper training and communication with the child. If a child is *tactile defensive* (resistant to being touched), avoid touching the student when redirecting him or her. Instead of physically attempting to control the child, make every effort to remove him or her from the situation or remove the "stimulus" (another child, a sound) from the student.
- Meet regularly with the student.
- Vary activities. When you teach a student with autism you will likely fall into a routine, which supports the child's need for consistency. Within that routine, however, find ways to expand ideas and activities, such as reading from trade books in addition to workbooks or a textbook.
- Incorporate art and hands-on activities into lessons.
- Identify other activities the student enjoys and use these in your teaching.

Using PECS graphics

For example, Boardmaker, the software program that accompanies the IntelliKeys keyboard, includes a set of PECS graphics to use with children with autism and related conditions. Another software program, Picture This (Silver Lining Multimedia), helps present real photos without ambiguous background clutter; these can be personal photographs that the child can easily identify. The DynaMyte communicator (DynaVox Systems), described in the chapter on physical disabilities, is also a popular tool for children with autism, and it can be incorporated into the PECS education method (see Figure 10.1).

Using speech-language technology

Technologies focused on assisting children with speech and language are also popular in programs for children with autism. For example, Earobics software (Cognitive Concepts) can help children develop speech skills and language strategies within a controlled environment. A group of researchers at the Perceptual Science Laboratory at the University of California, Santa Cruz (see **http://mambo.ucsc.edu/**) has developed a program to help a person un-

● FIGURE 10.1

Screen from an online demo by DynaVox Systems, showing PECS used as an overlay for a DynaVox keyboard. The window at the top left displays a sentence created with a word-prediction feature that highlights relevant picture keys when the user types the first letter of a word.

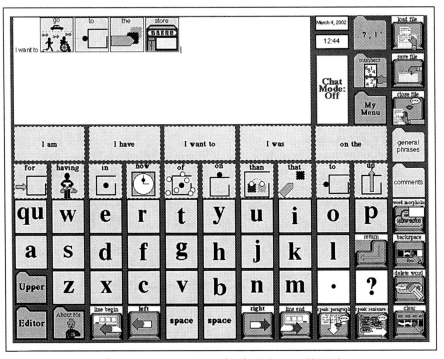

Source: Photo courtesy of DynaVox Systems LLC, Pittsburgh, PA (1-800-344-1778).

derstand communication by looking at the facial expressions of the speaker. The program uses a character named Baldi to illustrate the movements of a speaker when he is uttering a particular type of statement. Fast ForWord (Scientific Learning) has also been used successfully with autistic children because it develops letter/sound understanding through story analysis.

Students might also take advantage of traditional educational software packages, particularly those that offer immediate feedback and adequately break down the concept being taught. The computer may be a preferred method of instruction for some students with autism, because it limits both human interaction and the set of tasks or activities in each program. For example, with a program such as Mighty Math (Edmark), a child can work on a series of mathematics skills and receive instant feedback on progress. The Thinkin' Things Collection (also by Edmark) helps children learn how to observe situations and keep track of important information.

Other technologies that assist autistic children include these:

Using traditional software

• *Medication therapy.* Stimulant use has some positive effect on the interactions and communication skills of children with autism. In some cases this is the only special service the child receives.

Matthew McDonald

Matthew at home, happily watching a video and relaxing.

Matthew McDonald was born about three weeks before his due date. His mother had a fairly normal pregnancy, and although Matthew was small, he seemed to be reaching all the developmental milestones at the "right" times. At about age two and a half, Matthew started in a preschool program at a new, small, private school close to his mother's work. He seemed to do well there. The only boy in the program, he was more mechanical than the other students, but because both the teacher and the classroom aide had little experience with young children, they mostly attributed the difference to his being a boy.

After Matthew had spent about a year in the program, however, the teacher showed increasing concern about his lack of interaction with the other children, as well as about the way he often repeated phrases over and over again. He had a few toys that he played with all the time, including a model "Thomas the Tank Engine" that he carried with him at all times. When asked to put down his "Thomas," he sobbed and became withdrawn. Once, he left his "Thomas" in the car when his mother dropped him off, and this resulted in a major tantrum in school.

Matthew's mother hesitated to take him to a specialist. She felt the teacher had nothing positive to say, constantly picked on her son, and treated him differently from the other children. Unfortunately, this may have been the case. Eventually, though, Matthew's parents took him to their pediatrician, who recommended a developmental specialist and a language therapist. The developmental specialist, after evaluating Matthew both at home and at school, identified some areas of concern. She recommended that Matthew receive a full evaluation by a psychologist. The speech-language therapist found that Matthew had a large vocabulary and good articulation, but seemed unable to carry on a conversation or use language to obtain what he needed. The psychologist and her team gave Matthew a range of tests and assessments. Although his intelligence score was in the normal range, Matthew showed some language problems and unusual reactions to interactions. After more evaluation, the psychological team explained to Matthew's parents that he had a pervasive developmental disorder, and the best diagnosis was Asperger's syndrome.

By the time all the assessment and evaluation had taken place, Matthew was four years old. His parents worked with the local school system to locate a private school that focused mainly on children with learning disabilities. Although Matthew had no learning disabilities as far as anyone knew, this program could offer him structure and a supportive environment.

Matthew continues in that program today. He receives regular speech therapy and sensory-integration therapy—a technique used to help children regulate their own activity level. His language is good, and he needs no special communication technology, but he uses the computer to work on mathematics. He works with traditional mathematics software such as Math Blaster (Knowledge Adventure) as well as with Access to Math (Don Johnston) to review basic math facts. He has just started using an AlphaSmart keyboard, which aids his keyboarding and helps him understand sentence structure without worrying about how to shape letters. He uses Kid Pix software (Broderbund) to express his ideas and creativity as well as work on basic fine motor skills.

Another technological device Matthew uses both at home and at school is his LeapPad (LeapFrog Enterprises, **http://www.leapfrog.com/**). The LeapPad has several books (workbooks) that he inserts to work on basic reading skills. Matthew's current favorite is the reading workbook that includes characters from the movie *Monsters, Inc.* The sturdy LeapPad can be taken in the car and gives him an opportunity to focus on a task and work independently.

- *The Squeeze Machine.* Created by Temple Grandin, author of *Thinking in Pictures,* the Squeeze Machine was originally designed to calm cattle during transportation. The machine similarly can help people with autism calm down. Its mechanical "squeeze" is carefully controlled so that the person grows used to the touch and comfortable with it. Then this level of comfort with touch can theoretically be transferred to the touch of another human being.

- *Facilitated communication.* Facilitated communication is a process by which a person with autism works with a "facilitator" to communicate ideas. The facilitator holds the student's arm gently as he or she types out sentences on a nonelectronic communication board (typically, letters laid out in an alphabetic or QWERTY format on a piece of cardboard or plastic). Though the facilitator's role is simply to steady the arm of the person typing, this process has roused a large degree of controversy. Critics wonder who is communicating—the child or the facilitator? (To read more about this controversy, see Jacobson, Mulick, & Schwartz, 1995, available online at **http://www.apa.org/journals/jacobson.html.**)

ᴅEAF-BLIND IMPAIRMENT

The U.S. Department of Education (2000) reports that approximately sixteen hundred children who are both deaf and blind participated in special education programs during the 1998–1999 school year. According to the IDEA definition, children who are **deaf-blind** have

Definition of deaf-blind

> auditory and visual impairments, the combination of which creates such severe communication and other developmental and learning needs that they cannot be appropriately educated in special education programs solely for children and youth with hearing impairments, visual impairments, or severe disabilities, without supplementary assistance to address their educational needs due to these dual concurrent disabilities.

A child who is labeled as deaf-blind is rarely both totally blind and totally deaf. He or she typically has some degree of residual hearing or sight that determines appropriate services. For example, many children who are deaf-blind have some remaining sight that allows them to see enlarged object up close. Or they may have enough residual hearing to take advantage of hearing aids or other amplification devices.

Not all causes of deaf-blindness are known. Some cases arise from accident, such as a head injury, or from illness contracted during childhood. Often, though, the problem begins before the child is born; for example:

- *Rubella.* If a pregnant woman contracts rubella, the infant may suffer from hearing, visual, and heart problems.
- *Usher's syndrome.* A genetic disorder, Usher's syndrome seems to account for 50 percent of the population of people identified with deaf-blindness.
- *CHARGE syndrome.* CHARGE is a complex syndrome of unknown origin that causes lesions in the eye, heart defects, breathing problems, deafness, and stunted growth. (Resources for Further Investigation at the end of this chapter offers leads to information about this condition.)

P RINCIPLES AND PRACTICE | The Experience of Deaf-Blindness

Helen Keller is probably the best-known example of a person who was deaf-blind. Helen was born with sight and hearing, but after a childhood illness she lost both. Her story, portrayed in the movie *The Miracle Worker* and much more accurately in her own book *The Story of My Life*, reveals the unique experience of a person who is deaf-blind.

Living without the ability to see and hear may at first seem limiting, but focusing on the three remaining senses of touch, smell, and taste may give the child a fine appreciation of the world, especially of small details. The child may interpret certain experiences in a deeper way than those of us who focus on looks and sounds. For example, Helen Keller wrote eloquently in her book about tastes. One passage about eating walnuts conveys such detail that it makes the reader hungry! For example, Keller writes of her lessons outdoors:

> We read and studied out of doors, preferring the sunlit woods to the house. All my early lessons have in them the breath of the woods—the fine, resinous odor of pine needles, blended with the perfume of wild grapes. Seated in the gracious shade of a wild tulip tree, I learned to think that everything has lesson and a suggestion. . . . I felt the bursting cotton-bolls and fingered their soft fiber and fuzzy seeds; I felt the low soughing of the wind through the cornstalks, the silky rustling of the long leaves, and the indignant snort of my pony, as we caught him in the pasture and put the bit in his mouth—ah me! how well I remember the spicy, clovery smell of his breath! (Keller, 1903).

In addition, children with Down syndrome may be born with deaf-blindness, as may those with prenatal AIDS and fetal alcohol syndrome. Maternal drug abuse and other prenatal traumas can also produce deaf-blindness.

The child who is deaf-blind depends to a large degree on others for help with movement, orientation, communication, and many simple tasks. Because the aide, interpreter, or assistant has significant control over the child's experiences, the best guides and helpers are those willing to share a wide range of life experiences with the child.

● The Needs of a Child with Deaf-Blindness

A child who is deaf-blind has major challenges involving communication and mobility. Many useful techniques provide help.

Communication ● Without hearing, speech is difficult to produce and understand. Sign language and speech reading (lip reading) require sight. Therefore the child who is deaf-blind often learns tactile sign language.

Tactile sign language

Tactile sign language resembles other sign languages, but the receiver's palm becomes the receptor. The "speaker" traces signs into the palm of the "listener." Grab a friend and try tracing a letter into his or her palm. With your friend's eyes closed, see if she or he can make out which letters you are tracing. You'll see that with practice a person can become adept at this manner of communication. In fact, this is how some members of the deaf community "whisper"—they sign into each other's hands to prevent others seeing what they are saying.

Tactile sign language involves much more than letters. In fact, children who learn tactile sign languages (as well as other sign languages) typically learn signs for words, phrases, and ideas first, and later they learn the abstract idea of a written language system that relies on letters.

In addition to tactile sign language, some people with deaf-blindness rely on speech reading—accomplished by placing a hand on the speaker's face or near the mouth. Braille books and scanners can give a child access to text, and human interpreters can assist with receptive and expressive language.

Other communication possibilities, especially for those with significant residual hearing or sight, include these:

- American Sign Language
- Large-print writing and reading
- Picture symbols
- Object symbols
- Text-to-speech communication devices
- Touch cues

Determining the best communication technique for the student who is deaf-blind requires careful consideration of the child's strengths and weaknesses. It is important to keep in mind that the child *can* communicate. As a teacher, you can strongly support and encourage a full range of expression. Allow time for the child to take a turn in discussions and state his or her opinions.

Mobility ● Mobility is the other major challenge to people with deaf-blindness, who usually require some assistance, as well as orientation training and support, to move about. Obviously, all people should enjoy being able to move and work in any environment, and specific techniques can help the person who is deaf-blind enjoy this freedom.

Learning to navigate

Orientation and mobility specialists can help teachers and parents design spaces to help the child operate without difficulty. As the child learns to navigate these familiar spaces, he or she builds confidence and self-esteem. In public spaces, people who are deaf-blind often maneuver with the help of a cane or a guide dog. Guide dogs may be especially helpful because the dog can use both its sight and its hearing to assist its master. Trained working animals also provide companionship and may help by performing some physical tasks. Typically, dogs such as golden and Labrador retrievers make the best working animals, given their disposition and faithfulness to their masters. However, because guide dogs can be distracting in schools, a human buddy or interpreter may be a better option. Again, any decision on the best techniques and supports must consider the particular interests and abilities of the student.

● Technology for Students Who Are Deaf-Blind

A range of low- to high-tech technologies can help the person who is deaf-blind. At the low-tech end, simple bumpers on sharp edges of furniture or walls can keep a person from serious injury. Higher-tech options include these:

- Vibrating pager-like instruments can alert the student to focus attention on the teacher or remind the student about homework assignments and after-school activities.

- TeleBraille machines work similarly to teletypewriters: text is transmitted over telephone lines. Instead of appearing on a screen, the text is revealed in Braille on a decoding machine. Students can use school TeleBraille machines to read web pages or any other computer-based text, such as a CD-ROM encyclopedia.

- A visual ring signaler, hooked up to a lamp or light fixture, can make the light blink when a school bell rings. A similar device might be connected to an intercom system.

Technology for students with some hearing

People who are deaf-blind may take advantage of amplification devices or hearing aids. Hearing aid technology has made remarkable advances over the past quarter-century. Hearing aids are much smaller, last longer, and can sample sound fifty times per second. Modern hearing aids have the ability to make loud sounds soft and soft sounds louder. The student who is deaf-blind with some degree of hearing might also use a tool such as the Braille Lite note-taker from Freedom Scientific (Figure 10.2). This tool can allow a student to take notes during class lectures and access them later.

Technology for students with some vision

Those who have residual sight may use technological aids such as magnification devices that greatly magnify text or images on screen or page. Speech-to-text technology can also assist the person with some sight but limited

● FIGURE 10.2

The Braille Lite notetaker

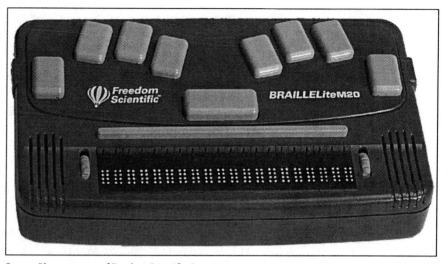

Source: Photo courtesy of Freedom Scientific, Inc.

hearing by providing printed versions of the spoken word. In addition, large-print textbooks and concrete, three-dimensional objects in the classroom help partially sighted students understand ideas presented.

Medical technologies also hold promise for people who are deaf-blind. Cochlear implants (described in chapter 7) may be an attractive choice for some people. Eye surgeries can help with cataracts and astigmatisms. In the Retinal Implant Project, a research program underway at Harvard Medical School's Massachusetts Eye and Ear Research Center, a silicone-chip eye implant is being used to restore vision for patients suffering from some leading causes of blindness.

You may wish to revisit chapters 7 and 8 on students with hearing disabilities and visual impairments to review further technological options.

MULTIPLE DISABILITIES

As indicated earlier in this book, the categories that we use to define children with exceptionalities are not always distinct and clear-cut. Often, children have **multiple disabilities,** and to assist them, we must keep in mind their full range of needs, focusing on what they can do in terms of the "big picture." Some disabilities seem to be *co-morbid;* that is, they often exist together. For example, children with Down syndrome, whose primary difficulty might be a developmental delay, often have a variety of health problems such as kidney failure or lack of coordination.

● Interventions for Students with Multiple Disabilities

One common set of multiple conditions involves learning disabilities and attention disorders, such as ADHD. In this case, children first need behavior modification, and in some cases medication, to help with their behavioral problems before their learning strategies and skills can be addressed.

Appropriate intervention for students with other types of multiple disabilities obviously depends on the particular conditions involved. Speech and communication are often the focus of treatments, as well as mobility training and support. Most students with multiple disabilities also need two kinds of transitional support: (1) assistance and training in transferring skills and strategies learned in school to home and other environments and (2) help in moving between educational programs, such as from a high school setting to a school-to-work program.

Early intervention is customary

Early intervention is typical for children with multiple disabilities, and this involves long-term relationships among teachers, parents, occupational and physical therapists, psychologists and psychiatrists, medical doctors, and other specialists. Functional skills (such as life skills and adaptive skills) most often are elements of the individualized education program (IEP).

Arranging the classroom for a child with multiple disabilities may require special consideration. In addition to providing for mobility and access to support materials, you should make every attempt to incorporate the child into regular classroom activities. Interaction with peers is critical for the child's social and emotional development.

P RINCIPLES AND PRACTICE — Deciding How to Focus Interventions

Those who work with children with multiple disabilities often have difficulty determining which condition should be the main focus of intervention. For example, a child who is physically ill may also need special education services to help with a learning disorder. The child's health is the first priority, but sometimes school services or tutoring can help the child focus on something other than the illness. In fact, many children (and adults) with terminal illnesses develop severe depression.

In such cases, helping a child overcome depressive feelings may then become the main focus of interventions, and doctors may agree to do less invasive treatments for the health condition.

These are tough decisions. No parent or teacher should attempt to set priorities for the child without consultation and support—and without the child's consent, to the greatest degree possible.

● Technology for Students with Multiple Disabilities

In addition to analyzing the particular capabilities of a student with multiple disabilities, teachers and specialists should seek tools that provide multiple supports. For example, a communication device such as the DynaMyte is useful in a wide variety of setting and situations. Helping a student succeed with this tool can increase other skills as well, such as social skills and self-confidence. Similarly, the most valuable adaptive tools are those that find use both inside and outside the classroom—for example, specialized writing instruments. If the student needs a wheelchair, the best choice is one that works well under various conditions. Rather than having several expensive wheelchairs—one for school, one for sports, one for travel—the student may derive the most benefit from a lightweight, sturdy sports wheelchair that suits all settings.

Providing tools with multiple uses

In general, the technologies most useful for a child with multiple disabilities fall into these categories:

- *Computerized communication systems.* Communication tools that have multiple settings and choices for sound output, such as the DynaMyte from DynaVox Systems, accommodate a wide range of conditions.
- *Switches and adaptive tools.* Tools that can be adapted to a range of tasks, such as an extendable grasping clamp, have great value for a child with multiple disabilities.
- *Voice-activated technologies.* Any appliance or tool that responds to voice commands can be helpful. For example, a student with limited mobility can be aided by a computer that can be turned on and off with voice commands.

SUMMARY

Autism and Asperger's syndrome are examples of pervasive developmental disorders (PDD). All types of PDD involve impairments in social interaction and communication as well as a tendency to engage in repetitive, restricted patterns of behavior. Some children with PDD can function in mainstream environments; others need treatment in residential centers. Educational programs often include some method of behavior modification, such as applied behavior analysis, Lovaas, or TEACCH. In any case, you should maintain high expectations for a child with PDD. Apply rules consistently, expose the student to new situations, and use varied, hands-on activities to engage the student in learning.

Deaf-blindness refers to a combination of hearing and visual impairments that creates severe needs in communication and learning. Nevertheless, most students with deaf-blindness have some degree of sight or hearing or both. Typically, communication and mobility are the major challenges for children with this diagnosis. They often use tactile sign language to communicate, and they do best in classrooms arranged so that they can navigate with confidence. Technological aids include vibrating pager-like devices, TeleBraille machines, and visual ring signalers. Students with some vision or hearing often benefit from more common technologies, such as a hearing aid, a magnification device, or a speech-to-text device.

Children with multiple disabilities typically require training in speech, communication, and mobility. They also need support in making transitions from school to home and from one educational setting to another. If the condition involves a learning disability combined with an attention disorder—a common type of multiple disability—the student will likely need behavior modification before the learning issues can be addressed. The most valuable technologies for children with multiple disabilities are those useful in a variety of settings—for instance, communication tools, adaptive devices, and all-purpose wheelchairs.

KEY TERMS

autism (p. 202)
pervasive developmental disorders (p. 202)
behavior modification (p. 205)
deaf-blind (p. 211)
tactile sign language (p. 213)
multiple disabilities (p. 215)

RESOURCES FOR FURTHER INVESTIGATION

Autism and Related Conditions

Autism.
http://kidshealth.org/kid/health_problems/brain/autism.html
This site from KidsHealth has nicely broken down information about autism as well as first-person accounts. It is designed for children, so the terminology is not overly jargon ridden. The site does a good job of allaying fears about the disorder and explaining elements in kid-friendly language.

The Autism/PDD Resources Network.
http://www.autism-pdd.net/
> This site is nicely organized, with many resources for parents and teachers alike. One link provides access to information about schools for autistic children; another provides a great resource for designing the IEP; yet another has detailed information about educational techniques and effectiveness. The site also offers information about working with insurance groups and planning for college.

Autism Research Institute.
http://www.autism.com/ari/contents.html
> The Autism Research Institute, based in California, has a nice website with information, including a useful checklist for teachers and links to research in the institute's quarterly newsletter, *Autism Research Review International.* Links go to editorials about the treatment of autism and clinical research, including the Lovaas and TEACCH methods.

Autism Society of America.
http://www.autism-society.org/
> The Autism Society of America offers much support material for parents, families, and teachers. Dedicated to both research and advocacy, the society has information about current thinking and research in the field. The website has a splendid information section under the link "What Is Autism?" In the Resources section, be sure to check the treatment comparison chart that describes methods such as Lovaas and TEACCH.

Center for the Study of Autism.
http://www.autism.org/
> The center's website has a large list of resource materials, including links to detailed information about different educational interventions and different types of therapies and medications, as well as links for siblings and support groups. You might enjoy the link to "Teaching Tips for Children and Adults with Autism," written by Temple Grandin, a professor of animal science at Colorado State University who is autistic.

Lovaas Institute for Early Intervention (LIFE).
http://www.lovaas.com/
> This website for the Lovaas Institute offers information about training in the Lovaas method and about relevant books and films.

Deaf-Blind Impairment

American Association of the Deaf-Blind (AADB).
http://www.tr.wou.edu/dblink/aadb.htm
> The AADB is a national advocacy group that promotes better opportunities and services for people with deaf-blindness. The AADB website is part of DB-LINK, listed below.

CHARGE Syndrome Foundation.
http://www.chargesyndrome.org/
> The CHARGE Syndrome Foundation has information about the syndrome as well as links to local chapters and the annual conference. One link is to Minnow's CHARGE page, a parent's website that explains what CHARGE is and offers a discussion-based support group.

DB-LINK: The National Information Clearinghouse on Children Who Are Deaf-Blind.
http://www.tr.wou.edu/dblink/
> The DB-LINK website offers links to numerous resources about deaf-blindness, including useful fact sheets.

Helen Keller National Center for Deaf-Blind Youths and Adults (HKNC).
http://www.helenkeller.org/national/
> HKNC is a residential program for children who are deaf-blind as well as a national program that provides evaluation, short-term comprehensive vocational rehabilitation training, work experience training, and assistance to deaf-blind clients for job and residential placements.

Hilton/Perkins Program, Perkins School for the Blind.
http://www.perkins.pvt.k12.ma.us/hiltperk.htm
> The Hilton/Perkins program, part of the Perkins School for the Blind, provides consultation, training, and technical assistance to programs throughout the United States and in developing countries. Emphasis is on program development for multidisabled blind and deaf-blind infants, toddlers, and school-aged children.

Usher's Syndrome.
http://deafness.miningco.com/library/weekly/aa062397.htm
> This site has some good background information on Usher's syndrome and how it can affect vision and hearing. Some links to other resources are included.

Multiple Disabilities

TASH.

http://www.tash.org/

TASH (once The Association for Persons with Severe Handicaps, a name no longer in use) is an organization of parents, teachers, and people with severe disabilities dedicated to advocacy and education. The TASH website has links to local chapters and conferences, as well as information on where to find research articles.

TECHNOLOGY FOR STUDENTS WHO ARE GIFTED AND TALENTED

FOCUS QUESTIONS

As you read this chapter, think about the following:

- Who is a gifted and talented student, and how do I identify such students in my classroom?

- What sorts of services do schools provide for students with gifts and talents?

- In what ways can I accommodate these students in my classroom?

- What technology applications might I use in my classroom for gifted and talented students, and how could these applications benefit other students as well?

Students identified as gifted and talented have unique and often overlooked classroom needs. These students need ways to enrich familiar academic territory, as well as a strong foundation of academic rigor across the curriculum. Technology can be a vehicle for these students to develop their academic strengths to a greater extent than previously possible. Students in gifted and talented programs use technologies such as the Internet and robotics, for example, to enrich both their academic experiences and their social learning.

Defining the Gifted and Talented Student

On the Fox network special program *The Smartest Kid in America,* young contestants in a televised knowledge bee answer questions about a range of topics as they compete for a trust fund of $150,000. If you've watched this show, or one like it, you were probably impressed by the ability of these ten- to twelve-year-olds to complete complex mathematical calculations in their heads, answer involved questions about world geography, and remember precise historical facts. You may have wondered, "If this child were in my classroom, how could I challenge him?" ("Him" is used here because, at the time of this writing, all the winners have been white males.) You may also think: "Is this a typical gifted child?" "How did he learn all this information, and why?"

Diversity of gifted students

The fact is, *The Smartest Kid in America* is not a representative picture of the gifted and talented student. Gifted children come in both sexes, from all ethnic and cultural backgrounds, and from every socioeconomic class. As a teacher, challenge yourself to encourage the gifts and talents within all your students—and additionally to seek out those with exceptional abilities and aptitudes, particularly children who don't look like the stereotypical "smartest kid."

In gifted and talented education (sometimes known as GATE), the term *gifted* often refers to a person with high intellectual or academic ability. The term *talented* often designates high ability in an artistic or athletic field. These terms tend to blur together, however. More important is the question of how you can identify a student with special gifts and talents.

● Identifying Giftedness

In the past, many professionals considered the child with an IQ score above 130 gifted, and everyone under 130 not. Today, however, identifying the gifted child in your classroom is much more complicated, both because of our understandings about the limits of IQ testing and because of the wide variety of intelligences and talents that exists in our society. In the past sixty-five years new theories about intelligence, ability, and talents have provided the rationale for offering an enriching academic program to a more diverse and complex classroom of students. Our current beliefs about intelligence make identifying giftedness not only more complicated, but also more equitable to girls and to nonwhite students.

Before we explore current trends in identifying gifted and talented students, it should be noted that federal law holds no mandate to provide services for these students. However, about half of the states (some with and some without funding set aside) have incorporated giftedness into their special education programs. To find out if your state provides special education for children with gifts and talents, visit **http://ericec.org/fact/stateres.html**. This web resource from the Council for Exceptional Children provides links to gifted organizations in each state.

The fact that gifted education is not always a funded part of the school program means that, depending on the state in which you teach, a gifted or talented child in your classroom might not receive the same level of educational support as a student with a disabling condition. It will most likely be up to you to identify the child's strengths and to design and present appropriate materials, while continuing to make sure that all students receive appropriate instruction. If you are teaching in a district that provides a program for gifted and talented children, students may be pulled out for resource room enrichment exercises, or you may have the support of a specialist in gifted education. Whether or not you have such support, you will be challenged with providing appropriate activities for the gifted students without injuring the self-esteem of the others.

Tracking

Many teachers create a **tracking** system in their classrooms, especially in the area of reading: that is, students are separated into different groups (tracks) according to their apparent ability or achievement level in the subject. You probably remember being placed in reading groups in elementary school and knowing which children were in the "high" and "low" groups. Perhaps you were in the eagle group, and you felt sorry for those children in the chickens or pigeons. If you were in the pigeons, you were probably aware of your rank and were embarrassed about your lack of reading skills. Children are alert to and sensitive about their achievement in the classroom. It is important for teachers and children to respect each child's individual differences. For this reason, many teachers prefer to use heterogeneous (mixed) groups. If you must use some form of grouping or tracking based on ability, be sure to talk to your students about their strengths and to give each of them an opportunity to excel.

Identifying real giftedness in the classroom is hard. Parents will be the first to tell you how precocious their child is, but it is your responsibility to identify which of the bright students in your class are in need of enhancements to the curriculum. Among many models of intelligence, none offer a prescribed method for testing students for the presence of a gift or talent. Let's examine some different theories of intelligence and how they can be used to help you evaluate your own students.

Theories and Measures of Intelligence ● Beginning in 1921, Lewis Terman conducted a major longitudinal study of gifted individuals. He identified a large group of children (1,528 in all) who had received an IQ score of 135 or better on Terman's revised Binet-Simon Scale (called the Stanford-

Binet Scale) (Hothersall, 1990). When Terman started his longitudinal study, the average age of the subjects was eleven (Terman, 1926). The group was assessed periodically over the next fifty years by Terman (Terman & Oden, 1959) and his colleagues (Sears, 1977; Sears & Barbee, 1977). The overall results from Terman's work indicate that high IQ scores are associated with high academic performance, marital happiness, career success, and high overall life satisfaction.

Challenges to IQ tests

With such backing from research, many educators were happy to use standard IQ tests such as the Stanford-Binet and the Wechsler Intelligence Scale for Children (WISC) as the sole measure of giftedness, giving children a score that ranked them in relation to other children. Even in the early years, however, some dissent arose. One of the first theorists to challenge the idea that traditional IQ testing alone can determine giftedness was Paul Witty. Witty (1936) suggested that any student "whose performance is consistently remarkable in any potentially valuable area" should be considered gifted or talented. Witty's work provided support for looking at ways to evaluate student knowledge beyond intelligence testing.

A major criticism of the original intelligence theories is that they focused on the abilities necessary for school success, but little else. In the 1960s psychologists began to expand their definition of intelligence to include *different types of intelligence,* rather than differentiating between underlying components of intelligence as a single attribute. Researcher Howard Gardner (1983) says that we should understand intelligence by asking "How are you smart?" rather than "How smart are you?" According to Gardner's theory of **multiple intelligences,** people possess some level of intelligence in at least seven areas:

Gardner's multiple intelligences

1 Linguistic intelligence: ability to communicate through language
2 Logical-mathematical intelligence: ability to solve numeric and/or reasoning problems
3 Spatial intelligence: ability to perceive and mentally manipulate objects
4 Musical intelligence: ability to perceive or create rhythmic musical patterns
5 Bodily-kinesthetic intelligence: ability to control motor movements
6 Interpersonal intelligence: ability to understand others and function effectively in social situations
7 Intrapersonal intelligence: ability to self-monitor and develop a sense of identity

In recent years, Gardner has proposed two additional types of intelligence: the aptitudes displayed by the naturalist and the existentialist (Gardner, 1999).

Gardner's argument contains a couple of points that help frame his concept of intelligences:

- All types of intelligence are equally important, though many (such as music and bodily-kinesthetic) are not assessed on traditional intelligence tests
- Some individuals may be superior in one or more of these areas and yet have extreme deficiencies in other areas.

This second idea helps to explain the existence of individuals with highly specific academic learning disabilities, such as reading disorders and mathematical disorders (Kirk, Gallagher, & Anastasiow, 1997).

Renzulli's three factors of intelligence

Joseph Renzulli has offered another multipart model of intelligence. Renzulli (1986) defines giftedness in terms of three factors: (1) above-average ability; (2) high degree of task commitment; and (3) creative or original thinking schemes. Gardner's and Renzulli's theories both fit well with the ideas behind the Universal Design for Learning, discussed earlier in the book. All students need access to materials that allow them to enhance their strengths and make accommodations for their weaknesses.

Today, many researchers and educators agree that giftedness is multifaceted. In addition to the skills measured by IQ, it includes creativity, memory, motivation, physical dexterity, leadership, sensitivity to the arts, and more. Students are frequently identified for gifted and talented education not with an IQ test, but by using informal assessment tools, interviews, and recommendations from teachers, administrators, and fellow students. To bring these many ideas about intelligence and giftedness together, the National Association for Gifted Children designed the chart shown in Figure 11.1. This chart illustrates five sets of characteristics that gifted students might possess.

Spotting the "critical mass" of giftedness

Table 11.1 offers a simple checklist that you can use to identify a gifted student in your classroom. Understand that most students will have one or more of the characteristics listed, and a gifted child may not have *all* of those listed. What you are looking for is a significant "critical mass" of behaviors in which this student engages. You may want to keep a copy of this list near your desk and mark how often your students' behaviors match the list. If you mark the checklist over time (rather than simply filling it out in one sitting), you may notice behaviors in some students that you overlooked before. Also, you may want to use this list after students have engaged in a novel experience or after a field trip to a new environment, rather than only in your most "traditional" classroom setting.

Identifying Giftedness in Students from Underrepresented Groups ●

If you look into the classrooms and programs designed for gifted children, it is clear that gifted students are not evenly recognized and valued across all groups in society. Giftedness is clearly underidentified among students with physical and/or learning disabilities, as well as those from

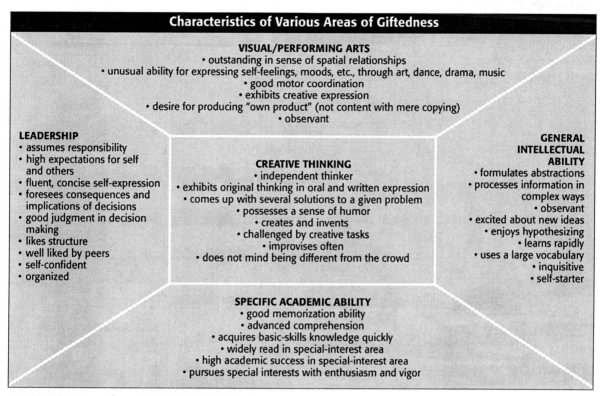

Characteristics of Various Areas of Giftedness

VISUAL/PERFORMING ARTS
• outstanding in sense of spatial relationships
• unusual ability for expressing self-feelings, moods, etc., through art, dance, drama, music
• good motor coordination
• exhibits creative expression
• desire for producing "own product" (not content with mere copying)
• observant

LEADERSHIP
• assumes responsibility
• high expectations for self and others
• fluent, concise self-expression
• foresees consequences and implications of decisions
• good judgment in decision making
• likes structure
• well liked by peers
• self-confident
• organized

CREATIVE THINKING
• independent thinker
• exhibits original thinking in oral and written expression
• comes up with several solutions to a given problem
• possesses a sense of humor
• creates and invents
• challenged by creative tasks
• improvises often
• does not mind being different from the crowd

GENERAL INTELLECTUAL ABILITY
• formulates abstractions
• processes information in complex ways
• observant
• excited about new ideas
• enjoys hypothesizing
• learns rapidly
• uses a large vocabulary
• inquisitive
• self-starter

SPECIFIC ACADEMIC ABILITY
• good memorization ability
• advanced comprehension
• acquires basic-skills knowledge quickly
• widely read in special-interest area
• high academic success in special-interest area
• pursues special interests with enthusiasm and vigor

● FIGURE 11.1   Characteristics of gifted students
Source: National Association for Gifted Children, "Parent Information" (http://www.nagc.org/ParentInfo/index.html).

non–English-speaking backgrounds, minority cultural groups, and families of low socioeconomic status.

A multifaceted approach to identifying giftedness will reduce the number of students improperly excluded from gifted and talented programs. Maker and Nielson (1996) have devised what they believe is a culturally neutral, twelve-point checklist for giftedness, shown in Table 11.2. You can adapt this list to your own classroom needs, perhaps by combining it with elements from Figure 11.1 and Table 11.1. Freeing your assessments from cultural and socioeconomic bias will help you spot children whose gifts might otherwise be neglected.

It is also important to recognize that what one culture considers gifted another might not. Ask yourself: How do a group's cultural norms and the behaviors it values translate across cultures? For example, you might perceive as gifted a student who is outgoing in a classroom. However, students from some

Identifying students often excluded

Cultural variations in gifted behavior

● TABLE 11.1

Classroom checklist for identifying gifted and talented students

❏	Learns easily with little need for repetition
❏	Has wide general knowledge
❏	Has vocabulary in advance of age peers
❏	Has an excellent memory
❏	Is intense and persistent in tasks
❏	Is self-directed and independent
❏	Is well-informed in unusual areas
❏	Is inquisitive and sometimes skeptical
❏	Has an adult-like sense of humor
❏	Is a perfectionist in tasks completed
❏	Demonstrates advanced artistic ability
❏	Demonstrates advanced dramatic ability
❏	Demonstrates advanced musical ability
❏	Demonstrates advanced mathematical ability
❏	Demonstrates advanced physical ability
❏	Is creative and inventive
❏	Has a wide range of interests and abilities
❏	Shows imagination and originality
❏	Shows a high level of empathy and sympathy
❏	Reads a great deal independently
❏	Shows a high level of task commitment
❏	Prefers the company of older children
❏	Plays games with sophisticated, complex rules

Source: Adapted from the Checklist of Learning and Behavioral Characteristics Common to Gifted and Talented Students, from Exceptionally Able Children, 1997 (revised), Education Department of Western Australia, East Perth. Available at **http://www.eddept.wa.edu.au/ centoff/gifttal/giftiche.html.**

● TABLE 11.2

Culturally neutral checklist for identifying giftedness

❑	Communication/ Expressiveness	Outstanding ability to share thoughts or emotion through actions, media, sounds, symbols, or words
❑	Humor	Keen sense of absurd, bizarre, and entertaining ideas and actions
❑	Imagination/ Creativity	Peculiar capacity for flexible and alternative use of ideas, processes, or materials
❑	Inquiry	Inquisitive exploration, observation, or experimentation with events, ideas, feelings, media, objects, sounds, or symbols
❑	Interests	Fervent, sometimes unusual, passionate, sometimes fleeting
❑	Intuition	Sudden recognition of corrections or deeper meanings without conscious or long term awareness, or reasoning
❑	Learning	Ability to acquire sophisticated understandings with amazing speed and apparent ease
❑	Memory/Knowledge/ Understanding	Unexpected capacity to integrate, retain, retrieve, and utilize information or skills
❑	Motivation	Determined to know, create, do, feel, or understand
❑	Problem-solving	Exceptional ability to bring order to chaos through the invention and monitoring of course to a goal; enjoyment of challenges
❑	Reasoning	Spectacular ability to think things through and consider the implications and alternatives; rich, highly conscious, and goal-oriented thought
❑	Sensitivity	Unusually perceptive or responsive to experiences, to feelings, and to others

Adapted from table in Kanevsky, L., Maker, C. J., Nielson, A., & Rogers, K. B. (1994). Brilliant behaviours. In C. J. Maker & A. Nielson (Eds.), *Principles and curriculum development for the gifted.* Austin, TX: PRO-ED; reprinted in C. J. Maker, & A. Nielson (Eds.), (1996). *Curriculum development and teaching strategies for gifted learners,* 2nd ed. Austin, TX: PRO-ED.

Native American cultures find it rude to speak out of turn; for them, this behavior conflicts with cultural norms of interdependence and collective decision making (Florey & Tafoya, 1988). If you stay aware of cultural norms, you will see giftedness within the context of culturally appropriate behaviors.

● Dual Exceptionalities

Gifted students with disabilities are often called "twice exceptional" or students with **dual exceptionalities.** For example, a large subset of students with

Children who have both gifts and disabilities

learning disabilities have intelligence scores or other talents in the gifted range (Willard-Holt, 1999). These twice-exceptional students need remediation activities. At the same time, they need opportunities to promote their individual strengths and talents, to express and develop their giftedness. Beckley (1998) names at least three groups of students whose dual exceptionalities are underidentified:

1 Students who have been identified as gifted, but are having difficulties in school and are seen as underachievers. These students may never have had any type of assessment to evaluate learning problems.
2 Students who have identified learning disabilities, but whose giftedness has never been identified. This may be due to the limits of traditional assessment instruments or to the students' poor test-taking skills.
3 Students in traditional classrooms who have not been identified to receive services for either giftedness or a learning disability. This group is the largest of the three, and it seems that these students have skills and difficulties that obscure each other.

When you plan for the educational needs of students with dual exceptionalities, focus on developing their strengths, interests, and superior intellectual capacities while providing logical remedial experiences. For example, a student with a learning disability may struggle with decoding, but may be able to compose impressive stories and essays using speech-to-text software. Don't let a focus on disability prevent you from recognizing the student's strengths and helping him or her develop them to the maximum.

EDUCATIONAL APPROACHES FOR GIFTED AND TALENTED STUDENTS

Acceleration vs. enrichment

Gifted and talented students have a variety of academic needs. Often the instructional programs designed to meet these needs emphasize either acceleration or enrichment. **Acceleration** means moving a student more quickly through the curriculum. **Enrichment** can be thought of as allowing a student to dig deeper in the content. For example, in an acceleration program, you might have a first-grader working in multiplication and fractions, concepts that are typically part of a third- or fourth-grade math curriculum. In an enrichment program, you might have the student apply mathematical skills to related topics in architecture or computer programming.

The choice of enrichment or acceleration for a student should be made on an individual basis. Simply because a child is good at computation doesn't

TECHNIQUES FOR YOUR CLASSROOM

To Accelerate or Not?

The stereotype of a gifted child may be the thirteen-year-old college grad or the five-year-old concert pianist—young people who have advanced to adult environments. Yet jumping so far ahead is often traumatic. Social and psychological drawbacks can make skipping even one school grade a poor solution for many students. Developmental theorists such as Jean Piaget tell us that all children go through sequential stages of development, and "skipping" stages is impossible (Kuther, 2000). Asking a child to assume a more mature social role by skipping a grade level is often more detrimental than helpful.

Nevertheless, many schools still choose to accelerate a child by having him or her skip a grade or take advanced coursework. You may have attended a high school that provided advanced placement courses or an honors curriculum. These curriculum accelerations are popular for students with gifts and talents in specific areas, such as math or language. Programs in elementary schools sometimes partner with local colleges to allow young students to attend classes or have a professor mentor the students in specific academic areas.

The types of acceleration programs available to students are variable, and two factors are equally important:

- Select academically rigorous programs that provide appropriate challenges for the student.
- Making sure that the child's social development and contacts with students of the same age continue.

As a teacher, you can "accelerate" the curriculum in your own classroom while allowing the student to work on age-appropriate social skills.

---

mean she will enjoy a college-level mathematics course that involves reasoning and logic—she might simply want the chance to do even more computations. Working with the student and parents to select the appropriate acceleration or enrichment program requires careful monitoring and ongoing thinking.

Even without a special gifted and talented program, you can provide appropriate and challenging material to all your students within the walls of your classroom. If your instructional techniques are diverse and filled with alternatives, you will reach a wide range of skills and challenges. One simple way to provide differentiation in the classroom is to organize **cooperative groups** for different subjects. Cooperative grouping goes beyond simply putting students in heterogeneous groups; it requires that students and teachers understand their roles and responsibilities in a cooperative environment (Slavin & Cooper, 1999; Johnson & Johnson, 2000). Students must be individually accountable and participate in group goal setting. When this happens, research shows, cooperative grouping results in better performance across a variety of

Cooperative groups

ability levels, including gifted students (for example, Kenny, Archambault, & Hallmark, 1995; Kulik & Kulik, 1992; Rogers, 1998).

▶ *Problem-based learning*

Another classroom-based teaching technique that works well with students with gifts and talents is **problem-based learning**. The idea behind problem-based learning is that students study real problems while learning basic and related skills (Stepien & Gallagher, 1993). Problem-based learning challenges students to use higher-level thinking skills (see Dalton & Smith, 1986) and to work with "real issues." Problem-based learning on a larger scale includes programs such as the Illinois Mathematics and Science Academy (**http://www.imsa.edu/**), where students explore real scientific problems both in residence and online.

▶ *Independent study*

Another technique that works with these students is **independent study** (Cohn, 1988; Howe, 1990). Independent projects can range from giving the student personalized enrichment or acceleration projects to guided independent study in related topics. Most teachers probably offer some degree of independent study for students who move quickly through classroom materials, but incorporating goal setting and individualized assessment can make this technique more effective.

The three techniques just mentioned are only a partial list of instructional methods that may prove effective for the gifted students in your classroom. For more information on teaching students with gifts and talents, be sure to examine sites such as GT World (**http://www.gtworld.org/**) and the other resources listed at the end of this chapter. Now let's consider how technology can support your work with gifted and talented students.

GIFTED EDUCATION AND TECHNOLOGY

Not every gifted child is interested in technology. Gifted children are as diverse as any other group of children, and only a subgroup will be interested in the computers themselves. View their technology use as you would any other student's: as a tool to provide appropriate instruction. As described in the previous section, many instructional techniques work well with gifted students, and technology can support all of them.

However, some students (whether gifted or not) are particularly interested in computers and technology. Your class may include some "computer geeks" who are eager to focus on high-tech explorations. For that reason, this section will suggest techniques for using advanced projects with students who have a special interest and talent in technology, as well as ways to use technology to enrich and accelerate the curriculum for other gifted and talented children.

● Academic Software Tools

Computer programs can enrich or accelerate student learning. SimCity (Maxis), for example, provides an enriching experience for students who want to apply understandings of planning, organization, and urban living. From the perspective of Bloom's taxonomy (chapter 2), computer applications like this can move students to a higher level of thinking as they apply their basic knowledge to a new situation (Dalton & Smith, 1986). Other software programs, such as Return of the Incredible Machine: Contraptions (Sierra), and the Strategy Challenges Collection (Edmark), allow students to build and solve complex puzzles and problems and challenge one another.

Using software to enrich or accelerate

Computer programming can provide an enriching activity for the student with aptitude in mathematical relationships and logical thinking. The process of learning a programming language, from Basic to C++ to Java, invites the student to apply mathematical skill to a systematic language. It goes without saying that developing skills in computer programming can be a valuable asset in finding a job after graduation. Programming itself allows a curious, creative student to design new applications within a relatively fixed environment.

A natural outcome of a fundamental understanding of programming is the field of robotics. Robotics has a long history in educational technology, thanks to the work of Dr. Seymour Papert at MIT. Papert's work on children's use of programming languages (such as LOGO, the language he created; see **http://www.microworlds.com/**) has guided researchers since the 1970s to think about the potential of computers as an alternative to traditional teaching. Papert's book, *The Children's Machine*, lays out how computers can be a tool for students to create new worlds and tap higher-level thinking. A notable current application is Lego Mindstorms™, a set of materials and programming tools that students can use to create gadgets from simple moving vehicles to complex, multitasking robots. Lego Mindstorms includes both software and building materials. These tools provide a problem-based environment in which students solve problems and discuss possible solutions in a natural and challenging process that helps them realize real-life applications of learning. This use of robotics fits with Universal Design for Learning theories as well as alternative theories of intelligence such as Gardner's theory of multiple intelligences.

Robots that students can create

Other software, such as Math Mysteries and PrimeTime Math, both from Tom Snyder Productions, provide advanced practice and application of skills to word problems and real-life situations. Calculators may also benefit mathematically gifted students who use graphing features and check complicated calculations.

● Accelerated Education Through the Internet

Distance education

The Internet is a popular choice for both teachers and parents to find accelerated materials. For example, students can sign up to take an advanced-level course through a distance education program. The Illinois Mathematics and Science Academy (**http://www.imsa.edu/**) allows students to take college-level courses in astrophysics or geometry. Stanford University, through its Education Program for Gifted Youth (**http://www-epgy.stanford.edu/**), offers courses for students as early as elementary school.

Commercial entities also offer accelerated study programs at sites such as the one maintained by Riverdeep Interactive Learning (**http://www.riverdeep.net/**). Here you can enroll in online courses and download software for use in mathematics, science, and language arts.

● Enriched Education Online

Expanding the curriculum

Some websites provide student enrichment activities. Sites such as Odyssey of the Mind (**http://www.odysseyofthemind.com/**) provide experiences and competitions through which students with gifts and talents can expand what they are doing in the regular classroom. Through Johns Hopkins University's Center for Talented Youth (**http://www.jhu.edu/gifted/**) students can enroll in online enrichment courses in mathematics and writing, offered throughout the year. At the Center for Science Education at the University of California at Berkeley Space Sciences Laboratory (**http://cse.ssl.berkeley.edu/SEGway/**) students can go through self-paced lessons on everything from light to space science.

● Summer Enrichment Programs

High-tech summer institutes

Many of the online education programs described above, such as Stanford's Education Program for Gifted Youth and the Center for Talented Youth at Johns Hopkins, offer residential summer institutes for gifted children. These programs include both enrichment and acceleration elements, and most have a technological focus. The University of Pennsylvania in Philadelphia offers the Six-Nation Gifted Student Program (**http://www.gse.upenn.edu/intl/gifted.html**), where students from six countries work together over four weeks on an international science and technology program on the university's main campus. Students who need a summer challenge can also engage in simulated astronaut training at Space Camp (**http://www.spacecamp.com/**) or

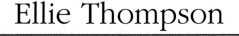

PROFILE

Ellie Thompson

Ellie gives a presentation with teachers from her school on a website they designed collaboratively.

Ellie Thompson, thirteen, is an eighth-grader at a Catholic school in Washington, DC. She is president of the student council and active in sports and music. She loves R&B and hip-hop music; her favorite recording artist is Lil Zane. During the summer, Ellie participated in a workshop with teachers from her school to learn how to design multimedia websites. Ellie's musical and technical talents inspired the team members from her school to use audio files as a main multimedia element in their web project.

Learning has always been easy for Ellie. The public school she attended from kindergarten to fourth grade had no program for gifted and talented students, so her parents decided to move her to a nearby private school where she could have more academic challenges. Her public school teachers agreed that she was definitely a bright student, and she tested well on measures of intelligence and aptitude, but the closest public-school gifted program would have meant a thirty-minute bus ride and little interaction with students from her neighborhood. Ellie is now taking advanced coursework in math, history, and literature, and she plans to take the advanced placement exams in these areas before she heads off to college.

Ellie's use of technology parallels that of other students her age at the school. However, after the summer website workshop, she now pursues more Internet-based activities, such as developing her own website and one for the school newspaper using advanced web-design software. She is also looking into taking some college courses over the Internet, "just to see what they are like."

learn the ins and outs of computers from programming to hardware assembly at National Computer Camps (**http://www.corpcenter.com/ncc/**).

● Multimedia and Hypermedia Productions

Authoring applications such HyperStudio (Knowledge Adventure), Macromedia Director (Macromedia), or a basic web design tool give gifted students outlets for creative expression of their ideas. Users create stand-alone productions or web pages that can include text, graphics, animations, and sound. While they express themselves creatively, students simultaneously enrich their learning and improve their technology skills. For example, if a student creates a multimedia production on comets, she is engaging in an enrichment activity to supplement classroom study as well as developing advanced computer skills.

Table 11.3 shows examples of activities involved in creating an instructional website and developing its content. Each activity relates to one of Gardner's multiple intelligences. Using multimedia and hypermedia design in this way can provide an outlet to expand the depth and breadth of knowledge for all students, including those with gifts and talents.

Enrichment + creative expression

● TABLE 11.3

Creating a web page: sample activities related to multiple intelligences

Type of Intelligence	Web Development Activities
Linguistic	Writing content Gathering background information on content area
Logical-mathematical	HTML coding
Spatial	Page layout Graphics organization
Bodily-kinesthetic	Use of mouse, scanner, digital camera
Musical	Flow of information Creation of MIDI files or other audio files
Interpersonal	Working with others for assistance with technical matters and content
Intrapersonal	Selecting the content of each page Providing personal history about the developer
Naturalist	Using sense of design elements and style

SUMMARY

Although federal law does not mandate special provisions for students with gifts and talents, many states do offer services for these children as part of their special education programs. However, the concept of what constitutes a gift or talent has changed greatly in recent decades. Most current thinking about intelligence holds that it consists of numerous elements or, as Howard Gardner puts it, of multiple intelligences. In addition to the skills measured by IQ tests, giftedness may include creativity, memory, motivation, physical dexterity, leadership, and sensitivity to the arts.

As a teacher, be especially aware that programs for gifted education usually fail to include a representative proportion of students from minority cultures and lower socioeconomic backgrounds. Make an effort to identify the special talents of students from such groups and to become aware of how a student's culture may affect his or her display of what you consider "giftedness." Also be aware that some students have dual exceptionalities; that is, they have special gifts *plus* a disability, and one of these may mask the other.

Traditional educational arrangements for gifted and talented students include acceleration, enrichment, or a combination of the two. Common instructional techniques include the use of cooperative groups, problem-based learning, and independent study. All of these approaches can be supported by carefully chosen technology.

Software applications can challenge students to solve problems and guide them to higher-level thinking. Computer programming and robotics explorations can enrich mathematical learning and help students understand the real-life applications of their skills. Internet courses, sponsored by universities and by commercial developers, offer both acceleration and enrichment opportunities for talented students. Multimedia and hypermedia design projects, such as creating a web page with text, graphics, and sound, can help students expand intelligence in many areas, from the linguistic and logical to the interpersonal.

KEY TERMS

gifted (p. 223)
talented (p. 223)
tracking (p. 224)
multiple intelligences (p. 225)
dual exceptionalities (p. 229)
acceleration (p. 230)

enrichment (p. 230)
cooperative groups (p. 231)
problem-based learning (p. 232)
independent study (p. 232)

RESOURCES FOR FURTHER INVESTIGATION

Online Resources

Center for Problem-Based Learning.
http://www.imsa.edu/team/cpbl/cpbl.html
   This site provides a thorough overview of problem-based learning, as well as information about creating challenging problems and examples. A nice site for both enriching and accelerating the curriculum.

ERIC Clearinghouse on Disabilities and Gifted Education.
http://ericec.org/gifted/gt-menu.html
   The ERIC Clearinghouse gathers and disseminates professional literature, information, and resources on the education and development of individuals of all ages who are gifted. The website offers fact sheets, articles, and a variety of other resources.

Gifted Resources Home Page.
http://www.eskimo.com/%7euser/kids.html
   This site contains links to publications and articles, enrichment programs, talent searches, summer programs, and other resources.

GT Home Page.
http://www.millville.cache.k12.ut.us/tag/
   This is a guide to articles, publications, schools, and programs as well as fun challenges for students.

GT World.
http://www.gtworld.org/
   Resources for and about giftedness.

Hoagies' Gifted Education Page.
http://www.hoagiesgifted.org/
   An extensive site that features research about gifted students, information for parents and teachers, and lists of both print and Internet resources. Be sure to check the great list of online activities and recommended software under the "Hoagies' Kids" link.

Invention & Design.
http://jefferson.village.virginia.edu/~meg3c/id/id_home.html
This site, which promotes a better understanding of the principles of the invention and design process, includes a set of active learning modules that employ a "hands-on" approach.

Math Forum.
http://forum.swarthmore.edu/
Hosted by Swarthmore College, this site includes mailing lists, discussion areas, ask-an-expert services, an Internet Mathematics Library of resources, and a challenging Problem of the Week.

MegaMath.
http://www.c3.lanl.gov/mega-math/welcome.html
This project makes "unusual and important" mathematical ideas accessible for elementary students—a good source of enrichment ideas and activities.

National Association for Gifted Children.
http://www.nagc.org/
Among other online resources useful for parents and teachers, the association offers links to articles or abstracts from two of its journals, *Gifted Child Quarterly* and *Parenting for High Potential.*

Odyssey of the Mind.
http://www.odysseyofthemind.com/
Competitions sponsored by Odyssey of the Mind use creative and divergent problem solving. The website includes sample problems, information about developing skills for creative thinking, and profiles of great thinkers in history.

Product Resources

HyperStudio. Torrance, CA: Knowledge Adventure.
http://www.hyperstudio.com/

Lego Mindstorms. Billund, Denmark: Lego Company.
http://mindstorms.lego.com/

Macromedia Director. San Francisco: Macromedia.
http://www.macromedia.com/software/director/

Return of the Incredible Machine: Contraptions. Bellevue, WA: Sierra.
http://sierra.com/

SimCity. Walnut Creek, CA: Maxis.
http://thesims.ea.com/us/

Tom Snyder Productions. Watertown, MA.
http://www.tomsnyder.com/
Publisher of Math Mysteries and PrimeTime Math.

Strategy Challenges Collection. Redmond, WA: Edmark.
http://www.edmark.com/

Print Resources

Gardner, H. (1983). *Frames of mind: The theory of multiple intelligences.*
New York: Basic Books.

Gardner, H. (1999). *The disciplined mind: What all students should
understand.* New York: Simon & Schuster.

Gardner, H. (1999). *Intelligence reframed: Multiple intelligences for the
21st century.* New York: Basic Books.

Maker, J. (1993). *Critical issues in gifted education: Programs for the gifted in
the regular classroom.* Austin, TX: PRO-ED.

Papert, S. (1993), *The children's machine: Rethinking school in the age of the
computer.* New York: Basic Books.

Zappia, I. A. (1989). Identification of gifted Hispanic students: A multi-
dimensional view. In C. J. Maker & S. W. Schiever (Eds.), *Critical issues in
gifted education, vol. 2: Defensible programs for cultural and ethnic minorities*
(pp. 19–26). Austin, TX: PRO-ED.

Organizations

Center for Talent Development
School of Education and Social Policy
Northwestern University
617 Dartmouth Place
Evanston, IL 60208-4175
(847) 491-3782
http://ctdnet.acns.nwu.edu/
The center offers programs for identifying, nurturing, and developing the
gifts of students ages four to eighteen. It provides publications and conferences, as well as summer academic opportunities for gifted students.

Center for Talented Youth
Johns Hopkins University
3400 N. Charles Street
Baltimore, MD 21218
(410) 516-0337
http://www.jhu.edu/gifted/
> The center at Johns Hopkins provides out-of-school educational opportunities, research on gifted students, conferences, publications, and other resources. Johns Hopkins is also home to a talent search and to summer programs for gifted children.

National Research Center on the Gifted and Talented (NRC/GT)
University of Connecticut
2131 Hillside Road, Unit 3007
Storrs, CT 06269-3007
(860) 486-4676
http://www.gifted.uconn.edu/nrcgt.html
> This center at the University of Connecticut conducts and disseminates qualitative and quantitative research on gifted education. Resources available include a newsletter and other useful publications that can be shared with parents and fellow teachers.

TECHNOLOGY IN EARLY CHILDHOOD SPECIAL EDUCATION

FOCUS QUESTIONS

As you read this chapter, think about the following:

- What is early childhood special education?

- What sorts of children receive special education in their early years?

- If I plan to teach older children, why should I be concerned about early childhood special education?

- How does a teacher become certified to work with this population?

- What resources are available to parents and teachers of young children?

Young children with exceptionalities have a set of needs different from older children's. A student identified as having an exceptionality at a young age is likely to have a more severe form of the condition and to need more intensive assistance. In addition, because the young child's world centers more on family than on school, services must incorporate the needs of the whole family. This chapter presents techniques that early childhood special educators find useful and discusses the ways in which technology can serve infants, toddlers, and preschoolers with exceptionalities.

WHAT IS EARLY CHILDHOOD SPECIAL EDUCATION?

ECSE defined

Early childhood special education (ECSE) is a system of early intervention programs for the youngest children with disabilities and their families. ECSE is based on the premise that early and comprehensive intervention maximizes the developmental potential of infants and young children with disabilities (McDonnell & Hardman, 1988). Early childhood special education can also be defined as special education programming for children who have disabilities that can be documented at an early age.

● The Basics of ECSE

Likely candidates for ECSE

Under IDEA, the term *early childhood special education* refers to children ages 3–5, while infants and toddlers are placed in what is called *early intervention* (Danaher, in press). For simplification in this chapter, early childhood special education refers to children ages birth to five. Children receiving ECSE generally have the most severe types of exceptionalities—disabilities more profound than those identified later in childhood. For example, a student who qualifies for ECSE might be a child living in a hospital intensive care unit or one who has obvious birth defects. Children with Down syndrome,

---

P RINCIPLES AND PRACTICE | The Rise of Early Childhood Education

As a classroom teacher in elementary, middle, or high school, you should keep in mind the importance of a good start in the educational system. To succeed in school, all children must enter kindergarten with basic skills and beginning literacy. For that reason, early childhood education has become a well-established area of discussion and research in the field of education.

Maria Montessori opened one of the first early childhood education centers in Rome in the early twentieth century, and European nations have long been implementing such programs for the education of their youngest citizens. In 1968, for example, Italy established a law providing for the education of all children of ages three to five. In

the small town of Reggio Emilia, for example, an integrated, child-based curriculum and environment have become models for the rest of the world. Many U.S. states have established early childhood education programs for all children, or are in the process of doing so. With so many families in need of day care for young children, this trend is sure to continue.

The law already requires early childhood interventions for children with exceptionalities. Programs for children with disabilities should not only follow principles established for all young children; they should also be flexible enough to focus on each child's individual needs.

children with autism, children with physical and motor impairments, and children with sensory conditions (such as deafness or blindness) are likely candidates for an ECSE program. In the year 2000, 205,769 children received ECSE services a cost of $375 million (U.S. Department of Education, 2000).

ECSE programs are designed to deliver a program of services ranging from identification of a disability to physical and developmental therapy, both at school and at home. If you have become familiar with early childhood education in any way (for instance, by working in a preschool or day care center), you know that the "education" of young students focuses on helping children to engage in developmentally appropriate play and activities. ECSE does the same, but the children in this system need specific assistance in reaching each developmental milestone.

All children in early childhood special education have individualized education programs (IEPs). The learning goals and objectives based on needs identified through formal testing by both medical and educational personnel assist early childhood special education center staff in helping the child to acquire skills that children of similar age already have.

⬤ Criteria for Receiving ECSE Services

The Early Intervention Program for Infants and Toddlers with Disabilities was established by Part C of the Individuals with Disabilities Education Act (IDEA). Under the law, states must provide services to any child "under 3 years of age who needs early intervention services" because the child:

(i)   is experiencing developmental delays, as measured by appropriate diagnostic instruments and procedures in one or more of the areas of cognitive development, physical development, communication development, social or emotional development, and adaptive development; or

(ii)   has a diagnosed physical or mental condition which has a high probability of resulting in developmental delay. (20 U.S.C. §1432(5)(A))

A state also may provide services, at its discretion, to at-risk infants and toddlers. An at-risk infant or toddler is defined under Part C as "an individual under 3 years of age who would be at risk of experiencing a substantial developmental delay if early intervention services were not provided to the individual" (20 U.S.C. §1432(1)).

Variations by state

Although it sets these general guidelines, the federal law allows individual states to determine the specific definition of "developmental delay" and the criteria of eligibility for services. Hence criteria vary widely, as shown by the sample criteria from six states in Table 12.1.

State	Required Level of Developmental Delay	Serve "At-Risk" Children?	Notes
Arizona	50% delay in one or more areas	No	If child is not eligible after evaluation, state offers continued tracking of child's development with the Ages and Stages Questionnaire and assists family in identifying needed community resources.
California	Significant difference between expected level of development and current level of functioning as determined by a qualified multidisciplinary team (MDT), including parents; atypical development determined by informed clinical opinion	Yes (biological and environmental risks)	High risk is determined by the MDT; it can stem from a combination of two or more biological factors or from the fact that a parent has a developmental disability.
Kansas	25% delay or a deficit of 1.5 standard deviations in one or more areas; or 20% delay or 1 standard deviation in two areas; or clinical judgment	No	Tracking, monitoring, and services for at-risk students are based on local discretion and funding.
New Jersey	33% delay in one area; 25% delay in two or more areas	No	Law requires reporting children with birth defects to special child health registry, and case management.
North Carolina	1.5 standard deviations in one area or 20% delay in months from birth to 36 months; atypical development	Yes (biological and environmental risks)	The at-risk category, called "high risk potential," requires three risk indicators. Atypical development is defined to include "substantiated physical, sexual abuse, and other environmental situations that raise significant concern regarding a child's emotional well-being."
West Virginia	A substantial developmental delay or atypical development in one or more areas, determined by an MDT including parents, and supported by observation, measurement, and/or clinical study	Yes (biological and environmental risks)	List of established conditions; at-risk category requires at least four risk factors; list of such risk factors included.

● **TABLE 12.1** Identification criteria for ECSE in six states

Source: Adapted from "State and jurisdictional eligibility definitions for infants and toddlers with disabilities under IDEA" by J. Shackelford, 2000, *NECTAS Notes,* No. 5 (April), revised, Table 1. Chapel Hill, NC: National Early Childhood Technical Assistance System.

P RINCIPLES AND PRACTICE | Child Find

In addition to developing standards for including children in ECSE, states must also find these children in the first place. Child Find is a state-run program designed to identify children with disabilities as early as possible, as required by IDEA. The program is administered by state departments of education in a variety of ways. For example, when a child is born with an exceptionality, the nurse may contact a local Child Find office and start the process of helping the new parents. Once a child is identified, he or she can be included in ECSE to the degree needed. A child with a developmental disorder such as Down syndrome might become part of an ECSE classroom; a child with a physical impairment might begin to receive physical therapy and be outfitted with adaptive tools and toys.

The process of initiating support and gathering resources does not always follow this pattern, however, and the Child Find system itself is not perfect. Not all children with exceptionalities are identified early enough to receive services before they enter school. For information on Child Find, call the National Information Center for Children and Youth with Disabilities (NICHCY) at 1-800-695-0285.

T HE EDUCATIONAL PROGRAM IN ECSE

Most early childhood programs are *noncategorical,* which means that the program serves children with a variety of disabilities rather than those in particular categories of disability. When the law providing service to these young children was enacted, many school systems designed inclusive programs that offered day care for "average" students as well as for children with exceptionalities. Serving an inclusive group helps to defray the cost of programs that often require specialized facilities and specially trained staff.

Most children who need early childhood special education have moderate learning delays in more than one area of development. Many, therefore, receive related services such as speech-language therapy, occupational therapy, and physical therapy. Parent education and home assistance are also included in the program for all ECSE students.

ECSE rationale

Although students might reach developmental milestones on their own at home, early childhood special education is designed to give them a head start. The staff of an early childhood special education center provides direct instruction in skills such as communication, exploration, movement, play, and socialization. These skills are essential for all children, and regular early childhood teachers also focus on them. The difference in early childhood special education is that the students learn these skills in a more focused manner.

Without such specialized intervention, many children in ECSE would not acquire the skills they need for kindergarten.

● Elements of an Early Childhood Special Education Program

Early childhood special education programs differ just as any set of classrooms or schools might. The following elements, however, are common to most programs, either because of IDEA regulations or because they have proved fundamental to program success.

Children without disabilities often included

Inclusion ● As mentioned, many states developed inclusion programs as they worked on establishing ECSE. That is, young children with exceptionalities were included in the same programs as children without disabilities. This approach can help a young child with an exceptionality interact with "age-appropriate" models of behavior. It can also lead to a more successful inclusion program once the child moves on to kindergarten.

IEP and IFSP integrated

Integrated IEP and IFSP ● Like other children in special education, a child placed in ECSE will have his or her own IEP. In addition, he or she will have an **individualized family service plan** (IFSP). The IFSP focuses on providing services to the family as a whole, integrating the child's needs at home and outside school. The goals and objectives of these two plans are typically designed simultaneously. They share overlapping activities and use related services. The team that helps create the IFSP can include an ECSE teacher, related service personnel, the regular program teacher, and family members.

Emphasis on activities of daily life

Natural Environments ● Because the ECSE focuses on helping children reach developmental milestones, the activities typically seem normal and natural. If you visit an ECSE center, you will likely see an emphasis on various facets of daily life. For instance, you may find a "household" area, where children can "play house"—wash dishes, care for dolls, clean, and shop. You may notice a major focus on eating—preparing for snack time, cleaning up afterwards.

You may also see many outlets for children to exercise their creativity by playing dress-up or acting out life situations. The importance of working on both fine and gross motor skills means that you will see tables with puzzles to work on and opportunities for outside play. When you visit any early childhood center, for children who are disabled or not, keep in mind that play is the work of children, and they should be active and enjoying themselves.

The classroom itself will be designed with the child in mind. Typically you will find small chairs and tables, open shelves, and low countertops. All areas of the room will be accessible and easy to maneuver in.

Preparing children for school

Readiness Curriculum   ●   In addition to a focus on development, an ECSE program is designed to prepare children for success in school. Literacy readiness—helping children prepare to read and communicate through writing—is a significant element of the curriculum. In addition to reading books, children will be encouraged to paint (in order to develop skills that will help them hold a pencil), figure out patterns and organize information, and communicate about what they are working on. To prepare for mathematics, children will count and sort shapes. They will also be learning to work with others and follow directions.

3–5 children per teacher

High Teacher-to-Student Ratio   ●   ECSE programs usually have a high teacher-to-student ratio. Some children with severe medical problems may require the help of two adults. Most programs have about three to five children for every teacher. Although this allows for individualization and personal attention, it also requires a large staff.

Parent Leadership   ●   Parents play a vital role in the education of all children, particularly of young children with exceptionalities. Parents' participation in the classroom and school experiences is one of the most significant elements in a successful program. Not only do parents need to learn about how their child is learning, they need to learn how to be advocates for their child in the future.

Parents volunteer

In a successful program, parents typically volunteer in the classroom and transfer techniques from the school into the home environment. Parents who take such a leadership role can have a significant impact on the long-term success of their children.

As with other children in special education, ongoing evaluation is vital. Regular meetings of the whole IEP and IFSP team are necessary, and these should include parents as well as teachers, related service personnel, and (when necessary) doctors.

● Problems in ECSE Programs

The above elements common to ECSE programs have positive effects. However, in two areas ECSE programs often fall short.

Diversity   ●   Many ECSE programs lack adequate populations of young children from minority backgrounds and lower socioeconomic status. The

Problems in assessing minority children

problem of diversity arises from our lack of a good way to assess and locate minority children with disabilities. An exception is Head Start, in which minority groups are actually overrepresented. Head Start programs are not designed specifically to serve children with special needs, but in many states students with identified special needs are incorporated into Head Start programs.

Professional Development for Teachers ● Ongoing professional development is paramount in the field of early childhood special education. Teachers must learn about the disabilities represented in their classrooms, about strategies for helping children learn and interact with others, about health care issues, and about working with families. ECSE teachers are the first line of school staff involved with these children, and it must be a priority for administrators of ECSE programs to make each child's experience as positive and effective as possible. Investment in ongoing professional development supports this goal and provides teachers and caregivers with the skills needed to provide quality assistance.

Nevertheless, though we are beginning to recognize the importance of early childhood education in general, salaries and professional opportunities for ECSE teachers are not impressive. As the focus on early development continues, we can hope that early childhood education teachers will receive the status and respect they deserve.

More technology training needed

Technology for ECSE—the subject of the next section—is one area where teacher professional development is crucial. Researchers have found that ECSE teacher training with computers not only encourages technology use, but promotes intelligent decision making about technology and its integration into the curriculum (Judge, 2001).

TECHNOLOGY IN ECSE CLASSROOMS

Before we address ways that technology finds use in ECSE, it should be noted that a great deal of controversy surrounds the use of technology (particularly computer technology) with young children, with and without disabilities. Jane Healy, author of *Failure to Connect: How Computers Affect Our Children's Minds—For Better and Worse,* wrote in an article, "most normally developing young children (which I define as roughly under age 7) are better off without today's electronic companions" (Healy, 1998). In 2000 the Alliance for Childhood published a report called *Fool's Gold: A Critical Look at Computers in Childhood* (Cordes & Miller, 2000), which outlined the ways in which using computers could be damaging to children, particularly in the area of physical development. The report is available at **http://www.allianceforchildhood. net/projects/computers/computers_reports_fools_gold_contents.htm.**

Nevertheless, most schools and organizations realize that computers do have a place in early childhood education. In a statement by the National Association for the Education of Young Children (NAEYC), executive director Mark Ginsberg said that computers can be used just like any other instructional tool, with careful adult supervision and moderation (Ginsberg, 2000). As you consider ECSE uses for technology, think back to the principles for technology use presented at the beginning of this book. Each time we make a decision about technology use, we must be sure it is in the best interest of the child.

● Technology for Communication

Communication is probably one of the most important elements of an ECSE program. Teachers and caregivers focus on helping a child develop all types of communication skills, from listening, speaking, and gesturing to reading and writing. Language and nonverbal communication are major tools in development that allow us all to express ideas and develop thinking strategies (Das, 1995). Language and communication skills allow children to learn, form social relationships, express feelings, and participate in everyday activities.

In ECSE, communication takes many forms. Helping a child make a choice or control a switch by kicking her feet is one way to assist that child in communicating. Helping a young child with exceptionalities to express wants and needs in several ways might be considered a major step in communication. Often teachers or parents find it difficult to work with *these* children because their progress is so slow. But a special education teacher considers these small victories times for celebration, and you will learn to appreciate slow, steady progress as a wonderful thing. Looking for ways that a child can begin to express him- or herself will help you focus your energy and passion.

Assistive and adaptive technologies

The same types of assistive and adaptive communication technologies discussed in earlier chapters apply to early childhood programs. For example, a device like the one shown from Frame Technologies in Figure 12.1 enables a child to record words and phrases and then press a button to replay them. You can see that the device has large buttons and pictures associated with each word or phrase. For a young child, the labels can include the names of teachers and classmates, routine activities in the classroom, and snack choices. Again, the objective in using this tool is to help the child make choices and express ideas. The device pictured in Figure 12.1 runs on AA batteries and is very durable (an important consideration for use with young children!).

● FIGURE 12.1

Voice-in-a-Box preschool edition, an augmentative communication device from Frame Technologies

Source: Photo courtesy of Frame Technologies.

Easy-to-use communication devices

The DynaMyte keyboard (DynaVox Systems), mentioned in chapter 9, is another popular tool for young children with exceptionalities at home and at school; it allows a student to speak by pressing large touch-screen buttons. The TalkTrac Wearable Communicator from Ablenet is a small communication device that holds up to seventy-five seconds of messages and is worn on the wrist. The One-Step Communicator, also from Ablenet, has only two large buttons for the child who needs a larger target or simpler choices.

Boardmaker overlay software from Mayer-Johnson (Figure 12.2) is another communication device. The teacher and student can work together to set up the device, using pictures and phrases created by the child. Boardmaker also works as a replacement for the traditional computer keyboard. Other tools that may support communication in the classroom include IntelliPics, IntelliTalk, Overlay Maker, and IntelliKeys keyboard, all from IntelliTools.

● Technology for Literacy

During the first years of life, children learn that printed language can convey information and accomplish many different goals. This idea is taught directly in ECSE. For example, young children play at using printed language by writing and receiving letters, often composed of pictures, scribbles, and drawings. Children's scribbles and drawings are, in fact, the first steps in learning to write. Children learn to read through their comments, questions, and repetitions of words they have heard in stories. In ECSE, teachers find ways for all children to read and write using these early forms. An effective ECSE

● FIGURE 12.2

Sample overlay created using Boardmaker

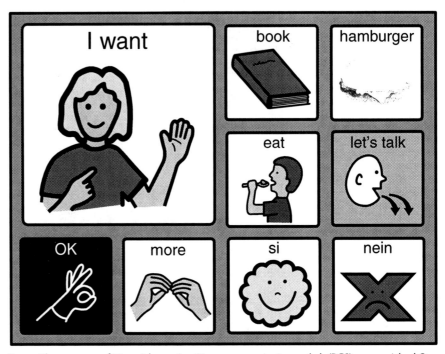

Source: Photo courtesy of Mayer-Johnson, Inc. Picture communication symbols (PCS) are copyrighted © 1981–2002 Mayer-Johnson, Inc., and are used with permission.

environment has books that are easy to hold and share and makes painting and drawing a routine part of the day.

Technology to support literacy development in early childhood can include such traditional educational software as the following:

Useful literacy software

• Reader Rabbit Toddler (The Learning Company)
• The JumpStart series (Knowledge Adventure)
• The McGee series (Lawrence Productions)
• Dr. Seuss Preschool (The Learning Company)
• The House Series and Thinkin' Things (Edmark). Children too young to use a mouse can use these two programs with IntelliKeys and the Instant Access Overlays from IntelliTools.

Other programs such as Kid Pix (Broderbund) allow children to use painting and drawing tools to create impressive-looking products. Kid Pix has plenty of tools with which the child can import clip-art pictures and add sounds. The program helps promote self-esteem through immediate success. Kid Pix can be incorporated into the curriculum as well: for example, you can have a child draw a picture with Kid Pix and then tell a story about it.

Logan Salcedo

Logan's school day allows plenty of time to play outdoors and to develop gross motor skills, as well as cooperative social skills.

Logan Salcedo was born in 1998 with no apparent problems. When he was about eighteen months old, though, his mother and grandmother noticed that he used language in a limited way. He was more likely to use gestures and grunts to communicate. His gross motor skills seemed normal, but not his fine motor control; he had a difficult time holding a crayon or paintbrush—unlike his brother Jamie, who at age two could reprogram the family's clocks and remote controls.

When his mother took Logan to the family pediatrician for his eighteen-month checkup, the doctor recommended that Logan see a speech therapist and developmental pediatrician, as well as an ophthalmologist for a vision exam. After watching Logan interact with other children in the office, the developmental pediatrician recommended that Logan return for a series of tests and that his mother take home several surveys of behavior to share with family and caregivers. The speech-language therapist evaluated Logan's expressive and receptive language and concluded that he seemed somewhat behind what was expected for children his age in both areas.

MRI scanning revealed that Logan had somewhat abnormal brain function. Based on this information, the developmental pediatrician diagnosed Logan with pervasive developmental disorder (PDD). Although he could not isolate a particular cause for Logan's developmental problems, he encouraged Logan's mother to help the child as much as she could. The pediatrician believed that Logan could attend school with other, normal children as long as he got a good head start and support at home.

Logan's mother worked hard to find out all she could about her son's condition, and then she worked with the local public school to find a program that might help him. At age three, Logan entered an early childhood program at a school not far from his home. Now he attends school every weekday from 8:30 a.m. to 3:00 p.m. In the mornings he participates in an inclusion program with other children, some of whom have developmental delays. In the afternoons he receives intensive speech and language therapy. Befitting his age, Logan also has a chance to nap at school.

Each morning, the children in Logan's child development center engage in "lifeplay" with real objects. They wash dishes in the playhouse; they purchase milk and bread in the classroom store, using a cash register with real coins and bills. The children also play with puzzles and paint and maintain an impressive garden. During this morning period, computer use is rather limited, though the classroom does have one Macintosh computer that the children can use for Kid Pix and an Elmo in Grouchland game.

In the afternoons, Logan's technology use becomes more intensive. His speech teacher has him using a Voice-in-a-Box communicator not only to help him communicate, but to increase his vocabulary and fine-motor skills. Logan's use of this communication tool is being carefully monitored, because his teachers and his family are encouraging him to communicate verbally. Older exceptional children at this center use the DynaMyte communication device and the IntelliKeys keyboard with Boardmaker overlays.

● Technology for Mathematics

Young children learning mathematics need to use concrete manipulatives and to work with adults and others, particularly when using the computer. A young child should never sit in front of the computer alone; rather, he or she should talk with a friend or teacher about the work and have concrete objects to use in figuring out problems.

Useful math software

Software programs such as Kid Pix and the Thinkin' Things series encourage organizational thinking and communicating ideas—both important elements to communicating about mathematics. Other programs such as the JumpStart series and Dr. Seuss Preschool provide direct presentation of counting and patterning activities.

Two programs specifically designed to teach mathematics to young children are Trudy's Time & Place House and Millie's Math House by Edmark. Both programs can be used with specialized keyboards, and they encourage children to talk about their experiences with others.

SUMMARY

Early childhood special education (ECSE) provides both school and home services for children with disabilities from birth to five years of age. Usually children who receive ECSE have relatively severe disabilities; some states also provide services for infants and toddlers who are deemed at risk of substantial developmental delays. ECSE helps children develop age-appropriate skills in areas such as communication, movement, and socialization.

A child in ECSE has an individualized family service plan (IFSP) as well as an individualized education program (IEP), and these two are typically integrated so that services to the family support those given to the child, and vice versa. ECSE classrooms focus on ordinary daily activities (such as playing house) in addition to school readiness skills. Many such programs incorporate children without disabilities as well as those who need special help. The teacher-to-student ratio is generally high, and parents are encouraged to assist in the classroom. The problems facing ECSE programs include a lack of diversity among the students and insufficient professional development for teachers.

Communication skills are a major component of ECSE programs. A variety of communication technologies, such as devices that record words or phrases and replay them at the touch of a button, can be useful for children in ECSE. Traditional educational software such as the Reader Rabbit and JumpStart series can help children develop literacy and mathematics skills. Drawing and painting should be part of the daily routine, and programs such as Kid Pix can help children express their creativity and boost their self-esteem. Math learning requires concrete manipulatives and adult assistance for a child who is working at a computer.

KEY TERMS

early childhood special education (p. 243)
individualized family service plan (IFSP) (p. 247)

RESOURCES FOR FURTHER INVESTIGATION

Online Resources

Early Childhood Collection, National Center to Improve Practice in Special Education Through Technology, Media, and Materials.
http://www2.edc.org/NCIP/library/ec/toc.htm
> The Early Childhood Collection at the NCIP has a selection of materials and links concerning the use of technology in early childhood special education.

Head Start Information and Publication Center.
http://www.headstartinfo.org/
> This site provides information and resources related to Head Start programs in each state. The site also includes links to information about how children with exceptionalities are included in Head Start programs.

National Association for the Education of Young Children (NAEYC).
http://www.naeyc.org/
> The NAEYC is a professional organization of early childhood educators. At the organization's website you'll find information about working in early childhood programs and about the organization's standards for those programs. You may be interested in reading the NAEYC's position statement on inclusion.

National Early Childhood Technical Assistance System (NECTAS).
http://www.nectas.unc.edu/
> NECTAS, based at the University of North Carolina at Chapel Hill, includes organizations and programs that focus on providing early childhood services for children with exceptionalities. This website offers a great deal of information about the law that provides for ECSE, links to research and effective practices, and information about workshops for parents and providers.

Zero to Three: National Center for Infants, Toddlers and Families.
http://www.zerotothree.org/
> The Zero to Three website has information about child development and about caring for young children. Excellent charts of child physical, motor, and language development help identify normal and abnormal differences among children. The document *New Visions: A Parent's Guide to Understanding Developmental Assessment* (included in full on the website) offers a wealth of useful information.

Product Resources

Ablenet, Inc. Minneapolis, MN.
http://www.ablenetinc.com/home.html
   Maker of the TalkTrac Wearable Communicator and the One-Step
   Communicator.

Boardmaker. Solana Beach, CA: Mayer-Johnson, Inc.
http://www.mayer-johnson.com/software/index.html

DynaMyte. Pittsburgh, PA: DynaVox Systems.
http://www.dynavoxsys.com/

Edmark. Redmond, WA.
http://www.edmark.com/
   Publisher of software such as Trudy's Time & Place House, Millie's Math
   House, and Thinkin' Things.

Frame Technologies. Oneida, WI.
http://www.frame-tech.com/
   Maker of Voice-in-a-Box.

IntelliTools. Petaluma, CA.
http://www.intellitools.com/
   Maker of IntelliPics, IntelliTalk, Overlay Maker, and the IntelliKeys
   keyboard.

JumpStart series. Torrance, CA: Knowledge Adventure.
http://www.knowledgeadventure.com/

Kid Pix. Novato, CA: Broderbund.
http://www.kidpix.com/

The Learning Company. Novato, CA.
http://www.learningcompanyschool.com/
   Publisher of Reader Rabbit Toddler and Dr. Seuss Preschool.

McGee series. Galesburg, MI: Lawrence Productions.
http://www.voyager.net/lawrence/

Print Resource

Sandall, S., McLean, M., and Smith, B., (Eds.). (2000). *DEC recommended practices in early intervention/early childhood special education.* Denver, CO: Division for Early Childhood, Council for Exceptional Children. Available at **http://www.dec-sped.org/**.

CHOOSING TECHNOLOGY BY CONTENT AREA

 he chapters in part 2 of this book will help you prepare your-self for teaching children with exceptionalities in your class-room. Keep this book on a nearby shelf to refresh your memory about the specific educational, social, and developmental needs of a child with learning disabilities, a developmental delay, or a sensory impairment. Some types of technologies, be they software programs, adaptive tools, or pieces of equipment, are useful for children with a wide range of exceptionalities.

The concept of Universal Design for Learning, discussed throughout this book, is worth mentioning here again. If you think of software as yet another way to present information, universal design principles can guide you in selecting software programs that may have multiple uses in your classroom. These uses can range from giving students a multimedia presentation of information (with sound, graphics, and animation) to providing for a way to individualize the instructional pace of a lesson. The idea of providing appropriate accommodations for *all* your students can help you focus on how each student learns best and which types of technology make the most sense.

In this section of the book we identify some specific software and hardware tools of use in different curriculum areas for children with and without exceptionalities. Although these technologies are listed in the areas in which they are primarily used, they may have utility across the board and beyond the classroom.

READING

Reading is generally the most focused-on area of curriculum. It has also been the subject of intense debate for several decades. Should we first teach students how to decode words, or should we first focus on teaching children to understand the meaning of what they are reading? Should our approach emphasize phonics, whole language, or critical literacy?

One thing we have learned from the many arguments about learning to read is that no one way works best for all children. Some children just seem to pick up words and letter sounds from being read to; other children need concrete instruction in how to sound out words; still others need specific techniques for shaping their mouths and making certain sounds. This is true of students in both regular and special education. As a teacher, you must figure out what particular combination of techniques to use for the students in your classroom.

The programs and devices described below address many facets of reading. As you read the descriptions, keep in mind any specific needs of your students and make your selections carefully. As with all other sections of this book, this list is not complete, but rather describes various popular technological offerings to give you a sense of what is available.

Ace Detective *(MindPlay)*	Enhances reading comprehension skills by breaking down text into "clues" needed to solve a mystery. Contains some difficult vocabulary at even the easiest level and no built-in dictionary assistance.
Arthur's Birthday: **A Living Book** *(The Learning Company)*	Arthur and Muffy have planned birthday parties on the same day! The boys decide to go to Arthur's party, and the girls want to go to Muffy's party. Arthur and his friends work together to find a creative solution to their dilemma. Even though many of the activities are classified as reading skill builders, many also include comprehension and problem solving, making players apply what they learn in context. This is important to the student who may spend so much time and energy decoding that comprehension suffers. Also, placing the reading between appealing adventures reduces the possibility of fatigue.
ClueFinders Series *(The Learning Company)*	Builds students' knowledge of math, language arts, science, geography, and logical reasoning. Players pursue an open-ended exploration of paths through the rain forest.
Earobics *(Cognitive Concepts)*	Develops listening skills, including phonemic awareness, phonics, and auditory processing and linguistic concepts. Comprised of five multimedia games. Great for the child who is unaware of the sounds that make up words; also helpful for students with auditory and speech impairments, as well as a range of learning disabilities and developmental delays. Can help improve spelling and writing as well as reading.

eReader *(CAST)*	This software can allow the user to add spoken voice, text highlighting, and navigation to any computer-based text. Using this software, text from the Internet, any scanned-in document, or any word-processing program can be read aloud to a student or the teacher can mark it up to help the student learn to identify the important elements. Good for any student having trouble reading text, whether because of a sensory impairment (such as blindness) or because of difficulty in decoding. Other tools labeled "e-Readers" include downloadable books (purchased from online bookstores such as Amazon or Franklin Electronic Publishers) that a user can listen to using a Palm Handheld or HandSpring Visor.
FastForWord *(Scientific Learning)*	This series of programs aid language and reading skills through phonological awareness and reading comprehension. Because the student uses the software while on the Internet, the program constantly assesses the student's performance and can print out reports specifying exactly which tasks were difficult for the student. This feature allows for diagnostic-prescriptive decision making.
Franklin Pocket Dictionary *(Franklin Electronic Publishers)*	Franklin Electronic Publishers markets portable electronic tools of help to students with a variety of needs. The Bookman is a portable laptop-style keyboard connected to an LCD screen, with the entire text of a book on a small, snap-in module. One such module, the Pocket Dictionary, allows the user to type in a word to make a definition appear. Alternative cards can be added to this gadget, from a cookbook to games. The user must be able to type, spell, and read, but the Franklin dictionary series includes an option called "Confusables" that provides a wide list of possible words and definitions.
Kurzweil 3000 *(Kurzweil Educational Systems)*	The Kurzweil is probably the best-known text-to-speech equipment in special education technology. Kurzweil software, along with a scanner and computer, can "speak" any text for students with a range of perceptional and visual difficulties. For example, the student with difficulty in decoding can use the Kurzweil to maintain reading comprehension. The teacher can adapt scanned-in documents in many ways, from inserting text prompts ("Listen here, guys, this is going to be on the quiz") to allowing the student to take "notes" in the margins. The Kurzweil's major disadvantage is its price. Other text-to-speech applications are available, including some embedded in computer operating systems, such as Apple Computer's "speakable items."
Learning Center Series *(Davidson)*	Designed to teach parts of speech, subject-verb agreement, synonyms, antonyms, as well as math concepts such as area, perimeter, and fractions. Detailed online help and explanations aimed at reteaching basic concepts and providing drill and practice. A major drawback is the poor instruction on how to manipulate the games; students sometimes must guess whether to use the mouse or the keyboard. (An example is trying to open the shark's mouth in the Ocean game.)

Little Explorers Picture Dictionary *(Enchanted Learning)*	This is an online picture dictionary available at **http://www.enchantedlearning.com/ Dictionary.html.** For the child who can make out the sounds in words but lacks confidence regarding which spelling rule applies, the dictionary can be a source of confirmation and further information about the term itself. The website includes links to more information about many of the entries. Links to English-French, English-German, English-Portuguese, and English-Spanish dictionaries may be particularly helpful with young second-language learners.
Living Books Library *(The Learning Company)*	This series, which includes *Arthur's Reading Race, Stellaluna,* Dr. Seuss's *Green Eggs and Ham,* and others mentioned elsewhere in this list, provides reading immersion and introduces students to print concepts. Text is highlighted as it is read to encourage tracking from left to right. On-screen stories often are shorter than hard copies, making them easier to complete. Available in English and Spanish. A disadvantage for some students is the built-in option to "play" in the story—to click on objects or characters on the screen, which then "respond," often in silly ways that distract from the story and from comprehension.
READ 180 *(Scholastic)*	Each lesson begins with a video providing background information relevant to the text to improve comprehension. Offers "clickable" vocabulary words.
Reading Blaster *(Knowledge Adventure)*	Consists of several programs that teach reading through games at three difficulty levels: easy, medium, and hard. One such program creates word search and crossword puzzles based on word families *(an, id, ut).* Eight words are used per puzzle. Another program allows players to match sounds with the appropriate words. (For example, the word *hum* matches the sound of humming.) The "Read A Book" portion allows kids to read text along with the computer. Another section of the software, "Mystery and Explore," allows the player to roam an old mansion to find missing persons. Along the tour the player encounters text that, if read correctly, leads directly to the person. The purpose is to develop rhyming skills, build a sight vocabulary, and offer reading practice. Allows for individualized pace of instruction and reinforces sight word vocabulary. Several games have no text to follow during the reading of the story; these require good impulse control to avoid random responses.
Reading Pen *(Wizcom Technologies)*	This is a handheld scanner, shaped like a small remote control with a narrow scanning surface at one end. When the user scans a word from a printed document (at any size from six to twenty-two points), the word is read back to the user and a dictionary definition is provided. Helpful for any student studying difficult vocabulary.
Ruff's Bone: A Living Book *(The Learning Company)*	Another story from the Living Books series, which allows students to read an enjoyable book while developing thinking and problem solving skills.

Start-to-Finish Books (Don Johnston)	These books teach vocabulary words first, and then present stories that the student can read with a mastery of the vocabulary. The packages include a CD-ROM–based instructional element, paperback books, and audiocassettes. Because the collection is not designed with any particular age group in mind, an older student who is having problems with basic decoding will not be offended by "juvenile" characters or design.
WiggleWorks (Scholastic)	The WiggleWorks package includes numerous books, in both print and CD-ROM format. The user can listen to stories while the words are highlighted and pages are turned. The software allows users to add words to a vocabulary list, create their own endings to the stories, and customize the program to their own preferences in terms of speech, sounds, graphics, and text. WiggleWorks also comes in Spanish.

WRITING

Writing includes everything from learning to hold a pencil or use a word processor to writing different types of sentences, composing essays, research papers, and short stories—the list could go on. Handwriting and spelling are important skills for writers, and classroom teachers and physical and speech therapists alike develop techniques to improve both. Spelling in and of itself is a sticky point in the field of special education technology, because we all have stories of students who can use the spell checker to produce a perfectly spelled sentence that makes absolutely no sense. The following programs can all help with the process of teaching students to communicate effectively using the written word. (For programs that teach typing, see the later section on keyboarding.)

AlphaSmart 3000 (AlphaSmart)	An alternative to a traditional laptop computer, the AlphaSmart is a lightweight, durable keyboard that can store up to eighty pages of text. Students can load the text onto a computer, either to print it or to continue working with it. Great for students who have difficulty with handwriting. Has excellent large keys for little fingers.
AppleWorks (Apple Computer)	The program ClarisWorks for Kids helped organize the writing process and included "ideas" for listing, graphing, and clip art. Apple Computer, which now owns the rights to the program, does not intend to provide customer support for it. The adult version—now called AppleWorks—is still available, however, and is supported by the company. It includes an easy to use word processor, painting tools, spreadsheet, and database.
Co:Writer and Write:OutLoud (Don Johnston)	These programs use word prediction and text-to-speech technology to help produce written text. Co:Writer helps students who have phonological or word-retrieval problems to locate words and spell them correctly. Immediate feedback on writing through the text-to-speech reader allows for self-correction. Students can become over-dependent on this type of program, however, and may substitute words suggested by the program rather than pursue their own ideas.

Discovery School's Worksheet Generator	This web resource (at **http://school.discovery.com/teachingtools/worksheetgenerator/index.html**) will help you create vocabulary quizzes as well as math worksheets. Select the style of vocabulary worksheet you would like to create (for example, matching or fill in the blank), enter a list of vocabulary words separated by commas or spaces, and give your quiz a title. The site will generate a worksheet for you in the style you selected. You can either print out the quiz for your students or direct students to the website. You can also create worksheets using the scramble option (with the letters out of order) or word chop (with syllables separated) to make the worksheet a little more challenging. You may also want to examine some of the other teaching tools on the Discovery School website, such as the Puzzlemaker (mentioned later in the mathematics section) and the Clip Art Gallery. The website also offers a Quiz Center, which allows you to make quizzes to be taken off campus and graded for you (this service is free but registration is required).
Dragon Naturally Speaking *(Scansoft)*	Currently the best-selling voice-to-text software program on the market. Using the head-set and microphone that come with the program, the user speaks into the computer, and the software transforms the speech into text. Though it involves some training—and dictation is a different process from writing—the program helps both students who have difficulty using the computer because of physical limitations and those who have problems with decoding or word processing in general.
HyperStudio *(Knowledge Adventure)*	Can be used to support students as authors. Provides organizational support in creating a "stack" or a story (for a report, essay, etc.); offers easily available drawing tools, clip art, sounds, and animations. Can be used in conjunction with the student's own artwork, Inspiration software, word processors, the Internet, and other presentations to provide a complete "writing process." This program has a learning curve for both teachers and students, however, and it requires significant decision making and attention to details.
Inspiration *(Inspiration Software)*	Inspiration software—and its companion version for younger students, Kidspiration—allow the user to create visual diagrams (also known as semantic webs) of any information. Students can draw diagrams as they brainstorm about different topics, or use preformatted templates to complete specific types of writing exercises, such as compare-and-contrast essays. Kidspiration has an added speaking element, so the student can hear what he or she has selected.
Microsoft Word *(Microsoft)*	Today's most popular word processor, Word was not designed with children in mind. It has the advantage, however, of being available in many students' homes so that students can easily transfer files between home and school. Advanced editing tools, such as inserting comments and tracking versions of drafts, make modern word processors a valuable part of the writing process.
Storybook Weaver Deluxe *(The Learning Company)*	Designed to allow students to narrate and illustrate a story with preset backgrounds and images. Can load stories used in class. Students also can easily generate a story.
Thinking Things *(Snaith Primary School)*	The website for Snaith Primary School in East Yorkshire, England (**http://home.freeuk.net/elloughton13/index.htm**), has a wonderful set of resources and projects that support the writing process. Be sure to check out the Magnetic Poetry section, where you

	can recreate a classic poem or create your own. Includes many examples of student-designed websites based on different curricular areas, such as "Myths and Legends" and content about different countries.
The Writing Web Site *(Somers Elementary School)*	The Writing Web Site (**http://www.adv-energy.com/~chewie/writemain.htm**), based at Somers Elementary School in Somers, Connecticut, has a nice selection of writing samples and materials for students in grades one through five. The site provides definitions of different types of writing (for example, expository and narrative), examples of each type, and materials to support writing activities. Be sure to check out the prewriting organizers in many of the areas, which offer a worksheet-style breakdown of the writing process.
Your Notebook with Help from Amelia *(Pleasant Company/ Mattel)*	Designed to encourage writing a personal journal. Provides great visual stimulation through art tools, word effects, and a large writing space. "Amelia" interacts with the writer, increasing motivation. "Mind Your Own Beeswax" pages respect the privacy of the author. Offers no dictionary tool, however, and the sound effects may be distracting.

MATHEMATICS

Many math programs share the goal of enhancing mathematical skills within a game format. The graphics, characters, and pace closely approximate one of children's favorite pastimes—cartoons. A student can tackle the game requirements at his or her own pace. In addition, most such programs allow a player to store a partially completed game in order to continue during another session. Another positive feature of many math games is the variety of levels they offer. Of course, the child will eventually move on to other programs, but while he or she is working on one skill set, a variety of levels will offer new challenges and reduce the possibility of boredom.

Access to Math *(Don Johnston)*	Automatically generates addition, subtraction, multiplication, and division worksheets based on specified rules. Excellent program for students who need remedial assistance in math without distracting sound or graphics. The on-screen worksheets can be manipulated to show problems vertically or horizontally, and they can include help with math rules.
ClueFinders Series *(The Learning Company)*	ClueFinders (two boys, two girls) help solve a mystery in various content areas, including math and problem solving. The finders choose among paths to the solution. Along the way they confront math problems to solve in order to continue on their journey.

MATHEMATICS

Discovery School's Puzzlemaker	The online Puzzlemaker (**http://puzzlemaker.school.discovery.com/**) allows you to create a puzzle block in which students insert the missing numbers. You select the size of the block (from three-by-three to ten-by-ten) and the range of numbers, and the site then generates a block with missing numbers that follow a certain pattern. The student must figure out the pattern and complete the puzzle. Other math activities at the Discovery School website include Brain Boosters, which offer logic and problem-solving activities, and Riddle of the Sphinx, in which the user solves word problems while attempting to escape from the Sphinx.
Hot Dog Stand: The Works *(Sunburst Technology)*	This program focuses on math operations and estimation as the user helps run a small business.
Illuminations *(National Council of Teachers of Mathematics)*	Illuminations are online mathematics lessons (**http://illuminations.nctm.org/imath/index.html**) based on the National Council of Teachers of Mathematics principles and standards for teaching math. The lessons for different age groups and subjects are updated frequently and have nice supporting materials for classroom use.
Making Change *(Attainment Company)*	Designed to teach the concept of money and related math skills. Permits some random guessing to achieve correct results.
Math Arena *(Sunburst Technology)*	The Math Olympics (twenty different events) allow the student to work on array multiplication, coordinates, percentages, fractions, and some geometry.
Math Blaster Series *(Knowledge Adventure)*	Math Blaster players follow instructions to demonstrate understanding of numbers and number sense. For example, the instructions might say to color all multiples of four in blue or to color 50 percent of the multiples of three in purple. The programs provide practice with number patterns, addition, subtraction, estimation, multiplication, division, fractions, decimals, and percentages. They also include various options for keeping time and problem solving.
Math Forum *(Drexel University)*	The Math Forum website at Drexel University (**http://mathforum.org/**) is a wonderful collection of links to mathematics-related lessons and materials, including lesson plans, online calculators and activities, historical information relating to mathematics, and much more. The section called Ask Dr. Math offers a collection of common (and not-so-common) questions about math that students have asked. Is zero a prime number? Why or why not?
MathPad *(IntelliTools)*	This program uses an overlay on the IntelliKeys keyboard to produce basic mathematical symbols without the difficulty of typing on a traditional keyboard. The student can compute problems within a grid and receive help with strategies such as borrowing. Also adaptable for use with a mouse or switch.

Mighty Math Series (Edmark)	This series includes six CD-ROMs designed to give students practice in basic math skills through a game-like environment. For example, Zoo Zillions (kindergarten through second grade) presents basic math information such as number facts and three-dimensional shapes. In Calculating Crew, designed for third- through sixth-graders, superheroes lead the user through four activities to rehearse and strengthen basic math concepts.

KEYBOARDING

All students need typing skills, particularly those whose exceptionalities make handwriting difficult or impossible. The key to success with keyboarding programs lies as much in how they are used as in the content of the programs themselves. When a student is learning to type or is improving typing accuracy and speed, the best method is to provide a time of day, every day, for the student to practice. Fifteen minutes of typing practice, scheduled as the first task of the morning (especially when students arrive at uneven times), can be the best instructional method, no matter which software program is used. In this context, any program that offers specific instruction and feedback on finger placement is useful.

Kid's Typing (Bright Star Technologies)	Designed to teach accurate typing and improve typing speed. Offers assistance for students with fine motor difficulty. Provides immediate feedback. In some areas, errors are noted only in red, making visual perception of errors difficult.
Mavis Beacon Teaches Typing (The Learning Company)	The Mavis Beacon series of typing programs offers great lessons for anyone who needs to improve his or her word-processing skills. The Typing for Kids program has games and activities to support instruction.
Type to Learn (Sunburst Technology)	Teaches keys, finger placement, correct posture, and other keyboarding skills through games. This keyboarding program is of particular benefit to the student who has a less-than-average prognosis for fine motor skills, yet needs an effective means of written expression. The program also correlates typing keys and fingers with signed language, helping to build connections among the various forms of communication.

LOGICAL THINKING

Although it is rare to find "logical thinking" listed as a specific objective in a student's IEP, teachers often focus on helping students learn how to think. Problem solving, classification, organization of ideas, and sequencing are underlying skills for mathematics, reading, and writing. Although students often best learn problem solving through interactions with other students in real-life activities, some software programs can help them prepare for such encounters by providing support and encouragement. As a teacher, you might supply connections between the software and the classroom by asking questions such as this: "Look what you figured out in this program. Can you think of a problem like this in our class?" The following game-like programs have the added benefit of practice in basic computing skills.

Chess Academy (Chess Academy Software)	Anyone who plays chess will tell you that chess skills have a lot of application to the real world. This particular program does a nice job of teaching the novice about chess, with good graphics and a wide range of levels. Other popular programs include ChessBase and Chess Assistant. Numerous online chess programs have differing degrees of instruction and graphics. One with a good deal of instruction can be found at **http://www.50chessgames.freeserve.co.uk/**.
Logical Journey of the Zoombinis (The Learning Company)	Popular among kids of all ages, this program includes a series of twelve logic/problem-solving games in which students create their own characters to engage in adventures. Focuses generally on mathematical thinking, but it also helps with sequencing, recognizing similarities and differences, and organization. A lot of fun, too.
Online games and activities using Shockwave and Flash	Online games are tremendously popular with kids of all ages and both genders. They use modern animation and are typically based on current trends. At **http://www.shockwave.com/sw/games/**, for example, you will find a broad series of games designed to be played over the Internet, either alone or with others. For younger students, Playhouse Disney (at **http://www.playhousedisney.com/**) and PBS Kids (at **http://www.pbskids.org/**) use Flash software to present games and activities based on popular television programs.

These games do require you to download the Flash or Shockwave player if it is not already installed on your computer, and faster Internet connections generally result in better performance. Of course, many games have no educational value. But some, including classic board games and traditional arcade games, provide nice ways to work on problem-solving or logical-thinking skills. Many websites that use Flash or Shockwave also allow students to produce their own puzzles, music videos, and other computer-based creations. The student develops skills by using the software itself (selecting elements, designing the interface, and doing basic visual programming). |
| Thinkin' Things Collection (Edmark) | Develops problem-solving skills; allows for experiential learning. Audiovisual tutorial provides easy instruction, but the high number of variables in each game can be overwhelming. |

SOCIAL STUDIES

IEPs for students with exceptionalities often overlook the social studies and instead focus on language and math skills. But the context and real-life application of these areas of study make for the "stuff" of life. In a problem-based teaching curriculum, for example, a social studies problem will involve students in applying a variety of skills learned in reading or math class. For children with any type of exceptionality, working in such real-life contexts encourages them to make logical connections among curriculum areas.

Classroom Connect Quest Channel	The idea behind the Quest Channel (online at **http://www.mayaquest.com/**) is to engage students in real-time, real-life explorations of continents or countries. Through online activities, students follow a group of explorers who are traveling through a particular region. Students log in as a class to learn where the explorers are on a given day, to track their travels on a classroom map, and to learn about the people in the region. Classroom activities and online discussions allow teachers and students to interact. This is a "fee" program, but you can sign up for a free two-week trial to see what you think of it. This activity might allow the student who has trouble getting to school to participate in a classroom activity without being physically present in the classroom.
Encarta Encyclopedia *(Microsoft)*	Using an encyclopedia is an important research skill for students to master. Asking the right questions can help students learn to contextualize information and understand categories—and may help with social skills as well. The Encarta Encyclopedia is a great example of the functions that technology can add to traditional information. This encyclopedia has movies, pictures, sounds, and activities to help the user understand the concepts he or she is investigating. The software also includes a terrific outline format that helps the student understand a research topic in relation to other topics. The Encarta Encyclopedia comes bundled with the Encarta Researcher, a tool to assist students in taking notes and keeping references, not only from the CD itself but from Internet sources as well. Like most other current CD-ROM encyclopedias, the Encarta links to the Internet to help the student find the most current information.
Geography programs *(Comp Ed)*	Comp Ed, Inc., offers numerous free geography selections, downloadable from **http://www.schoolexpress.com/**, that provide basic information about different states, countries, and continents. These work well to shore up students' knowledge about a geographical region they are studying.
Neighborhood Map Machine *(Tom Snyder Productions)*	This program allows the user to create different neighborhood scenes and play games within those scenes. The student uses tools such as grids and symbols to design the environment and employs problem-solving techniques to complete the game. The program offers basic instruction on directions (north, south, east, and west) as well as on traffic signs and symbols.
The Oregon Trail *(The Learning Company)*	This adventure game has students embark on a virtual journey across the United States on the Oregon Trail. Students must first select an occupation (doctor, carpenter, banker), decide what time of year to leave, and then buy supplies for the trip. They travel across the United States in a covered wagon, encountering challenges such as rivers, illness, and crime. The program not only helps students understand the challenges of the early American pioneers, but it develops strategic decision-making skills as well.

SimCity and other Sim software *(Maxis)*	These simulation-based programs are popular for good reasons: the graphics and animation are excellent, and students can be creative and rational in creating everything from towns to worlds to people. The user designs his or her "world" and uses problem-solving skills to handle real-world problems that arise (such as economic slowdown, natural disasters, crime). The programs offer excellent ways to teach about communities, leadership, government, and interpersonal relations.
Where in the World Is Carmen Sandiego? *(The Learning Company)*	The Where Is Carmen Sandiego? series, which includes a variety of individual titles, invites users to follow Carmen Sandiego in her criminal adventures. Students track down Carmen on the basis of clues about where she and her accomplices are hiding. From this game-type environment students can learn geography, cultural information, and map reading.

SCIENCE

Like social studies, science is too often neglected in the IEPs of students with exceptionalities. Not only is science instruction important in itself, but the sciences allow for meaningful application of reading, writing, and problem-solving skills.

The following list includes two sets of stand-alone lessons, but it focuses primarily on the Internet, which is full of wonderful materials for teaching science— more so than for any other curriculum area. The information in online science lessons is generally up to date and is often presented by scientists themselves, rather than watered down for "educational" purposes. The immediate feedback and interactivity of many web-based lessons provide an excellent learning environment for a student with an exceptionality.

Arty the Part-Time Astronaut	An online set of instructional activities and games (at **http://www.artyastro.com/artyastro.htm**) designed to teach about space. The Timeline activity is an excellent way to show how time is different on the other planets. Nice supporting documentation.
Interactive Frog Dissection	The Interactive Frog Dissection (**http://curry.edschool.virginia.edu/go/frog/**) is a great example of the Internet's instructional utility. This self-paced tutorial allows the user to conduct a complete frog dissection without ever smelling the formaldehyde! Excellent feedback in the quiz section. A nice option for students who cannot be on campus or who need additional reinforcement of the concepts.
Science Learning Network	The Science Learning Network (**http://www.sln.org/**), sponsored by the National Science Foundation and Unisys Corporation, offers a wide range of web-based materials for teaching science, nicely organized by subject and intended grade level.

Science Seekers *(Tom Snyder Productions)*	In this series of science lessons students learn basic scientific principles while engaged in real-life problems such as conservation, environmental issues, and protection of endangered species. The programs have great instructional support for the classroom, but they are fast-paced at some points and may need some framing by the teacher.
Virtual Labs *(Edmark)*	The Virtual Labs series provides students with materials and information to conduct laboratory experiments on the computer instead of in person. These programs may be especially useful to reinforce information from a traditional lab or for the student who missed the original lab presentation.

SOCIAL AND LIFE SKILLS

Students usually learn social skills best when the lesson is as similar as possible to the social situations in which they will need the skills: person to person and in realistic settings. However, computer- or video-based instruction in social skills can be especially useful to the student with an exceptionality. Direct instruction in the target skill, individualization, and reinforcement are all reasons why you might select one of the following items.

Basic Coins *(Attainment Company)*	This program presents instruction on the U.S. currency system, including specific instruction in giving change for different dollar amounts. The program is not directed at any one age group, so it is useful for students young and old who need help with this life/vocational skill.
Gaining Face *(Team Asperger's)*	This software program (available at **http://ccoder.com/GainingFace/**) is designed to teach facial expressions and recognition of different emotional states. First, you select a male or female face, age, and ethnicity. Then you can select a "mood" (such as "distracted," "excited," or "shocked") and see how that mood is depicted through facial expression. You can also guess a mood based on the facial characteristics and compare the ways in which different moods might be expressed. The program includes a proficiency quiz to check for understanding. Created for students with Asperger's syndrome and autism, this can be helpful for any student who needs help with understanding expressions.
Life Skills and Work Skills videos *(Attainment Company)*	Multipart videos such as *Plan Your Day, Home Cooking,* and *Everyone Can Work* are designed to teach a variety of essential skills. Videos can be useful in providing models of appropriate behavior in real life settings.

Life Skills CD-ROMs *(Attainment Company)*	Titles in this series include *Grooming for Life, Personal Success,* and *Keeping House.* One title, *Community Success,* is designed to teach appropriate social interactions. All the CDs in this series give specific instruction in looking for social cues and present information within real-life contexts.
SpeakEasy Communication Aid *(AbleNet)*	Augmentative and assistive communicators can help students with social skills by allowing them to ask questions, share ideas, and take turns. The SpeakEasy is a small, easy-to-use communicator that may be helpful to students with physical difficulties as well.

COMMUNICATION

Students with exceptionalities may have specific needs in speech or language, or they may require additional help with expressive or receptive communication. Any technology that helps a student successfully communicate ideas and make choices can have an enormous impact in the classroom.

Boardmaker *(Mayer-Johnson)*	This software program allows the user to design overlays for the computer keyboard to help students make specific selections or share ideas.
DynaVox and DynaMyte communicators *(DynaVox Systems)*	Students with communication problems and those with limited mobility and dexterity can use these state-of-the-art alternative and augmentative communication devices. The communicators can be programmed with many key phrases. Overlays can be personalized to the user's needs and to specific techniques (such as the PECS systems used by people with autism).
Earobics *(Cognitive Concepts)*	As noted in the reading section, this program helps develop listening skills by offering specific instruction in the elements of language. With headphones on, students listen to lessons about blends, letter sounds, and accent, accompanied by visual and textual information. The program has proved successful when other traditional ways of teaching decoding and speech skills have failed.
IntelliKeys Keyboard *(IntelliTools)*	This keyboard is designed to use overlays to help a student input information into a computer. The overlays (either preformatted from the company or designed with Boardmaker for an individual student) allow the user to "type" on a larger surface area or make selections from a set of choices. This valuable tool works well for writing skill building, too.
Learn to Speak Series *(The Learning Company)*	This software series is designed to teach basic vocabulary and conversation in a variety of languages, including English. Students learning English benefit from the software's voice recognition and English word pronunciation help.

LINK Keyboard *(Assistive Technology)*	This keyboard looks similar to the AlphaSmart (listed in the Writing section) but has voice output as well. Users can type and hear the words read back to them, or they can use the voice output to communicate with others. The device can be connected to a telephone or mounted on a wheelchair.
TTYs and TDDs	Teletypewriters and telecommunication devices for the deaf continue to be especially useful for the student with a hearing impairment. These tools allow a user to communicate with others via traditional telephone lines. They are helpful for students with other communication difficulties as well.

part

III

TOOLS FOR EDUCATORS

When you do find time to work on the computer, you'll find it a valuable resource to support your teaching.
(Amy Young)

13

TECHNOLOGY FOR MANAGING AND COMMUNICATING STUDENT INFORMATION

FOCUS QUESTIONS

Using appropriate software and hardware can help you provide educational services for exceptional students with greater ease and less paperwork. This chapter presents advances in technology that assist with activities such as assessment of abilities and disabilities, monitoring of student learning objectives and individual education plans, and communication among parents, specialists, and teachers.

As you read this chapter, think about the following:

- What role will I play in the IEP process?

- What assessments do students with exceptionalities undergo?

- Who is responsible for information gathered about the student, and how is such information shared with parents and others?

- What role does technology play in this aspect of special education?

DEVELOPING INDIVIDUALIZED EDUCATION PROGRAMS (IEPs)

Importance of documenting, organizing information

As a classroom teacher, one of your main responsibilities will be figuring out what your students have learned and how they are progressing and sharing this information with others. Teachers of students with exceptionalities must document this process carefully and maintain well-organized records in order to determine whether the child's needs are being met. The process of developing an individualized education program (IEP) begins as soon as a child has been identified as having potential special needs. Once the IEP is created, the child will be constantly monitored for changes in progress and performance. Only in this way can we know whether the child is in the right setting and is receiving all the services he or she may need.

Technology can help organize and focus all the paperwork and communication necessary to make this program work. The following sections look at several stages in the process.

● Initial Observations and Discussions

The first stage in developing an IEP is to identify a student as having a need for special education. The process of identifying a student can start when a parent expresses a concern, or a pediatrician observes a delay in development, or a teacher spots a learning difference. In many cases, exceptionalities go unidentified until a child enters the classroom. For instance, you might notice that a child squints to look at the board and share this fact with her parents. After a visit to the optometrist, she might return to school with glasses. As a teacher, your job is to be observant, take good notes, keep good records, and communicate with parents. Although this chapter focuses on managing this process for students with exceptionalities, some of this material will help you better track performance and changes in *all* your students.

Assessment begins only after parents give the school permission to evaluate their child for an exceptionality. As a teacher, you will speak with the parents about your observations, but first, take a moment to consider their point of view. Their perfect child has gone off to school, and now this teacher—with twenty-four other students in his or her class—finds a problem with the child. Such discussions work best when you remember to "sandwich" your critique of the child's performance with more positive remarks:

Tips for speaking with parents

- Start off with something good you've noticed about the child: how he shares his toys, how coordinated she is on the playground.

- Next, present your concern: she seems to struggle when I ask her to read out loud, he could not remember the process for regrouping.
- Then offer another positive: I love having him/her as part of our classroom.

With each step, be sure to give concrete and specific examples. Don't say, "He's not good in math." Instead, say, "When it comes time to do math, he starts to seem frustrated with the concept of regrouping and starts acting out in class." Never make judgments, just share information. When you approach parents with mostly negative information about their child, you put them in a defensive position, making it difficult to start the working relationship that is in the best interests of the child.

● Assessment

Assessment is an ongoing and recurring event for children with exceptionalities. Various assessment instruments measure students' behaviors: how they solve problems, how they sound out words, how they start an addition problem. Before we discuss the types of assessments available, it is important to address the limitations of all assessments.

Remember that assessments are estimates

Assessments offer an *estimate* of what a child knows or how she solves problems. In the best use of assessment, therefore, the tester carefully watches the subject and asks her why she did this or that. All tests, observations, and evaluations are limited by human variability: the student may be having a bad day, or he may not be interested in the test activity, or he may not like the evaluator. Keep these issues in mind when you look at any test result. Ongoing reflection is the key!

Once parents give their permission for assessment, students typically take a **battery of tests**—a set of tests designed to assess performance in a wide range of areas. Depending on the results of initial assessments by the special education or regular classroom teacher, an educational psychologist, a neuropsychologist, and an audiologist might test a given student to clearly map his or her unique learning profile. Another child might test with a speech and language therapist and the school psychologist.

Typical measures in a battery of tests

A standard testing battery includes a measure of intelligence, such as the Wechsler Intelligence Scale for Children, third edition (WISC-III), or the Stanford-Binet; a measure of achievement, such as the Woodcock-Johnson or the Wide Range Achievement Test (WRAT); and measures of emotional functioning and behavior, such as sentence-completion tests and parent/teacher rating scales. The examiner typically selects additional tests based on the initial information gathered.

For example, when a parent shows concern that a child has a learning disability, an educational psychologist will typically conduct at least eight different types of assessments, from intelligence testing to talking with the student about what he or she thinks of school. The diagnosis of a learning disability usually occurs over several days of testing at different times of day and using different types of assessment instruments. Areas of assessment include intelligence, reading, perception (visual, auditory, figure/ground), academic achievement, mathematics, written language, and social behavior.

● The Role of Technology in Assessment

Technology is becoming increasingly important in many assessment processes. Most college students are familiar with computer-based tests. The Graduate Record Examination (GRE), the Scholastic Assessment Test (SAT), and many other admission and placement tests are available for computer-based administration.

Administering tests on a computer

When a younger student takes a test on the computer, such as the Integrated Visual and Auditory Continuous Performance Test (IVA), the child sits in front of the machine and types his or her responses to stimuli on the screen. During computerized administration, the teacher or psychologist stays nearby to observe and to help the child if necessary.

Computerized testing makes the results available more quickly. A student who takes a test on a computer might also be able to use a screen reader to hear the questions read aloud or use a speech-recognition system to "write" his or her essay.

Even when the child takes a test without a computer, psychologists frequently use scoring and interpretation software to analyze test results. For example, the Woodcock-Johnson, a measure of academic achievement administered by psychologists and teachers, can be both scored and interpreted with accompanying software.

With computer scoring and interpretation, the psychologist types in the raw scores from the child's answers on the test, and the scoring software produces standardized scores, including the child's percentile rank (his score in relation to how other children score on this test), a grade-level equivalency (his placement in a ranking of other students, with an assigned grade level), and other relevant information. The interpretation part of the software package might include such information as the "type" of reading difficulty the child is experiencing and objectives that should be included in the child's IEP.

EVALUATING How useful are computerized scoring and interpretation?

Computerized scoring and interpretation have advantages and disadvantages. While computer-scored protocols can be more accurate and the scoring

PRINCIPLES AND PRACTICE

High-Stakes Testing and Students with Disabilities

As a practicing or prospective teacher, you are well aware that most schools in the United States participate in rounds of testing that range from statewide assessments and national instruments such as the Iowa Basics to local school evaluation programs. Test results appear in local newspapers, and they often become tools to judge teacher and school performance. A great deal of current discussion regards the effectiveness of these tests and the wisdom of basing high-stakes decisions—such as school funding, student promotion from grade to grade, and career advancement for teachers—on the test results.

In Oregon, Virginia, and many other states, students must take a proficiency examination in order to graduate from high school. When a student with a learning disability takes one of these exams with accommodations (such as a longer testing time), he or she may receive a so-called IEP diploma instead of a regular high school diploma. In an Oregon court case filed in 1999, a group of students and their parents, calling themselves the Advocates for Special Kids, sued the Oregon Department of Education for discrimination and violation of the Americans with Disabilities Act, citing as one issue the use of IEP diplomas (*ASK v. Oregon State Department of Education,* 1999). By the time a settlement was reached in 2001, the judge had declared that awarding an alternative diploma amounted to discrimination.

The details of the Oregon settlement were based on the report of a "blue ribbon panel" of experts that examined the issue of fair testing for children with learning disabilities. The panel's report (which can be found at the Oregon Department of Education website, **http://www.ode. state.or.us/sped/index.htm**) clearly stated that a student should receive any accommodations during testing that he or she received in normal instructional situations. Other states, as well as national testing groups such as the College Board, which administers the SAT, are now readjusting their testing policies to meet these guidelines.

The implications for students with learning disabilities are substantial. When the rules established in Oregon are followed, students with disabilities can elect to take the typical final proficiency examination given to all students; they can then apply to colleges or for jobs without any special indication of their exceptionality. Students with learning disabilities believe that this process gives them a chance to start a job or be accepted to college on an "even playing field" with other students.

process is more efficient than hand scoring, the scoring of some tests involves judgment calls best made by someone who has an overview of the child's academic history and testing behavior. Further, interpretation of test results is, at its best, a combination of accuracy and scientific and clinical knowledge on the part of the interpreter. Computerized interpretation alone is insufficient to understand the many factors that enter into a child's test performance. Evaluators often choose to use the computer's interpretation as one piece of data among many when evaluating a student, making sure that all the available data converge to support their conclusions.

● Software for Developing the IEP

After the assessment has taken place, the next step is to develop the IEP. The assessment process tells us the student's current level of performance; conversations with parents and other team members help us decide where to go from there.

Software can be extremely useful in IEP development. IEP software has been used since the early 1980s, and these programs have an ambitious agenda. Most serve three related purposes:

1 They produce official forms.

2 They contain databases that maintain histories of student needs, goals, interventions, and objectives.

3 They serve as authoring resources, offering banks of commonly used IEP goals and objectives.

Examples of IEP software

One current example of IEP software is IEPplus (SUNGARD Pentamation), which produces IEPs and incorporates staffing and budgeting information. Another program, IEPMaker (Chalkware Education Solutions), is a FileMaker Pro template that includes thousands of goals and objectives for academics, communication, fitness, language, motor skills, and social skills.

IEP software offers potential advantages for schools and students (Smith & Kortering, 1996). Computer-assisted IEPs allow improvements in efficiency, closer matching between levels of performance and goals, and more options for parent and teacher participation. Potential drawbacks, however, include an emphasis on efficiency over substance and the risk that the resulting IEP will be less individualized and therefore less tailored to the unique needs and goals of the student. In using any IEP software, your challenge is to make sure that the team, not the software, is creating the IEP.

Regardless of the software used, most school systems use an IEP template for all students so that teachers and administrators know where to look for relevant information. For example, as the child's math teacher, you want to be able to go directly to the math objectives to determine in which math group you'll place the student. The speech-language pathologist will go directly to the information about language use and needs. The school administrator must track when and where the student is receiving needed services. A uniform IEP format speeds each to his or her information area.

● Monitoring Student Progress with Technology

Once IEP goals have been established, they must be monitored on a regular basis. Here, too, software can be an important tool. Programs such as Accelerated Reader (Renaissance Learning) help assess and report on student reading progress and identify weaknesses. Renaissance Learning has also developed software called Surpass to assess student preparedness for state standardized tests.

Integrated learning systems

Many schools use *integrated learning systems,* mentioned early in this book. These network-based instructional and assessment programs provide instructional support and practice for students and also help track how students are doing. Students who use an integrated learning system log on to the computer and complete activities at their own rate. The system records the student's work and provides printouts with which the teacher can determine how the student is progressing. Examples of integrated learning systems include SuccessMaker (NCS Learn) and CompassLearning Mathematics (CompassLearning). Many school districts have custom-designed integrated learning systems matched to state standards and tests.

Using an electronic gradebook

Teachers often find that an **electronic gradebook** works well for managing grades and student scores. This software organizes assignment and test scores and helps calculate overall grades. For example, many school districts have adopted Grade Machine (Misty City Software) to help track student grades and report them to parents.

Keep in mind that teachers assess *all* students in the classroom throughout the year. Most teachers assess students informally by tracking specific skills students use in classwork and homework. In many cases, the best information about student success comes from, for example, notes you keep on a student's explanation for solving a math problem or on behavior during a playground conflict. This is as true for students with disabilities as for all other students.

COMMUNICATING WITH PARENTS AND STUDENTS

Developing a supportive learning environment requires the full cooperation of your students and their parents, and this requires close communication. Technology can help you communicate effectively.

● Email

Email communication is commonplace in education, and many school systems provide email capacities for teachers. Email offers you the opportunity to communicate with parents in important ways. Teachers are probably the only professionals who don't have phones on their desks but they often have computer access. Email allows parents and students to contact teachers at any time of day and allows teachers to reply when they have time.

Making email work for you

Although email can be useful, it can easily be abused. You may choose to have parents and administrators use your school email address and give friends and relatives another address for personal use. In this way, you can more clearly define for yourself when you are working and when you are not. Another technique is to develop some sort of policy for how often you will check email and reply. You might want to tell students and parents that you don't check email on the weekends or after eight at night.

● Websites

School websites can be full of valuable information for parents and other interested parties. For example, the school's site can post messages about special events and the school calendar, provide information about district and state standards, and share important phone numbers.

Using a class website

Many classes have developed their own websites that might be shared via the school's main site, as long as personal information about the students is not included. Teachers can post homework assignments on the class website and provide a calendar of class activities. In addition, some schools have "webcams" that allow the user to see a live video stream of what is going on in the school cafeteria or on the playground.

Joyce Epstein (2001) suggests six types of involvement that help teachers create better community relationships. These include

1 Parenting: assisting parents with child rearing and understanding development.
2 Communicating: talking about the student's progress. This involves communication both from school to home and from home to school.
3 Volunteering: creating schedules that allow parents and community members to be involved in class activities.
4 Learning at home: helping parents create and implement learning activities at home.

TECHNIQUES FOR YOUR CLASSROOM

Information Sharing on the Web

Within the school community, web-based technologies support many types of information sharing. For example, SchoolSpace software (described later in this chapter) allows the teacher to input information with an Internet browser. The teacher could theoretically access this information from home as well, with proper identification and password.

Technology of this sort raises questions related to parents' access to information. For example:

• Should parents be able to log on to the school's system and track their children's activities and progress?
• Will web technologies become an intrusive "Big Brother" presence? Are we far away from having webcams in our classrooms that allow parents to log in and watch?

Already, in fact, some student management systems allow students and parents to log in from home and check grades or absences.

Of course, we all want parents to be partners in their children's education. Each school system therefore must weigh carefully the amount of information available to parents via the Web.

As a teacher, be certain to remain professional in your communications; any communication or comments you might make about students, either by email or on a report, might be shared with others.

5 Decision making: allowing parents to participate in school governance.

6 Collaborating with the community: coordinating various types of services for parents.

You can readily see how web tools can assist in most or all of these forms of involvement.

SCHOOLWIDE NETWORKS

Think of the huge amount of data a school system collects and manages: attendance reports, test scores, medical information, grade report cards, and many other pieces of vital information. Information management for students with exceptionalities is even more important, because the law stipulates that schools must keep track of data about students with disabilities and manage the data in a fair and ethical way. How do school systems handle all this information?

The Lab School of Washington

The Lab School of Washington® offers a unique learning environment for students with learning disabilities.

The Lab School of Washington®, a private school for children with learning disabilities, has two campuses located in Washington, DC, and Baltimore, Maryland. The school is well known for innovative instructional techniques and use of the arts, based on the Sally L. Smith Methodology®. Ninety percent of Lab School graduates go on to college.

Students come from at least twenty different schools and school districts in Washington, Maryland, and Virginia. Although The Lab School maintains its own curriculum and standards, teachers and administrators must communicate with each child's home school district about the child's progress in this special placement setting. Each school district typically has a different IEP format, a different internal organization of personnel, and different opinions about how its students should be served. You can imagine the amount of work required for The Lab School to communicate with all these separate agencies. On a weekly basis, staff from The Lab School campus might meet with as many as twenty different groups of school officials, parents, psychologists, and lawyers from different school systems and states to determine, for example, if the Lab School is the best setting for a particular student or to review the child's IEP.

Technology plays a major role in the process. Each student's IEP is accessible through a schoolwide network of computers, allowing different groups to contribute and review information. The speech therapists may enter information from an assessment; the teachers may access information about a child's previous experiences; and the administration can track the specific regulations that apply to each child. Through this schoolwide network, professionals at the school share information and updates and manage a large set of information about each student.

One of the obvious priorities of this network is security, so the school maintains a completely separate network for Internet access and email. The school uses a software program similar to the GoalView product from Learning Tools International (**http://www.ltools.com/goalview/**), customized to meet the school's particular needs. Through this program, staff members manage students' IEPs and match activities to each district's specific documentation and forms.

ALLOWING All school personnel have access to network information

A schoolwide or districtwide network of computers often provides the answer. Networking software such as the Individual Planning System (Learning Tools International) allows teachers and related services providers to record and access student information. For example, psychologists can enter data about students; occupational therapists can input goals and recommended activities; speech and language pathologists can enter progress reports. Such networks help school personnel become much more efficient and organized.

Some school systems use computer technology to manage *all* areas of student information, from attendance to grade reports. For example, School-Space (Limitless, Inc.), a program used in some school districts in central Pennsylvania, was adapted to match the state's curriculum standards and schedule.

A schoolwide network is most likely to operate smoothly if everyone who uses it understands the software. The Schools Interoperability Framework (SIF), a joint project by education software companies, school district technology coordinators, and administrators, aims to standardize the specifications of education software to make data entry, exchange, access, and delivery a simpler and more effective process for educators. (For a description of the project, see **http://www.sifinfo.org/overview.html**.) In order to achieve this ease of communication, companies that create software for use in schools and universities would have to follow the guidelines and programming recommendations put forward by the Software and Information Industry Association (SIIA), the organization spearheading this initiative.

SUMMARY

As a teacher, you will often be the first to identify a student who needs special education. From that moment on, it is important to take good notes, keep good records, and communicate effectively with parents and specialists.

Before special-needs assessment can begin, parents must give their permission. Once parents have agreed to the process, the child will usually be given a battery of tests covering multiple areas of performance, such as intelligence, emotional functioning and behavior, and various aspects of academic achievement. Some tests are administered by computer, and many are scored and interpreted with computer software. Computer scoring and interpretation can be more accurate and efficient than manual methods, but the computer's results are not sufficient in themselves. Good evaluators use the computer's interpretation as just one piece of data among many.

Technology can also play an important role in creating the IEP. Software programs offer banks of goals and objectives to draw from, along with a convenient way to maintain databases and generate official IEP forms. Again, the software can improve efficiency, but it requires sufficient thought about the uniqueness of each student.

Once the IEP is created, technology can help track the student's progress. Stand-alone software programs assess student progress and report results. Integrated learning systems, set up to serve an entire school network, check progress, maintain records, and in some cases tie in with specific state standards. On a simpler scale, electronic gradebooks can help individual teachers deal with test scores, grading, and reporting.

Because of the vast amount of information to be collected and stored, schools increasingly rely on computerized networks that allow teachers and related services providers to record and access all types of student information: IEP goals, test scores, progress reports, recommended activities, and much more. These networks can serve either an individual school or an entire district.

Throughout the process of creating and implementing the IEP, communication with parents is vital. Email is an easy and effective tool for keeping in touch with parents. The school website—or a class-specific site, if you create one—can keep both parents and students apprised of important information.

KEY TERMS

battery of tests (p. 278)
electronic gradebook (p. 282)

RESOURCES FOR FURTHER INVESTIGATION

Online Resources

Council for Exceptional Children.
http://www.cec.sped.org/
The main page at CEC contains information about training and advocacy, as well as links to the divisions of this international organization of special educators. Two divisions, the Council of Administrators of Special Education and the Division for Research, may be particularly helpful on the topics of this chapter.

The IEP Process.
http://www.education-world.com/special_ed/iep/index.shtml
This section of the Education World site provides a nice set of links to resources about the IEP process, such as ERIC documents and other research articles, as well as companies that produce IEP software. You might also find other useful information in the "Special Education" section of Education World.

LD In Depth: Special Education.
http://www.ldonline.org/ld_indepth/special_education/
This area of the LD Online website provides some helpful material about the trends and processes of special education, as well as links to information about assessment. From here, you can also visit the IEP pages of the LD Online site, which offer more information specifically about the IEP process.

National Association of State Directors of Special Education.
http://www.nasdse.org/
NASDE is an organization of special education professionals focused on management of special education programs and advocacy on behalf of children with special education needs. The site provides information about IEP implementation and links to other organizations.

Office of Special Education Programs.
http://www.ed.gov/offices/OSERS/OSEP/
OSEP, an office in the U.S. Department of Education, provides information and data about special education throughout the United States, as well as information about grants and new legislation. You can also find links to research and local state special education offices here.

Product Resources

CompassLearning Mathematics. San Diego, CA: CompassLearning.
http://www.compasslearning.com/

Grade Machine. Kirkland, WA: Misty City Software.
http://www.mistycity.com/grademachine/

IEPMaker. Vacaville, CA: Chalkware Education Solutions.
http://www.iepware.com/

IEPplus. Bethlehem, PA: SUNGARD Pentamation Inc.
http://www.pentamation.com/

Learning Tools International. Santa Rosa, CA.
http://www.ltools.com/
   Maker of the Individual Planning System and GoalView software.

Renaissance Learning. Wisconsin Rapids, WI.
http://www.renlearn.com/
   Maker of Accelerated Reader and Surpass software.

SchoolSpace. Chicago, IL: Limitless, Inc.
http://www.schoolspace.com/home.htm

SuccessMaker. Tucson, AZ: NCS Learn.
http://www.ncslearn.com/successmaker/

Print Resources

Pierangelo, R. (1994). *A survival kit for the special education teacher.* New
   York: Center for Applied Research in Education. A great resource for general and special education teachers alike, this book provides detailed information about the IEP process, different tests, and related services and
   medications.

Pierangelo, R., and Jacoby, R. (1996). *Parent's complete special education
   guide.* New York: Center for Applied Research in Education. Another
   helpful resource, this book is organized from the parent's point of view and
   provides information about the IEP process and what to expect. Useful for
   teachers as well, it includes some background information about special
   education and different exceptionalities.

PRINCIPLES AND PROFESSIONALISM

As you read this chapter, think about the following:

- What should I remember about the principles for technology use in teaching?

- How do I keep up with new advances and approaches to using technology in education?

- What new education-related technologies are on the horizon?

- What can I do if one of my students perceives accommodations for students with exceptionalities as unfair?

This chapter is designed to sum up the previous chapters and help you keep in mind the main principles of the book. The chapter suggests ways for staying abreast of new trends and technologies and returns once more to the Universal Design for Learning as a model for working with all students in your classroom. Using the principles outlined in this chapter (and throughout this book) will help guide your implementation of technology.

Ⓐ RETURN TO THE PRINCIPLES

Let's look back at the four basic principles for technology use presented in the opening chapter of this book.

Principle 1: Technology Is an Instructional Tool ●

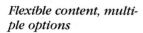

Technology: one of many options

The first principle of integrating technology into special education is to view technology as one of your many options when planning an educational program for a given student. Technology can enhance the many jobs that fill your day in the classroom—teaching lessons, addressing student needs, planning, writing reports, consulting with parents, and always seeking the right tool to help each of your students to learn.

Sometimes teachers see technology as just another task on their list of things to do. Throughout this book, we have countered that impression by examining ways in which technology can be an addition to your teaching "tool kit" that helps you and your students retrieve information, communicate, display knowledge, practice skills, and generally make learning more meaningful.

Principle 2: Fit Technology Choice and Use to Students' Individual Needs ●

Technology suited to each student's uniqueness

The first step is carefully assessing a student's learning needs. Then the available technology must be evaluated. Only then can you match the student to the appropriate technology tool.

You know that each of your students is unique. You plan lessons with them in mind, and you look to the latest research and teaching strategies to ensure that everyone in your classroom is learning. Technology, both hardware and software, works best when its use suits a particular student's strengths, weaknesses, and learning style. You and your students can avoid the frustration and failure of a bad fit with some planning and research on your part. When you have a sense of how a particular student learns best, you can use the information about specific disabilities and the guidelines for choosing software outlined in this book and make a successful match between the child and the technology.

Principle 3: Use Applications in Different Ways with Different Students ●

Flexible content, multiple options

As a teacher, you must know what technology tools are available, and you must be creative in using them. Inclusive classrooms challenge teachers to provide differentiated instruction, matching lessons and materials to students' different levels and styles of learning. Carefully chosen software applications can give you flexible content and multiple options to use with different students. You can simplify a lesson or enrich one by offering students

Anna Ellington

Anna reviews her reflection journal before preparing for the next day's lessons.

Anna has been teaching for six years in a public middle school in suburban Maryland. The student population at her school is average: that is, it is fairly diverse in terms of socioeconomic class, contains a representative sample of cultural and ethnic backgrounds, and has a representative population of students with exceptionalities. Anna has had approximately 10 percent of the students in her classroom labeled as having learning disabilities or attention-deficit problems. She also has students who take medication for depression and other emotional and behavioral problems. Moreover, many of Anna's students "struggle" in her reading and literature classes, not because of any identified exceptionality, but because she has high expectations and many students lack strong writing backgrounds.

Anna addresses her students' needs through a few simple adaptations in her classroom. She asks her students to keep track of their work in large notebooks with their names on them. She faithfully keeps up her own journal of her students and their progress, and this provides great insights into techniques that work or that fail. In general, she finds that her sixth and seventh grade students are poorly organized and lack initiative in their reading and writing activities. Rather than lament their limitations, she teaches them techniques and strategies to make them better writers. When she takes her students to the computer lab down the hall, she spends a good deal of time teaching them how to prepare to write or to do research.

With the help of Anna and the technology teacher, the students use Inspiration (concept-mapping software) to organize their ideas and their writ-

PROFILE CONTINUED   ing. They also use Encarta Researcher, an organizational tool in Microsoft's Encarta Encyclopedia, when they look at the encyclopedia or go online for research; this tool helps students focus on what a source is as much as what it has to say. Further, Anna guides the students in organizing their notes and ideas by having them make note cards on paper as well as with Three by Five notetaking software. In a few assignments, her students will prepare Power-Point presentations instead of traditional papers. PowerPoint helps students increase their visual and auditory literacy skills by connecting words to images and sounds.

Last year, Anna's advanced writing class included a student named Joseph who is blind. Working with the school's vision specialist, Anna located as many Braille books as she could. She also had the school librarian teach Joseph and her how to use a Kurzweil reader. Joseph used the device to scan printed books, save them on disk, and then listen to them read aloud at home and in the class. Anna has since used the same disks with other, sighted students lagging in reading. She also discovered a few years ago that recorded books can help interest students in reading assignments. She explains, "Middle school kids like to wear their Walkmans to look cool, so they don't mind so much that they are listening to Carl Sagan instead of Britney Spears."

Anna is a great example of a teacher who makes use of technology where it makes sense and who maintains her high expectations for all her students. Not surprisingly, both her approach and the content of her classes are popular with the students.

specific tools or helping them use particular aspects of a program. Your creative approaches toward lesson planning apply equally well when you consider innovative uses for the technology available at your school.

Principle 4: Avoid Overreliance on Technology; Balance Benefits and Drawbacks ● Sometimes a student may rely on an intervention instead of learning to do work on his or her own. When young swimmers first discover swim fins, they are often enthralled by how much faster and more smoothly they can move through the water. At first, the fins strengthen and develop important swimming muscles. Eventually, though, swimmers reach a plateau, and they actually lose ground in their ability to swim without fins. Good swimming teachers therefore avoid relying too much on fins. The same principle applies to educational technology.

Judgment call: costs versus benefits

Although a specific technological application can be an important spark to a child's interest or a boost to the child's self-esteem, you will want to evaluate the technology's costs as well as its benefits. Again, you must make similar judgment calls in other areas of instruction: for instance, when to abbreviate a child's assignment or to increase the level of difficulty; when to require more independence in a research project or to provide helpful leads and topic options. Approach technology decisions in the same way. As with much of your instructional planning, you can work with other members of a child's educational team to make these decisions.

Keeping Up with the Pace of Change

Need for ongoing professional development

Every teacher faces the challenge of keeping up with instructional, philosophical, and technological advances. Once you've graduated from your teacher education program, you may lose easy access to new theories and techniques being explored in your area of teaching. Ongoing professional development is a must; it will help you keep your skills honed, and it will offer opportunities to talk with others about your teaching and to reflect on your own practices. In fact, just about every state and school district requires continuing professional development, so you'll have opportunities to expand your repertoire through your school system.

Many teachers, however, find that keeping informed about innovation, especially in the area of technology, takes more than professional development workshops. Here are some other ways to stay well informed:

Signing up for updates

Join a Mailing List ● Many of the websites included in each chapter's Resources section offer email-based mailing lists. When you sign up, you'll receive weekly or monthly updates about the site or about the association's activities. For example, the group Equal Access to Software and Information (EASI) sends out alerts for its webcasts on technology in special education. These webcasts—Internet broadcasts involving specialists and technology innovators—can provide information on how people with exceptionalities are using state-of-the-art technologies. You may also enjoy a more general email-based list such as Action Alerts from the Association for Supervision and Curriculum Development (ASCD).

If you prefer paper-based, "snail mail" publications, a membership in a professional organization, such as the Council for Exceptional Children (CEC), entitles you to receive journals and newsletters about what is going on in special education. The Technology and Media (TAM) subgroup of CEC sends out both paper and email-based news updates, and this group's research can also be found on the Web.

Go to Conferences ● Look for local conferences in your field or in special education (CEC has many local chapters). Conferences often have a tech-

P RINCIPLES AND PRACTICE   Future Trends in Technology

Some technologies discussed in this book, such as face-to-face sign language teleconferencing via the Internet, may have had less educational exposure than time-tested tools such as recorded books. Yet as new technologies and gadgets emerge on the scene, creative teachers will find ways to make them work in the classroom.

Some technologies to keep an eye on in the future include

- *Voice-activated tools.* In the future, more and more tools will be controllable by voice. Voice-activated televisions, clock radios, and alarms already exist, as well as telephones that dial any number when the number or the person's name is spoken aloud, and dictation software that allows the user to speak to the computer in a normal tone and pace. Voice controlled devices will continue to be developed for both the educational and general consumer markets.
- *Sophisticated voice output devices.* New technology allows people with deafness to sign into a camera hooked to a computer (or telephone or even dish-

washer), and the signs will then be "voiced." Smaller communication devices with voice output are being developed as well.

- *Teleconferencing.* As Internet connections become faster and more widespread, you will see more use of video-based communication and real-time information sharing. This has implications for distance education, as well as for people who cannot participate in traditional ways in community forums, workshops, and classes.
- *Smaller, smarter, and faster tools.* Tools we now use will continue to become smaller and less intrusive, better able to anticipate what we want them to do, and faster at doing it.
- *Nanotechnology.* The field of nanotechnology focuses on microscopic robotic devices, some of which have the capacity to change the way the human body recovers from traumas and birth defects. It will not be long before we will be able to "cure" paralysis and brain dysfunctions by placing small instruments in a person's back or brain. Soon a student in your own classroom may be using such a device.

Local and national meetings

nology stand or at least a few sessions on how technology is being used. Your professional organization's national conferences are also a good way to find out how teachers like you are making use of technology. TAM usually has its annual meeting in January or February in some warm location, and that in and of itself may entice you to go!

Take a Class ● When you take courses that count toward your master's degree or provide continuing education units (CEUs, required for ongoing teacher certification in most states), be sure to select courses you find interesting and practical. Taking a web-design course may give you some ideas about integrating the Web in your classroom—and designers and communication professionals may offer perspectives different from the ways you've viewed technology in the past. A computer or technology class may provide you with good examples (and sometimes poor ones) of teaching about technology.

Where to find courses

The computer science department at your local community college may offer introductory or intermediate courses in new applications; even if these are not designed for teachers, you'll be able to transfer what you learn to the classroom. Of course, your friendly local college or school of education will offer a range of advanced coursework and often special-topics courses in your field. Accreditation requirements are moving schools and colleges of education to incorporate more and more technology into the coursework, so you may have the chance to see how teacher education faculty members make use of technology to support learning in their own disciplines.

Participate in a Summer Institute ●

Many summer workshops available

Who said teachers work only nine months a year? Teachers' summer plans often include organizing for the next school year (and of course recovering from the previous one). In addition, a summer institute or workshop may be just the place to learn new techniques, new technologies, and ways to integrate those technologies with different instructional techniques. For example, Intel holds summer technology integration workshops for teachers in which each participant receives a laptop at the end of the program. Other summer workshops in technology can offer support and funding for you or your school to purchase technology for the students. Many summer programs are available, so begin looking in early spring for the best ones.

Talk with Your Resident Special Education Teacher, Occupational Therapist, Physical Therapist, or Speech Language Pathologist ●

Brainstorming with specialists

Look for professionals who are well informed about uses of high-tech and low-tech tools in different settings. Ask them to brainstorm with you about applying these techniques to your classroom. Occupational therapist's classrooms often are full of simple accommodations, such as slanted work surfaces and better desk arrangements, that can help make any classroom more useful to students.

Join an Advocacy Group ●

Variety of groups to join

Your state most likely has a special education advisory board or other group that looks at the practices of special education in your school system. Go to that agency's public meetings, or even volunteer to sit on the board. Parent-support groups offer good opportunities as well; often they schedule speakers who inform the members about current trends and technological advances that relate to specific exceptionalities. Joining such a group can help you keep in touch with emerging best practices in the field.

Universal Design and the Issue of Fairness

In addition to the four basic principles summarized earlier, this book has focused on the idea of Universal Design for Learning as a way for you to think about managing technology use in your classroom. Behind universal design stands the principle that all students learn in different ways and that our job as teachers includes teaching our students *how* to learn. When you apply this perspective to technology use, you avoid isolating students with disabilities as "special" cases who need "special" technological aids. In essence, all of your students become special cases, because you adjust your instruction and your use of technology for each one.

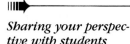

Are accommodations unfair?

Universal design can also help you with fairness issues. When you have a child who receives special accommodations in your classroom, other students may find the situation unfair. During tests, for example, if a student with a learning disability receives extra time and the assistance of a reader (either a human assistant or a technology-based reader), other students may ask you, "Why can't I do it that way? He's getting off easy." The student who uses a calculator may also feel as if he or she is "cheating" the system, and the student who uses a laptop in the classroom may feel separated from his or her peers by virtue of that special technology. Such problems are easier to deal with if you have some degree of individualization for all your students.

Sharing your perspective with students

When you use universal design, the process of adapting to individual student needs becomes an open one. In your classroom you make a point of making accommodations for everyone. You share with your students the understanding that technology is a tool that can help each of us reach our individual goals. You may allow one student to turn in a web page rather than a typical book report. Another student may receive the accommodations of substituting an email interview with a local newsmaker for traditional library research. Offering multiple options for everyone helps all students respect each other's differences.

SUMMARY

This chapter has reviewed the four core principles set out at the beginning of the book: (1) technology is an instructional tool, to be used like any other tool; (2) technology choices and uses must fit each student's individual needs; (3) software and hardware applications can and should be used in different ways with different students; and (4) technology's benefits and drawbacks must be balanced for each student.

Technology continues to develop at a rapid pace. In the near future, you can expect to see improvements in areas such as voice-activated tools and teleconferencing. To keep current on these advances, you can join mailing lists, go to conferences, take classes, participate in summer workshops or institutes, talk with special education teachers and other specialists, and join one or more advocacy groups.

The theory of Universal Design for Learning, which holds that all students learn in different ways, offers a way of thinking about the use of technology in your classroom, as well as a way of addressing the issue of fairness. You adapt your teaching and your use of technology for *all* students, not just the ones with disabilities. The universal design perspective reinforces the most important point of this book: the use of technology depends on understanding children's needs in terms of their individual learning characteristics.

RESOURCES FOR FURTHER INVESTIGATION

Online Resources

Association for Supervision and Curriculum Development (ASCD).
http://www.ascd.org/
The ASCD website has resources that you may find useful in your study of special education and technology. In the Reading Room, you'll find selected articles from the current edition of *Educational Leadership*, the organization's flagship journal. You can sign up to receive Action Alerts via email. The organization has conferences, research institutes, and materials useful for any area of education you are studying. Membership allows greater access to website materials and resources.

Equal Access to Software and Information (EASI).
http://www.rit.edu/~easi/
This website offers a useful mailing list and information about online courses, curriculum strategies, and research articles on adaptive and assistive technology.

Inclusive Education.
http://www.uni.edu/coe/inclusion/
At this site you'll find extensive discussion of the inclusion of special needs students in the typical classroom, as well as information about books, organizations, and websites related to the topic. The site is sponsored by the Renaissance Group, a consortium of universities working to reform teacher education.

IntelliTools Activity Exchange.
http://www.intellitools.com/shareyouractivities.html
> A great site for information about using the IntelliTools products, the Activity Exchange allows users to share activities they've created with IntelliTalk, Overlay Maker, ClickIt!, and IntelliPics. You can browse, preview, and download activities you're interested in.

Intel Teach to the Future.
http://www.intel.com/education/teach/index.htm
> Here you will find information about Intel's teacher workshops on using technology as well as links to educational materials that use Intel and Microsoft products.

News-2-You.
http://www.news-4-you.com/
> News-2-You is a weekly newspaper for users of augmentative communication as well as emergent readers. Communication symbols appear along with the text to allow symbol users an opportunity to read the news. The stories are simplified and easy for children to understand.

Technology and Media Division of the Council for Exceptional Children.
http://www.tamcec.org/
> TAM is an organization of researchers, teachers, and parents interested in how technology is used in special education. The website has links to research via the organization's e-journal as well as information about conferences and technological resources. When you sign up to be a member of TAM, you'll receive news updates in the mail.

HANDBOOK OF RESOURCES

The first two sections of this Handbook provide general guidelines for creating a class website with your students and helping students use presentation tools. Later sections offer handy Web resources divided into several basic categories.

For lists of software and hardware organized by specific areas of the curriculum, see the earlier section of this book "Choosing Technology by Content Area." Be sure also to check the textbook website, available through **www.cengage.com/education**, for more resources and recent updates.

● BUILDING A CLASS WEBSITE

Rationale

Building a class website with your students can help you reach a number of instructional goals. For example, it can

- Help students understand the concepts you are studying in class in greater detail
- Provide a project that culminates into a series of lessons
- Give students an alternative to a traditional paper or presentation

In addition to these curriculum-related benefits, building a website helps students learn technology-specific terminology, increase their technical proficiency, and develop design and presentation skills.

Building a website is a valuable activity whether the site is accessible on the Internet, available only to other people within the school, or even stored on a disk rather than posted on the Internet!

Materials

The technology you will need is not as complex as you might think. You can begin with the following materials:

- A computer with an Internet connection
- An HTML editing tool: either a web-authoring program (such as Netscape Composer, Microsoft Publisher, or Macromedia Dreamweaver) or a contemporary, full-featured word processor or "works" program that can save documents as HTML (for example, Microsoft Word and AppleWorks)
- An image-editing program (such as Adobe PhotoDeluxe or, on the high end, Adobe Photoshop)

Process

1. *Check your school system's Internet policies.* How much information can you post to a website? What kinds of information? What other restrictions may affect your project?
2. *Determine the purpose of your website.* Will the website share information about your class and the projects you are undertaking this year? Is it designed to showcase student work? Is it part of a research project—for example, a website that teaches about history?

3. *Plan the content and organization of your site.* Once you've determined the purpose of your project, you and your class should lay out specific goals for content and organization. What should be included on the site: pictures, information about students, research data? How should this material be organized? This is a good time to create a storyboard. Lay out on paper what the website will look like. What will the opening page be like? What type of menu will be included? How will you guide website "visitors" through the online information?

4. *Conduct research.* Your students can engage in many different types of research. For instance, the research process may include using the library, searching the Web for information about your topic, or taking pictures around the school. Be sure students keep careful records about where they found information.

    This is a great chance to teach students of any age about "fair use" and copyright issues. Share with your students the legal and ethical considerations concerning the copying of information, images, movies, and sounds from the Internet or from any other source. A great site to learn more about copyright issues can be found at **http://www.templetons.com/brad/copymyths.html**.

5. *Assemble and review your materials and information.* Before you begin construction of the actual website, gather together all the materials and information you have acquired. This might be a time to go back to your original storyboards and rethink some aspects of the site's organization. Perhaps you didn't find as much information in one area as you expected to, or perhaps you need to add a new category to your menu.

6. *Begin building the site.* This step will require you to determine responsibilities for each of your students, create teams to work on different sections, and determine timelines for the work. For step-by-step instructions on the details of building a website, look at one or more of these tutorials:

    http://www.american.edu/IRVINE/teach/webpage.html
    This is part of a lesson on building websites written by the author of this book. It's designed to be used with Netscape Composer.

    http://www.lissaexplains.com/
    The "Lissa Explains It All" site offers a tutorial on basic Web design, written for young students and applicable to any text editor.

    http://www.webdiner.com/webadv/
    The Web Diner has excellent instruction and a nice set of templates (designed to be used with any text editor) that can help you create a basic web page.

http://geocities.yahoo.com/
GeoCities, a website where you can post your own page, has great templates to help you get started.

http://hotwired.lycos.com/webmonkey/kids/
Webmonkey for Kids has a fine selection of lessons and links to downloadable programs.

7. *Evaluate your website.* You will want to include some sort of assessment element in your project. Perhaps students will give an oral presentation about their part of the site, explaining how they created it. You should also select some criteria for evaluating the website overall, such as those listed in chapter 2.

8. *Update your site.* If you decide to make your site available on the Internet, will it need to be updated at some point in the future? If so, you should come up with a plan for necessary updates.

● INTEGRATING TECHNOLOGY INTO THE CURRICULUM USING PRESENTATION TOOLS

Rationale

One of the main criticisms of technology use is that students are generally passive when they use traditional educational software. By having students use computers to *create* something, you engage them in active learning and help them think more critically about what they are studying. One such strategy is building a class website, as discussed above. Another is having students use a presentation tool, such as HyperStudio or Microsoft PowerPoint, to create a stand-alone presentation that shows what they have learned about a specific topic. The term *stand-alone* implies that the presentation does not depend on the child to explain orally the project; the presentation itself should contain all the information the child wants to convey. This strategy is easily connected to curriculum standards and it provides a permanent project that documents what the student has learned.

Materials

• One or more computers, preferably with Internet connections

• Any software that can create presentations (good examples for student use are HyperStudio, Microsoft PowerPoint, AppleWorks, and Kid Pix)

Process

1. *Establish guidelines for students.* After deciding on a subject area or project, develop a set of guidelines for the finished product. For example, how

long (how many screens) should the presentation be? What must be included in the way of academic elements (number of references, depth of research), design elements (pictures, sounds, and so on), and organization?

2. *Introduce the project to your students.* Give students details about what you expect, and have them brainstorm ideas. During this brainstorming process, you can have your students use a concept-mapping program like Inspiration to organize their ideas. Then, as they gather material during research, they can go back to Inspiration to fill in what they have discovered and develop an outline.

You may decide to develop a sample project that your students can use as a model or template. Students with little experience in designing their own projects may need this support. For some students, however, this technique can be limiting because they may simply follow your model rather than think of their own ways of presenting the material.

3. *Set a specific timeline.* How much time will students need to work on each element (research, organization, computer time)? Develop specific goals for each stage of the process. Give additional time to students who need it, or add additional criteria for students who move very quickly. This is a good opportunity to differentiate the curriculum (think about the principles of universal design).

4. *Have students work out on paper how they want the final project to look.* You may have a set of worksheets or a checklist you want them to use to make sure all required elements are included.

5. *Provide support for using presentation software.* Tutorials for appropriate software programs can be accessed through the website for this textbook. Other helpful sites include:

http://www.actden.com/pp
This is an excellent user's guide to Microsoft PowerPoint.

http://www.hyperstudio.com/
Click on "Library" to find a large set of user guides and sample projects for HyperStudio.

http://www.uvm.edu/~jmorris/kidpix.html
On this Kid Pix resource site, you'll find instructions for using "moopies," a presentation-type element of the Kid Pix program (great for younger students).

6. *Give students the opportunity to share their final projects.* You can arrange to have the projects presented to another class, during a school assembly, or during parent's night. Help students with self-evaluation and assessment of their projects.

● ONLINE DISCUSSION AND SUPPORT GROUPS FOR TEACHERS

Many states and school systems have local technical support groups, such as TechSETS (at **http://www.techsets.org/**), a resource group for people using and supporting technology in California schools. In addition, many areas have computer user groups, such as AMUG, the Arizona Macintosh Users Group (at **http://www.amug.org/**). As a member of such a group, you can access discussion boards and technical support resources for just about any problem or project. There are Microsoft Windows users groups in just about every area, as well as support groups for UNIX, Linux, and other operating systems. A quick Web search will help you find them.

For additional leads to discussion and support groups, check the sites listed below.

Disability Resources: Listservs (Discussion Groups).
http://www.disabilityresources.org/LISTSERVS.html
A part of the Disability Resources network, this page has a detailed listing of email-based discussion groups on a range of topics related to special education.

Email Discussion Lists and Electronic Journals.
http://www.edwebproject.org/lists.html
This site, part of the EdWeb project maintained by Andy Carvin, has a large set of email-based discussion lists with instructions on how to join the groups. Some groups may no longer be active; others will fill up your "inbox" in a matter of hours. Be sure to save the instructions on how to remove yourself from the discussion group in case such problems occur.

NetDay Compass.
http://www.netdaycompass.org/
This site is dedicated to connecting educators to technical support groups in just about every area of technology use. Here you can find links to discussion boards and listservs (email discussion groups) on topics ranging from using the Internet to configuring a network, and from getting funding for technology to making connections to standards.

● ONLINE CURRICULUM MATERIALS

The following sites offer a great variety of instructional resources. Many of the sites listed in the next section, "Information on Exceptionalities and Educational Programs," also make instructional materials available.

Bigchalk.
http://www.bigchalk.com/
Bigchalk offers a wide selection of lesson plans, information about exceptionalities, and support materials on topics such as classroom management. The site has links and homework helpers for students and parents as well.

The Copernicus Education Gateway.
http://www.edgate.com/
This site has links to curriculum materials, online courses, and instructional websites to support learning in a wide range of areas. There are also links to activities for students and support materials for parents.

Eisenhower National Clearinghouse.
http://www.enc.org/
With links and information about curriculum materials in math and science, as well as frequent news about education in general, the Eisenhower Clearinghouse offers a wealth of information that can support instruction.

International Reading Association.
http://www.reading.org/
The IRA website has information about critical literacy and other approaches to the teaching of reading, as well as recommendations of wonderful trade books for use in your classroom.

MarcoPolo.
http://marcopolo.worldcom.com/
This site represents a partnership between MCI WorldCom and a group of educational organizations (including the National Council of Teachers of Mathematics, the National Endowment for the Humanities, and the National Geographic Society) to provide standards-driven, Internet-based curriculum materials. The site is frequently updated, and you can sign up to maintain your own personal selection of materials that can then be accessed by your students from school or from home.

National Council for the Social Studies.
http://www.socialstudies.org/
The NCSS website has lesson plans and materials for teaching about the social studies across age groups, including nice materials on "teachable moments."

National Council of Teachers of Mathematics.
http://www.nctm.org/
The NCTM website provides links to excellent curriculum materials for teaching all levels of mathematics.

The New York Times Learning Network.
http://www.nytimes.com/learning/
The New York Times maintains a collection of lesson plans in areas ranging from American history to science and geography, all with links to current events and newspaper reports.

Project 2061.
http://www.project2061.org/
This website of the American Association for the Advancement of Science furnishes great links to materials that support the teaching of science at various levels.

Information on Exceptionalities and Educational Programs

DRM Guide to Disability Resources on the Internet.
http://www.disabilityresources.org/
This site, maintained by Disability Resources Monthly, has an extensive list of links on just about every topic related to special education. Each link is described in detail and evaluated. You can also find specific information and links to resources in your own state.

ERIC Clearinghouse on Disabilities and Gifted Education.
http://ericec.org/
ERIC offers information and fact sheets about exceptionalities and issues in special education, including links to discussion groups, organizations, and legislation.

The International Center for Disability Resources on the Internet.
http://www.icdri.org/
In addition to its various resources, this site has information about laws and policies concerning people with exceptionalities from throughout the world.

Office of Special Education and Rehabilitative Services.
http://www.ed.gov/offices/OSERS/
This main site of the U.S. Department of Education's Office of Special Education and Rehabilitative Services (OSERS) provides a range of information about programs, legislation, and funding, as well as a host of facts about special education.

In addition, the following sites, mentioned in various chapters of this book, provide handy resources for information on exceptionalities and branches of special education.

Ability OnLine. **http://www.abilityonline.org/**
Abledata: National Rehabilitation Information Center.
   http://www.abledata.com/
Alexander Graham Bell Association for the Deaf and Hard of Hearing.
   http://www.agbell.org/
American Academy of Child and Adolescent Psychiatry. **http://www.aacap.org/**
American Association of the Deaf-Blind.
   http://www.tr.wou.edu/dblink/aadb.htm
American Association on Mental Retardation. **http://www.aamr.org/**
American Council of the Blind. **http://acb.org/**
American Foundation for the Blind. **http://www.afb.org/**
American Printing House for the Blind. **http://www.aph.org/**
American Psychological Association. **http://www.apa.org/**
American Society for Deaf Children. **http://www.deafchildren.org/**
American Speech-Language-Hearing Association. **http://www.asha.org/**
The Arc. **http://www.thearc.org/**
Arthritis Foundation. **http://www.arthritis.org/**
Association for Education and Rehabilitation of the Blind and Visually Im-
   paired. **http://www.aerbvi.org/**
Association for Supervision and Curriculum Development.
   http://www.ascd.org/
Autism. **http://kidshealth.org/kid/health_problems/brain/autism.html**
The Autism/PDD Resources Network. **http://www.autism-pdd.net/**
Autism Research Institute. **http://www.autism.com/ari/contents.html**
Autism Society of America. **http://www.autism-society.org/**
A Blind Net. **http://www.blind.net/**
Center for Talent Development. **http://ctdnet.acns.nwu.edu/**
Center for Talented Youth. **http://www.jhu.edu/gifted/**
Center for the Study of Autism. **http://www.autism.org/**
CHARGE Syndrome Foundation. **http://www.chargesyndrome.org/**
Communication Disorders.NET. **http://www.communicationdisorders.net/**
Council for Children with Behavior Disorders. **http://www.ccbd.net/**
Council for Exceptional Children. **http://www.cec.sped.org/**
Council for Exceptional Children: Division of Learning Disabilities.
   http://www.dldcec.org/
Council on the Education of the Deaf. **http://www.deafed.net/**
Cystic Fibrosis Foundation. **http://www.cff.org/**
DB-LINK: The National Information Clearinghouse on Children Who Are
   Deaf-Blind. **http://www.tr.wou.edu/dblink/**
Deaf Resource Library. **http://www.deaflibrary.org/**
The Down Syndrome WWW Page. **http://www.nas.com/downsyn/**

Easter Seals. http://www.easter-seals.org/

Epilepsy Foundation. http://www.efa.org/

The Eunice Kennedy Shriver Center. http://www.shriver.org/

Exceptional Parent Magazine. http://eparent.com/

Federation of Families for Children's Mental Health. http://www.ffcmh.org/

Focus Adolescent Services.
http://www.focusas.com/BehavioralDisorders.html

Gifted Resources Home Page. http://www.eskimo.com/%7euser/kids.html

GT Home Page. http://www.millville.cache.k12.ut.us/tag/

GT World. http://www.gtworld.org/

Head Start Information and Publication Center.
http://www.headstartinfo.org/

Helen Keller National Center for Deaf-Blind Youths and Adults (HKNC).
http://www.helenkeller.org/national/

Hilton/Perkins Program, Perkins School for the Blind.
http://www.perkins.pvt.k12.ma.us/hiltperk.htm

Hoagies' Gifted Education Page. http://www.hoagiesgifted.org/

IDEA Practices. http://ideapractices.org/

The IEP Process. http://www.education-
world.com/special_ed/iep/index.shtml

Inclusive Education. http://www.uni.edu/coe/inclusion/

The International Dyslexia Association. http://www.interdys.org/

LD OnLine. http://www.ldonline.org/

Learning Disabilities Association. http://www.ldanatl.org/

Lovaas Institute for Early Intervention. http://www.lovaas.com/

The Listen-Up Web! http://www.listen-up.org/

Muscular Dystrophy Association. http://www.mdausa.org/

National Academy for Child Development. http://www.nacd.org/

National Alliance for the Mentally Ill. http://www.nami.org/

National Association for Gifted Children. http://www.nagc.org/

National Association for the Education of Young Children.
http://www.naeyc.org/

National Association of the Deaf. http://www.nad.org/

National Association of State Directors of Special Education. http://www.
nasdse.org/

National Attention Deficit Disorder Association. http://www.add.org/

National Center for Injury Prevention and Control.
http://www.cdc.gov/ncipc/

National Center for Learning Disabilities. http://www.ncld.org/

National Early Childhood Technical Assistance System.
http://www.nectas.unc.edu/

National Federation of the Blind. http://www.nfb.org/

National Information Center for Children and Youth with Disabilities.
   http://www.nichcy.org/
National Institute of Neurological Disorders and Stroke.
   http://www.ninds.nih.gov/
National Institute on Deafness and Other Communication Disorders.
   http://www.nidcd.nih.gov/
National Research Center on the Gifted and Talented.
   http://www.gifted.uconn.edu/nrcgt.html
The New York Institute for Special Education. **http://www.nyise.org/**
Special Education Resources on the Internet. **http://seriweb.com/**
Spina Bifida Association of America. **http://www.sbaa.org/**
Spinal Cord Injury Information Network. **http://www.spinalcord.uab.edu/**
Sports 'n Spokes. **http://www.sportsnspokes.com/**
United Cerebral Palsy Association. **http://www.ucpa.org/**
Usher's Syndrome.
   http://deafness.miningco.com/library/weekly/aa062397.htm
TASH. **http://www.tash.org/**
Zero to Three: National Center for Infants, Toddlers and Families.
   http://www.zerotothree.org/

● INFORMATION ABOUT TECHNOLOGY

Some of the following sites address issues of technology in general; others are oriented more toward practical tips for teachers and students.

Alliance for Technology Access. **http://www.ataccess.org/**
Assistive Technology Industry Association. **http://www.atia.org/**
Center for Applied Special Technology. **http://www.cast.org/**
Center for IT Accommodation. **http://www.itpolicy.gsa.gov/cita**
Closing the Gap: Computer Technology in Special Education and Rehabilitation.
   http://www.closingthegap.com/
Computers and ADD. **http://www.ncpamd.com/ComputersAndADD.htm**
Early Childhood Collection, National Center to Improve Practice in Special Education Through Technology, Media and Materials.
   http://www2.edc.org/NCIP/library/ec/toc.htm
EASI's K to 12 Education Technology Centre.
   http://www.rit.edu/~easi/ak12/k12.html
Easy Access to Software and Information. **http://www.rit.edu/~easi/**
Gallaudet University Technology Access Program. **http://tap.gallaudet.edu/**
Guide to Toys for Children Who Are Blind or Visually Impaired.
   http://www.toy-tma.org/industry/publications/blindcurrent/cover.html

IntelliTools Activity Exchange. http://www.intellitools.com/shareyouractivities.html

Intel Teach to the Future. http://www.intel.com/education/teach/index.htm

International Society for Augmentative and Alternative Communication. http://www.isaac-online.org/

Software to Go. http://clerccenter2.gallaudet.edu/stg/index.html

Tech Connections. http://www.techconnections.org/

Technology and Media Division of the Council for Exceptional Children. http://www.tamcec.org/

Web 4 Teachers. http://www.4teachers.org/

● SELECTED SOFTWARE, HARDWARE, AND TOYS

The following list gives the website (current as of the date of this book's publication) for the maker, publisher, or primary U.S. distributor of each product. Many products are also available through stores and other vendors.

Accelerated Reader. **http://www.renlearn.com/**

Access to Math. **http://www.donjohnston.com/**

AlphaSmart. **http://www.alphasmart.com/**

ALVA Delphi Braille Display. **http://www.aagi.com/**

Articulation I: Consonant Phonemes. **http://www.learningfundamentals.com/**

ASAP. **http://www.microtalk.com/**

AudioCalc-Talking Scientific Calculator. **http://www.blazie.com/**

Away We Go! **http://www.ScientificLearning.com/** or **http://www.scilearn.com/**

Basic Coins. **http://www.attainmentcompany.com/**

Boardmaker. **http://www.mayer-johnson.com/software/index.html**

Braille 'n Speak. **http://www.blazie.com/**

Community Success. **http://www.attainmentcompany.com/**

Computers at Work. **http://www.attainmentcompany.com/**

Co:Writer. **http://www.donjohnston.com/**

DigiCom. **http://www.greattalkingbox.com/**

Dragonfly Toy Company. **http://www.dftoys.com/**

Dragon NaturallySpeaking. **http://www.lhsl.com/naturallyspeaking/**

Dr. Seuss series. **http://www.learningcompanyschool.com/**

DynaMyte. **http://www.dynavoxsys.com/**

Earobics. **http://www.earobics.com/**

Encarta Researcher (part of Encarta Encyclopedia).
   http://www.microsoft.com/
Explorer Globe. http://www.leapfrog.com/
Fast ForWord. http://www.scilearn.com/
Franklin Language Master. http://www.blazie.com/
The Fun & Learn Phonics Bus. http://www.leapfrog.com/
HandsOFF! http://www.zygo-usa.com/handsoff.html
HyperStudio. http://www.hyperstudio.com/
Inspiration. http://www.inspiration.com/
IntelliKeys keyboard. http://www.intellitools.com/
IntelliPics. http://www.intellitools.com/
IntelliTalk. http://www.intellitools.com/
JAWS. http://www.hj.com/
JumpStart series. http://www.knowledgeadventure.com/
Kid Pix. http://www.kidpix.com/
Kurzweil 3000. http://www.kurzweiledu.com/
Laureate Special Needs Software. http://www.laureatelearning.com/
Lego Mindstorms. http://mindstorms.lego.com/
Macromedia Director. http://www.macromedia.com/software/director/
MAGic. http://www.hj.com/
Maltron adaptive keyboards. http://www.maltron.com/
MatchTime. http://www.attainmentcompany.com/
Math Mysteries. http://www.tomsnyder.com/
McGee series. http://www.voyager.net/lawrence/
Millie's Math House. http://www.edmark.com/
Monkeys Jumping on the Bed. http://www.donjohnston.com/
One-Step Communicator. http://www.ablenetinc.com/home.html
OPENBook. http://www.hj.com/
outSPOKEN. http://www.aagi.com/
Overlay Maker. http://www.intellitools.com/
Personal Success. http://www.attainmentcompany.com/
Phonics Alive! http://www.phonicsalive.com/
Phonics Based Reading. http://www.lexialearning.com/
Phonology. http://www.learningfundamentals.com/
PrimeTime Math. http://www.tomsnyder.com/
Proportional Reading. http://www.proportionalreading.com/
Reader Rabbit series. http://www.learningcompanyschool.com/
The Reading Edge. http://www.telesensory.com/
Reading for Meaning. http://www.tomsnyder.com/
Reading Pen. http://www.wizcomtech.com/products/readingpenII.html
Reading SOS. http://www.lexialearning.com/

Return of the Incredible Machine: Contraptions. http://sierra.com/
Road Runner. http://www.ostrichsoftware.com/
SimCity. http://thesims.ea.com/us/ and http://www.sc3000.com/
Simon Skills Pack. http://www.donjohnston.com/
SpeechViewer III for Windows. http://www-3.ibm.com/able/snsspv3.html
Start-to-Finish Books. http://www.donjohnston.com/
Storybook Weaver Deluxe. http://www.learningcompany.com/
Strategy Challenges Collection. http://www.edmark.com/
Surpass. http://www.renlearn.com/
TalkTrac Wearable Communicator. http://www.ablenetinc.com/home.html
That's a Fact, Jack! Read. http://www.tomsnyder.com/
Thinkin' Things. http://www.edmark.com/
Trudy's Time & Place House. http://www.edmark.com/
Turn and Talk. http://www.frame-tech.com/
Versatile Image Processor. http://www.jbliss.com/
Video Voice. http://www.videovoice.com/
Visual Voice Tools. http://www.edmark.com/prod/vvt/
Voice-in-a-Box. http://www.frame-tech.com/
Window Bridge. http://www.synthavoice.com/
Window-Eyes. http://www.gwmicro.com/
WinVision. http://www.artictech.com/
Working It Out Together. http://www.attainmentcompany.com/
WriteAway. http://www.is-inc.com/
Write:OutLoud. http://www.donjohnston.com/
ZoomText Xtra. http://www.aisquared.com/

● PROFESSIONAL TOOLS FOR TEACHERS

Center for Problem-Based Learning.
   http://www.imsa.edu/team/cpbl/cpbl.html
Evaluation Rubrics for Websites.
   http://www.siec.k12.in.us/~west/online/eval.htm
GoalView. **http://www.ltools.com/**
Grade Machine. **http://www.mistycity.com/grademachine/**
IEPMaker. **http://www.iepware.com/**
IEPplus. **http://www.pentamation.com/**
Individual Planning System. **http://www.ltools.com/**
Invention & Design.
   http://jefferson.village.virginia.edu/~meg3c/id/id_home.html
Web 4 Teachers. **http://www.4teachers.org/**

REFERENCES

Achenbach, J. (1996, December 4). Reality Check: You Can't Believe Everything You Read. But You'd Better Believe This. *The Washington Post*, pp. C01.

ACOT. (1996). *Integrating technology into classroom instruction.* Apple Classrooms of Tomorrow Research Series, Report No. 22. Cupertino, CA: Apple Computer.

American Academy of Pediatrics. (2001). Clinical practice guideline: Treatment of the school-aged child with attention-deficit/hyperactivity disorder. *Pediatrics, 108(4),* 1033–1044.

American Psychiatric Association. (2000). *Diagnostic and statistical manual of mental disorders,* Fourth Edition Text Revision (DSM-IV-TR). Washington, DC: American Psychiatric Press.

American Society for Autism. (2001). *Current interventions in autism: A brief analysis.* Bethesda, MD: Author. Available online at http://www.autism-society.org/packages/packages.html.

Bailey, G. D., & Bagby, R. (1998). Creating an educational website: Guidelines for technology leaders. Available online at http://www2.educ.ksu.edu/Faculty/BaileyG/html/web.creat.art.pdf.

Bandura, A. (1995). *Self-efficacy in changing societies.* New York: Cambridge University Press.

Bartlett, J. (1992). *Familiar quotations,* 16th ed. Boston: Little, Brown.

Beckley, D. (1998). *Gifted and learning disabled: Twice exceptional students.* Storrs, CT: National Research Center on the Gifted and Talented.

Bernthal, J. E., & Bankson, N. W. (1993). *Articulation and phonological disorders,* 3rd ed. Englewood Cliffs, NJ: Prentice-Hall.

Bialo, E. R. (1997). Open your eyes: The evidence is there! *Technology and Learning,* September, 1997.

Blaiwes, A. S., & Weller, D. R. (1978). *A computerized evaluation and training system (CETS) for recruit training commands: An overview.* NAVTRAEQUIPC-IH-307. DTIC No. ADA 133 106. Orlando, FL: Naval Training Equipment Center.

Blischak, D. M. (1999). Increases in natural speech production following experience with synthetic speech. *Journal of Special Education Technology, 14,* 44–53.

Bloom, B. S., Englehart, M. B., Furst, E. J., Hill, W. H., & Krathwohl, D. R. (Eds.). (1956). *Taxonomy of educational objectives: The classification of educational goals. Handbook I: Cognitive domain.* New York: McKay.

Boone, R., & Higgins, K. (1993). Hypermedia basal readers: Three years of school-based research. *Journal of Special Education Technology, 12(2),* 86–106.

Burgstahler, S., Wild, N., & Smallman, J. (2000). From high school to college to work: Students with disabilities in high tech fields. Technology and persons with disabilities. Paper presented at the Center on Disabilities 15th Annual International Conference, Los Angeles, March 20–25, 2000.

Carpenter, J. (1993). *Clark county social service school mediation program evaluation report.* Clark County, NV: Clark County Social Service.

Carpenter, J. (1994). *Clark county social service school mediation program evaluation report.* Clark County, NV: Clark County Social Service.

Catalano, R., Loeber, R., & McKinney, K.. (1999). School and community interventions to prevent serious and violent offending. Washington, DC: Office of Juvenile Justice and Delinquency Prevention.

Chalfant, J. C., & Van Dusen, M. V. (1989). Teacher assistance teams: Five descriptive studies on 96 teams. *Remedial and Special Education, 10(6),* 49–58.

Cognition and Technology Group at Vanderbilt. (1991). Integrated media: Toward a theoretical framework for utilizing their potential. Paper presented and published in proceedings of Multimedia Technology Seminar, Washington, DC, May 20–21, by the Center for Special Education Technology, Council for Exceptional Children, Reston, VA.

Cohn, S. J. (1988). Assessing the gifted child and adolescent. In C. J. Kestenbaum & D. T. Williams (Eds.), *Handbook of clinical assessment of children and adolescents* (pp. 355–376). New York: New York University Press.

Cordes, C., & Miller, E. (Eds.). (2000). *Fool's Gold: A Critical Look at Computers in Childhood.* College Park, MD: Alliance for Childhood.

Cranmer, T. W. (2000). Frontiers in tactile perception. *The Braille Monitor, 43(1).* Baltimore, MD: National Federation of the Blind. Available online at http://www.nfb.org/bm/bm00/bm0001/brlm0001.htm.

Crawford, D., & Bodine, R. (1996). *Conflict resolution education: A guide to implementing programs in schools, youth-serving organizations, and community and juvenile justice settings.* Washington, DC: Office of Juvenile Justice and Delinquency Prevention, U.S. Department of Justice, and Office of Elementary and Secondary Education, U.S. Department of Education.

Dalton, J., & Smith, D. (1986). Extending children's special abilities. Melbourne, Australia: Department of School Education, Victoria.

Danaher, J. (in press). *Eligibility policies and practice for young children under Part B of the IDEA, NECTAS Notes,* No. 6, rev. Chapel Hill, NC: National Early Childhood Technical Assistance System.

Das, J. P. (1995). Some thoughts on two aspects of Vygotsky's work. *Educational Psychologist, 30(2),* 93–97.

Dede, C., & Sprague, D. (1999). Constructivism in the classroom: If I teach this way am I doing my job? *Learning and Leading with Technology, 27,* 6–9.

Doctoroff, S. (1996). Supporting social pretend play in young children with disabilities. *Early Child Development and Care, 119,* 27–38.

Edyburn, D. L. (1999). Action research tools for assessing handwriting skills and enhancing handwriting instruction with technology. *Journal of Special Education Technology, 15(3).* 50–57.

Epstein, J. L. (2001). *School, Family, and Community Partnerships: Preparing Educators and Improving Schools.* Boulder, CO: Westview Press.

Fescer, F. A., & Long, N. J. (1998). *Life space crisis intervention.* Washington, DC: Center for Effective Collaborative and Practice, American Institutes for Research. Available online at http://www.air.org/cecp/interact/authoronline/april98/1.htm.

Fitzgerald, G. E., & Koury, K. A. (1996). Empirical advances in technology-assisted instruction for students with mild and moderate disabilities. *Journal of Research on Computing in Education, 28(4),* 526–553.

Florey, J., & Tafoya, N. (1988). Identifying gifted and talented American Indian students: An overview. Eric Document 296810. Las Cruces, NM: ERIC Clearinghouse on Rural Education and Small Schools.

Freeman, B. J. (1993). The syndrome of autism: Update and guidelines for diagnosis. *Infants and Young Children, 6(2),* 1–11.

Frith, U. (Ed.). (1999). *Autism and Asperger syndrome.* Cambridge, UK: Cambridge University Press.

Gable, R. A., Quinn, M. M., Rutherford, R. B., Jr., & Howell, K. W. (1998). Functional behavioral assessments and positive behavioral interventions. *Preventing School Failure, 42,* 106–119.

Gagné, R. M. (1985). *The conditions of learning* (4th ed.). New York: Holt, Rinehart and Winston.

Gardner, H. (1983). *Frames of mind: The theory of multiple intelligences.* New York: Basic Books.

Gardner, H. (1999). *Intelligence reframed: Multiple intelligences for the 21st century.* New York: Basic Books.

Ginsberg, M. (2000). Early childhood unplugged. Available online at Connect for Kids: Reference Room, http://www.connectforkids.org/resources3139/resources_show.htm?doc_id=40967.

Glanze, W. (Ed.). (1996). *The Signet Mosby medical encyclopedia.* Rev. ed. New York: Penguin.

Gooden, A. R. (1996). *Computers in the classroom—how teachers and students are using technology to transform learning.* San Francisco: Jossey-Bass.

Grabe, M., & Grabe, C. (2001). *Integrating technology for meaningful learning,* 3rd ed. Boston: Houghton Mifflin.

Green, G. (1996). Early behavioral intervention for autism: What does research tell us. In C. Maurice, G. Green, & S. Luce (Eds.), *Behavioral interventions for young children with autism* (pp. 29–44). Austin, TX: PRO-ED.

Greszko, K. (1988). Types of battery operated toys. Handout developed for the Technical Assistance Center No. 3, George Mason University, Fairfax, VA.

Hawkins, J., & Honey, M. A. (1990). *Challenges of formative testing: conducting situated research in classrooms.* Technical Report No. 48, ED319380. New York: Center for Children and Technology, Bank Street College of Education.

Hawkins, J., & Pea, R. D. (1987). Tools for bridging everyday and scientific thinking. *Journal for Research in Science Teaching, 24(4),* 291–307.

Healy, J. M. (1998). The "meme" that ate childhood. *Education Week, 18(6),* 56, 37.

Hilton-Chalfen, D. (1991). *Computers and students with disabilities: new challenges for higher education.* Available from Educational Uses of Information Technology, 1112 16th St., N.W., Suite 600, Washington, DC 20036.

Holzberg, C. S. (1997). The right stuff for young writers: A diverse collection of programs to develop kids' written expression. *Electronic Learning, 16(6),* 30, 36–37.

Hothersall, D. (1990). *History of psychology,* 2nd ed. New York: McGraw-Hill.

Howe, M. J. A. (1990). *The origins of exceptional abilities.* Oxford, England: Basil Blackwell.

International Narcotics Control Board. (1996). *Report of the international narcotics control board for 1995.* New York: United Nations.

Jacobson, J. W., Mulick, J. A., & Schwartz, A. A. (1995). A history of facilitated communication: Science, pseudoscience, and antiscience. *American Psychologist, 50(9),* 750–765. Available online at http://www.apa.org/journals/jacobson.html.

Johnson, D. W., & Johnson, R. (2000). Cooperation, conflict, cognition, and metacognition. In A. Costa (ed.), *Developing minds: A resource book for teaching thinking,* 2nd ed. Alexandria, VA: Association for Supervision and Curriculum Development.

Judge, S. L. (2001). Computer applications in programs for young children with disabilities: Current status and future directions. *JSET E-Journal, 16(1).* Available online at http://jset.unlv.edu/.

Kanner, L. (1943). Autistic disturbances of affective contact. *Nervous Child, 2,* 217–250.

Kauffman, J. M. (1996). Good? Better? Best? Empirical and ethical criteria for choosing and discarding practices. Presentation at Midwest Symposium for Leadership in Behavior Disorders, Kansas City, MO.

Keilitz, I., & Dunivant, N. (1986). The relationship between learning disability and juvenile delinquency: Current state of knowledge. *Remedial and Special Education, 7(3),* 18–26.

Keller, H. (1903). *The Story of My Life.* New York: Doubleday.

Kenny, D. A., Archambault, F. X., & Hallmark, B. W. (1995). *The effects of group composition on gifted and non-gifted elementary students in cooperative learning groups.* Storrs, CT: National Research Center on the Gifted and Talented.

Khang, S. W., & Iwata, B. A. (2000). Computer systems for collecting real-time observational data. In T. Thompson, D. Felce, & F. J. Symons (Eds.), *Behavioral observation: Technology and applications in developmental disabilities.* Baltimore, MD: Brookes.

Kinnaman, D. E. (1999, December). We're closer now: Can technology live up to its educational promise? *Curriculum Administrator, 60.*

Kirk, S. A. (1963). Behavioral diagnosis and remediation of learning disabilities. *Proceedings of the conference on the explorations into the problems of the perceptually handicapped child.* Evanston: IL: Fund for the Perceptually Handicapped Child.

Kirk, S. A., Gallagher, J. J., & Anastasiow, N. J. (1997). *Educating exceptional children,* 8th ed. Boston: Houghton Mifflin.

Kulik, J. A. (1994). Meta-analytic studies of findings on computer-based instruction. In E. Baker & H. O'Neil (Eds.), *Technology assessment in education and training.* Hillsdale, NJ: Erlbaum.

Kulik, J. A., & Kulik, C. C. (1992). Meta-analytic findings on grouping programs. *Gifted Child Quarterly, 36(2),* 73–77.

Kuther, T. L. (2000). Moral reasoning, perceived competence, and adolescent engagement in risky activity. *Journal of Adolescence, 23(5),* 599–604.

Lahm, E., & Morrissette, S. (1994). Zap 'em with assistive technology. Paper presented at the annual meeting of the Council for Exceptional Children, Denver, CO.

Lahm, E., & Nickels, B. (1999). Assistive technology competencies for special educators. *Teaching Exceptional Children, 32(1),* 56–65.

Lambert, N. M. (1988). Adolescent outcomes for hyperactive children: Perspectives on general and specific patterns of childhood risk for adolescent educational, social and mental health problems. *American Psychologist, 43,* 786–799.

Laurent Clerc National Deaf Education Center. (1999). Software evaluation guidelines. Available online at http://clerccenter2.gallaudet.edu/stg/how-to-evaluate.html.

Lewis, R. (1993). *Special education technology: Classroom applications.* Pacific Grove, CA: Brooks/Cole.

Lindsley, O. R. (1972). From Skinner to precision teaching. In J. B. Jordan & L. S. Robbins (Eds.), *Let's try doing something else kind of thing* (pp. 1–12). Arlington, VA: Council for Exceptional Children.

Lyon, G. R. (1995). Research initiatives in learning disabilities: Contributions from scientists supported by the National Institute of Child Health and Human Development. *Journal of Child Neurology, 10,* 120–126.

Maker, C. J., & Nielson, A. (1996). *Curriculum development and teaching strategies for gifted learners.* Austin, TX.: PRO-ED.

Marcus, L., & Schopler, E. (1994). Ethics and behavior therapy with children. In J. Hattab (Ed.), *Ethics and child mental health* (pp. 166–176). Jerusalem: Gefen Books.

McDonnell, A., & Hardman, M. (1988). A synthesis of "best practice" for early childhood services. *Journal of the Division for Early Childhood, 12(4),* 328–339.

Mesibov, G. (1995). A comprehensive program for serving people with autism and their families: The TEACCH model. In J. Matson (Ed.), *Autism in children and adults: Etiology, assessment, and intervention* (pp. 85–97). Belmont, CA: Brooks-Cole.

Musselwhite, C. (1986). *Adaptive play for special needs children.* San Diego: College-Hill Press.

National Association of the Deaf. (2001). What is wrong with the use of these terms: "Deaf-mute," "deaf and dumb," or "hearing-impaired"? Available online at http://www.nad.org/infocenter/infotogo/dcc/terms.html.

National Center for Education Statistics. (2000). *Postsecondary students with disabilities: Enrollment, services, and persistence.* NCES 2000092. Washington, DC: U.S. Department of Education, Government Printing Office.

National Center for Education Statistics. (2001). *Dropout rates in the United States: 1999.* NCES 2002114. Washington, DC: U.S. Department of Education, Government Printing Office.

National Center for Learning Disabilities. (2001). *LD basics.* New York: National Center for Learning Disabilities. Available online at http://www.ncld.org/info/index.cfm.

Nelson, L. K., & Masterson, J. J. (1999). Computer technology: Creative interfaces in service delivery. *Topics in Language Disorders, 19(3),* 68–86.

Newman, D. (1990). *Technology's role in restructuring for collaborative learning.* CTE Technical Report No. 8. New York: Center for Children and Technology, Bank Street College of Education.

NICHCY. (1999). *NICHCY briefing paper: Questions often asked by parents about special education services* (4th ed.). (LG1). Washington, DC: National Information Center for Children and Youth with Disabilities.

NICHCY. (2001a). Deafness and hearing loss. Fact Sheet No. 3, January. National Information Center for Children and Youth with Disabilities. Available online at http://www.nichcy.org/pubs/.

NICHCY. (2001b). Visual impairments. Fact Sheet No. 13, January. National Information Center for Children and Youth with Disabilities. Available online at http://www.nichcy.org/pubs/.

O'Riordan, K. (1999). Reading and literacy program targets special needs readers. Available online at http://www.mff.org/edtech/article.taf?_function=detail&Content_uid1=274.

Papert, S. (1980). *Mindstorms: Children, computers, and powerful ideas.* New York: Basic Books.

Papert, S. (1993), *The children's machine: Rethinking school in the age of the computer.* New York: Basic Books.

Pea, R. D. (1987). Cognitive technologies for mathematics education. In A. Schoenfeld (Ed.), *Cognitive science and mathematics education* (pp. 89–122). Hillsdale, NJ: Erlbaum.

Pea, R. D., & Sheingold, K. S. (Eds.). (1987). *Mirrors of minds: Patterns of experience in educational computing.* Norwood, NJ: Ablex.

Renzulli, J. S. (1986). The three ring conception of giftedness: A developmental model for creative productivity. In J. S. Renzulli & S. M. Reis (Eds.), *The triad reader* (pp. 2–19). Mansfield Center, CT: Creative Learning Press.

Rettig, M. (1987). Microcomputers in early childhood special education: Trends and issues. Paper presented at the National Early Childhood Conference on Children with Special Needs, Denver, CO.

Rogers, K. B. (1998). Using current research to make "good" decisions about grouping. *NASSP Bulletin, 82(595),* 38–46.

Rose, D., & Meyer, A. (2000). Universal design for individual differences. *Educational Leadership, 58(3),* 39–43.

Russell, T. L. (1999). *No significant difference phenomenon.* Raleigh: North Carolina State University.

Schank, R. C. (Ed.). (1998). *Inside multi-media case based instruction.* Boston: Erlbaum.

Schroeder, F. K. (1999). Braille usage: Perspectives of legally blind adults and policy implications for school administrators. Doctoral dissertation. Baltimore, MD: National Federation of the Blind. Available online at http://www.nfb.org/brusage.htm.

Schroeder, J. E., Hall, S., & Morey, J. C. (1985). Appendix M: Statistical results of the evaluation. In J. E. Schroeder, F. N. Dyer, P. Czerny, E. W. Youngling, & D. P. Gillotti (Eds.), *Videodisc interpersonal skills training and assessment (VISTA): Software and evaluation details,* vol. 4 (Research Note). DTIC No. ADA 166 867. Fort Benning, GA: U.S. Army Research Institute Field Unit.

Sears, P. S., & Barbee, A. H. (1977). Career and life-satisfactions among Terman gifted women. In J. C. Stanley & W. C. George (Eds.), *The gifted and the creative.* Baltimore, MD: Johns Hopkins University Press.

Sears, R. R. (1977). Sources of life satisfactions of the Terman gifted men. *American Psychologist, 32,* 119–128.

Slavin, R. E., & Cooper, R. (1999). Improving intergroup relations: Lessons learned from cooperative learning programs. *Journal of Social Issues, 55(4),* 647–664.

Smith, M. (1996). Strategies to reduce school violence: The New Mexico Center for Dispute Resolution. In A. M. Hoffman (Ed.), *Schools, violence, and society* (p. 256). Westport, CT: Praeger.

Smith, R., & Vokurka, J.F (1990). A software selection model for the special student. *Computing Teacher, 17 (5),* 36–38.

Smith, S. L. (1995). *No easy answers: The learning disabled child at home and at school.* New York: Bantam.

Smith, S. W., & Kortering, L. J. (1996). Using computers to generate IEP's: Rethinking the process. *Journal of Special Education Technology, 13,* 81–90.

Software Publishers Association. (1996). *Educational technology promotion guide.* Report No. EPT-96. Washington, DC: Software Publishers Association.

Solit, G., Taylor, M., & Bednarczyk, A. (1992). *Access for all.* Washington, DC: Gallaudet University.

Stepien, W., & Gallagher, S. (1993). Problem-based learning: As authentic as it gets. *Educational Leadership, 50 (7),* 25–28.

Stoll, C. (1995). *Silicon snake oil: Second thoughts on the information highway.* New York: Doubleday.

Sugai, G., & Horner, R. H. (1999). Discipline and behavioral support: Practices, pitfalls, & promises. *Effective School Practices, 17(4),* 10–22.

Tallal, P., Miller, S. L., Bedi, G., & Byma, G. (1995). Training with temporally modified speech results in dramatic improvements in speech perception and language comprehension. *Society for Neuroscience Abstracts, 21* (Part I), 421.

Terman, L. (1926). *Genetic Studies of Genius,* vol. 2. Stanford, CA: Stanford University Press.

Terman, L. M., & Oden, M. H. (1959). *Genetic studies of genius,* vol. 5: *The gifted group at mid-life.* Stanford, CA: Stanford University Press.

Tindal, G., & Nolet, V. (1995). Curriculum-based measurement in middle and high schools: Critical thinking skills in content areas. *Focus on Exceptional Children, 27(7):* 1–22.

Torgesen, J. K., & Barker, T. A. (1995). Computers as aids in the prevention and remediation of reading disabilities. *Learning Disability Quarterly, 18(2),* 76–87.

Torgesen, J. K., & Mathes, P. G. (1998). *What every teacher should know about phonological awareness.* Tallahassee: Florida State University, Florida Department of Education.

Turow, J., & Nir, L. (2000). *The Internet and the family 2000: The view from parents, the view from kids.* Report Series No. 33. Philadelphia: Annenberg Public Policy Center of the University of Pennsylvania.

U.S. Department of Education. (2000). *Twenty-second annual report to congress on the implementation of the individuals with disabilities education act.* Washington, DC: Government Printing Office.

Walton, J. P., Frisina, R. D., & O'Neill, W. E. (1998). Age-related alteration in neural processing of temporal sound features in the inferior colliculus in the CBA mouse model of presbycusis. *Journal of Neuroscience, 267,* 2117–2130.

Weinberg, W. A., Harper, C. R., Emslie, G. J., & Brumback, R. A. (1995). Depression and other affective illnesses as a cause of school failure and maladaptation in learning disabled children, adolescents, and young adults. Chapter 15 in *Secondary education and beyond: Providing opportunities for students with learning disabilities.* Pittsburgh: Learning Disabilities Association. Available online at http://209.24.177.194/articles/seab/weinberg/.

Willard-Holt, C. (1999). Dual exceptionalities. ERIC EC Digest #E574. Reston, VA: ERIC Clearinghouse on Disabilities and Gifted Education.

Wise, B. W., & Olson, R. O. (1994). Computer speech and the remediation of reading and spelling problems. *Journal of Special Education Technology, 12(3),* 207–220.

Witty, P. A. (1936, March). Exploitation of the child of high intelligence quotient. *Educational Method,* 298–304.

Woolsey, M. L., Gardner, R., III, & Harrison, T. (2001). The use of ecobehavioral assessment to identify the critical behavioral variables in two types of residential classrooms for the deaf. The Ohio State University. Paper presented at the 27th Annual Convention of the Association for Behavioral Analysis, New Orleans, LA.

Zernike, K., & Petersen, M. (2001). Schools' backing of behavior drugs comes under fire. *New York Times.* August 19.

Zito, J., Safer, D., dosReis, S., Gardner, J., Boles, M., & Lynch, F. (2000). Trends in the prescribing of psychotropic medications to preschoolers. *Journal of the American Medical Association, 283,* 1025–1030.

GLOSSARY

acceleration Moving a student more quickly than usual through the curriculum.

accessible web design Web page design that allows people with visual impairments access to the entire site content.

adaptive technology Technology tools that help modify the environment to aid a person with a disability.

American Sign Language (ASL) A true language (with its own syntax and grammar) that uses hand gestures and facial expressions in place of spoken words.

articulation disorder Inability to produce the sounds appropriate for one's age, or persistent substitution or omission of sounds.

assistive technology Technology tools used to increase, maintain, or improve the functional capabilities of a student with a disability.

attention deficit disorder (ADD) *See* attention-deficit/hyperactivity disorder.

attention-deficit/hyperactivity disorder (ADHD) A persistent pattern of inattention and/or hyperactivity-impulsivity, marked by symptoms such as difficulty sustaining attention and organization, excessive talking or fidgeting, and unusual forgetfulness.

augmentative and alternative communication (AAC) Communication assisted by tools or techniques that supplement, replace, or enhance conventional speech or writing.

authoring tool An application that enables the user to design a stand-alone product, such as a presentation or report, with multimedia or hypermedia components.

autism A developmental disability that significantly affects verbal and nonverbal communication and social interaction; frequently characterized by repetitive activities and stereotyped movements, resistance to environmental change or change in daily routines, and unusual responses to sensory experiences.

automatic speech recognition (ASR) Software technology that allows for the conversion of speech to text and vice versa.

bandwidth The amount of information that can be moved in a given amount of time over a telecommunications line; in other words, the speed of a connection.

battery of tests A set of tests designed to assess performance across a wide range of areas.

behavior modification A direct instructional approach that aims to teach a child to manage his or her own behavior and reactions to the environment through reinforcement.

Braille A text system in which raised dots represent letters and punctuation; the most popular text system among people with visual impairments.

central hearing loss Hearing impairment resulting from damage to the central nervous system, either in the nerves that occupy the pathways to the brain or in the brain itself.

cochlear implant A medical device that transmits sounds by electrically stimulating the nerve fibers in the cochlea (a fluid-filled tube in the inner ear); used with adults and children who have a profound sensorineural hearing loss in both ears and show no ability to hear speech through hearing aids.

communication board A simple, flat surface covered with buttons or pictures that a child can use to make a request or indicate his or her answer to a question. Some communication boards include a computerized voice.

communication disorder A disorder of speech or language, such as difficulty in pronouncing words, using the rules of syntax, or understanding the meaning of words and sentences.

concept mapping A visual method of presenting ideas and connections between ideas. Also known as *semantic webbing*.

conductive hearing loss Hearing impairment caused by disease or obstruction in the outer or middle ear. People with this type of hearing loss can generally make use of a hearing aid.

cooperative groups Heterogeneous groups of students who work together to accomplish shared learning goals.

curriculum-based measurement A technique of assessing students based on standards and ongoing evaluation, rather than by comparison to other students.

deaf-blind Having serious auditory and visual impairments that, in combination, create severe communication and other developmental and learning needs.

deafness A severe hearing impairment that impedes the child's processing of linguistic information through hearing, with or without amplification.

developmental delay A disability that causes a child to develop at a rate significantly below average and experience difficulties in learning and social adjustment. Delay can stem from a mental or physical impairment or both.

diagnostic process A process of selecting a treatment (in educational terms, an *instructional method*) through an evaluation of the individual's specific strengths and weaknesses.

direct instruction An instructional process that uses rapid pacing and choral group responses, based on scripted sets of instructional materials in areas such as reading, remedial reading, spelling, math, writing, and language.

Down syndrome A chromosomal disorder (the presence of an extra chromosome 21) that typically causes mental retardation as well as recognizable physical characteristics, such as a somewhat flattened skull.

dual exceptionalities Two exceptionalities occurring in the same individual; a term often used in reference to gifted students who have disabilities.

early childhood special education A system of early intervention programs for the youngest children with disabilities and their families.

electronic gradebook Software that allows easy input of assignments and tests and helps a teacher calculate overall grades.

emotional and behavioral disorders A general term for serious and persistent difficulties that can be described by a psychiatric diagnosis.

enrichment Providing a student with learning opportunities that extend or deepen the regular classroom experiences; in gifted education, an alternative to acceleration.

exceptionality A difference, representing performance either above or below average, in any area of functioning, including intelligence, academic skills, mobility, speech, language, and sensory skills.

fluency disorder Persistent interruptions in the flow of speech, such as stuttering.

fragile X syndrome A genetic disorder arising from a defect on the X (female) chromosome; the leading inherited cause of mental retardation.

frames Independent sections into which the content of a web page is divided—in effect, multiple web pages on a single screen.

freeware Free software that you can either download or run on the Internet.

functional behavioral assessment Assessment of the functional relationships between a child's behavior and the suspected causes of that behavior, required by IDEA for children whose behavior interferes with the educational process.

gifted Possessing high intellectual or academic ability; often used in combination with *talented,* with little distinction between the two terms.

hearing impairment An impairment in hearing, whether permanent or not, that affects a child's educational performance.

hypermedia Multimedia that allows the user to move in a nonlinear fashion from one segment of the product to another, as in links on a web page.

IDEA *See* Individuals with Disabilities Education Act.

inclusion The practice of placing students with exceptionalities in the regular classroom for the majority of the school day; also known as *mainstreaming.*

independent study A learning project that a student undertakes independently, with the teacher's approval and guidance.

individualized education program (IEP) A written statement, required by IDEA, indicating specific educational plans for a child with a disability; the statement is reviewed and revised on an annual basis.

individualized family service plan (IFSP) A written plan for a student who is receiving early childhood special education, including services to be provided to the family as a whole.

Individuals with Disabilities Education Act (IDEA) A federal law that provides for the education of persons with disabilities by the states.

integrated learning systems Computerized educational systems that offer personalized tutoring, monitor students' progress, and provide teachers with detailed reports.

interface The look and format of a software program or website—what a user sees when interacting with the program.

language disorder A difficulty in understanding and using speech or the written word; it can involve phonology, morphology, syntax, semantics, or pragmatics, or a combination of these.

learning disability A discrepancy between a student's ability (as measured by intelligence tests and other devices) and that student's actual performance. The specific problem may involve listening, speaking, reading, writing, reasoning, or mathematical abilities—or more than one of these areas. Although the cause of learning disabilities is not clear, they are presumed to arise from some sort of central nervous system dysfunction. The federal government uses the term *specific learning disability.*

least restrictive environment The phrase in IDEA indicating that students with disabilities will receive their education in an environment that allows them to interact with their peers to the greatest extent reasonable.

legally blind Having a visual acuity of 20/200 or less in the better eye, after correction, or a field of vision no greater than 20 degrees at the widest diameter.

low vision A degree of visual impairment in which the person can read with the help of large-print reading materials and magnification.

mainstreaming *See* inclusion.

manual communication An educational approach for children with hearing disabilities in which students learn to use sign language (usually American Sign Language) and fingerspelling.

mixed hearing loss Hearing impairment resulting from a combination of conductive and sensorineural losses so that the problem exists in the outer or middle ear as well as in the inner ear.

moderate visual impairment A corrected visual acuity between 20/70 and 20/160; typically people with such an impairment can make good use of visual aids.

morphology The system governing the way words in a given language are structured.

multiple disabilities A combination of two or more impairments that together create severe educational problems; officially the term excludes deaf-blindness, which is considered a separate category.

multiple intelligences The theory, made popular by Howard Gardner, that human intelligence can be divided into seven or more distinct areas.

notetaker Any accommodation designed to help a student take notes; technological devices used for this purpose include minicassette recorders, laptop computers, and stand-alone keyboards.

optical character recognition (OCR) Use of a scanner and software to recognize printed text and convert it to information that a computer can use.

oral communication An educational approach for children with hearing disabilities in which students learn to speak and to use speech reading as well as to use their residual hearing with the assistance of a hearing aid.

paraplegic A person with damage to the cervical nerves that manage the arms and legs, resulting in paralysis and loss of sensation.

partially sighted Having a visual impairment less severe than low vision; typically a person with partial sight may be able to see objects up close or far away and with corrective lenses may be able to function at normal levels.

personal digital assistant (PDA) A handheld electronic device, such as those made by Palm and Handspring, that includes a calendar, address book, and other organizational tools.

pervasive developmental disorders A category of disorders characterized by severe and pervasive impairment in several areas of development, such as social interaction skills and communication skills. The category includes autism and Asperger's syndrome, among other conditions.

phenylketonuria (PKU) A genetic disorder resulting in enzyme defects that lead to mental retardation and other developmental delays if the condition is not treated in infancy.

phonology The sound system of a language and the rules that cover sound combinations.

physical disability An orthopedic impairment, brain injury, or other health impairment that interferes with or substantially limits the student's ability to take part in routine school activities.

pragmatics In language, the ability to combine form and content to communicate functionally and in socially acceptable ways.

problem-based learning An instructional method in which students learn by developing solutions to authentic, "real world" problems.

profound visual impairment A corrected visual acuity of 20/500 or worse; a person with this degree of impairment cannot use vision as an educational tool.

project-based learning Using a project or problem as the central component of a lesson or series of lessons; this central project ties the curriculum together and provides "real-life," authentic opportunities for learning.

proxy server A software application that runs on the main server computer for the school or school system and blocks access to websites deemed inappropriate.

quadriplegic A person with damage to thoracic, lumbar, or sacral nerves causing loss of use of the trunk, legs, or pelvic organs.

remedial teaching A term often used for teaching students with disabilities or others with learning problems. The approach involves identifying the child's particular difficulties, determining what needs to be taught and how to teach it, and providing appropriate practice and feedback, while at the same time including the child in the normal planned curriculum as much as possible.

remedial technology Technology, typically software, designed to teach basic skills to a wider age group than might typically learn them: for example, basic literacy software for adults.

screen reader A device that reads aloud the text displayed on a screen.

semantics The meaning of words and sentences in a language; a student with semantic difficulties has trouble understanding what words and sentences mean.

sensorineural hearing loss Hearing impairment that results from damage to the sensory hair cells of the inner ear.

serious emotional disturbance A long-term behavioral or emotional condition that is strongly detrimental to learning; it can be marked by symptoms such as an inability to maintain good interpersonal relationships, inappropriate behavior or feelings under normal circumstances, and pervasive unhappiness or depression.

severe visual impairment A corrected visual acuity of 20/200 to 20/400; a person with such an impairment has difficulty seeing even with visual aids but can use vision to some degree in the learning process.

shareware Software that you can try out for free; if you decide to keep it and use it, you are supposed to pay a small fee.

Signed Exact English (SEE) A sign language in which the signs are similar to those of American Sign Language, but the word order follows that of American English.

specific learning disability *See* learning disability.

speech disorder A disorder involving articulation, fluency (the flow of speech), or voice (pitch, loudness, and so on).

speech reading Understanding speech by interpreting the movements of the speaker's lips and facial muscles (commonly known as lip reading).

standards movement The trend to establish sets of learning objectives and outcomes that all students should meet by a particular grade or age and to test students regularly to check progress.

syntax A language's system for combining words to form sentences.

tactile sign language A sign language in which the "speaker" traces signs into the palm of the "listener."

talented Possessing high artistic or athletic ability; often used in combination with *gifted,* with little distinction between the two terms.

talking books Books integrated with computer software in such a way that the student can choose to have all or parts of the story read aloud.

task analysis Breaking a task down into its smallest subtasks and strategies. Using task analysis, teachers can pinpoint exactly which part of a task is giving the student difficulty and determine how to teach the specific skills needed.

telecommunication device for the deaf (TDD) A machine that uses typed input and output, usually with a visual text display, to enable individuals with hearing or speech impairments to communicate using a telecommunications network.

telecommunications relay service (TRS) A system that allows for conversations between hearing individuals and those with hearing disabilities through the assistance of a third party, a relay operator.

teletypewriter (TTY) A device connected to a telephone that allows a person with a hearing disability to type in a message that can be read by another TTY.

temporally modified speech Speech is modified to make it slower or faster: for example, a software program that stretches out sounds to allow a child time to process and understand them.

testing accommodations Modifications to assessments and testing environments that allow students with disabilities to participate in standardized tests.

text telephone Any device that allows two-way conversations over a telephone network using typed text instead of spoken words.

text-to-speech software Software that allows the computer to pronounce (read aloud) an indicated word or set of words.

total communication An educational approach for children with hearing disabilities in which students learn both oral and manual communication.

total vision impairment *See* profound visual impairment.

totally blind Having little or no visual sensitivity to light at any level.

tracking The system of separating students into different groups (tracks) according to their apparent ability or achievement level.

Universal Design for Learning A theory of instructional design based on providing multiple ways of presenting information, having students engage in a variety of learning activities, and offering various options for assessment.

videoconferencing Communication by way of two computers, each with a small camera connected to it so that the users can see each other as they use sign language.

videophone A telephone-like device that allows two people to see each other and use sign language to communicate.

visual impairment Loss of vision that, even with correction, adversely affects a child's educational performance; a general term covering impairments ranging from mild to severe, including blindness. *See also* legally blind; low vision; partially sighted; totally blind.

voice disorder A disorder involving the quality, pitch, or intensity of a person's speech: for example, hoarseness or a tendency to speak too loudly.

voice recognition A system that allows the user to dictate to the computer through a microphone and to control the computer and other devices through the voice.

word prediction A process by which a computer suggests a word the user is typing on the basis of the letters already typed; the computer can then fill in the entire word, reducing the number of keystrokes required.

INDEX

CHOOSING TECHNOLOGY BY CONTENT AREA

T he chapters in part 2 of this book will help you prepare yourself for teaching children with exceptionalities in your classroom. Keep this book on a nearby shelf to refresh your memory about the specific educational, social, and developmental needs of a child with learning disabilities, a developmental delay, or a sensory impairment. Some types of technologies, be they software programs, adaptive tools, or pieces of equipment, are useful for children with a wide range of exceptionalities.

The concept of Universal Design for Learning, discussed throughout this book, is worth mentioning here again. If you think of software as yet another way to present information, universal design principles can guide you in selecting software programs that may have multiple uses in your classroom. These uses can range from giving students a multimedia presentation of information (with sound, graphics, and animation) to providing for a way to individualize the instructional pace of a lesson. The idea of providing appropriate accommodations for *all* your students can help you focus on how each student learns best and which types of technology make the most sense.

READING

Reading is generally the most focused-on area of curriculum. It the subject of intense debate for several decades. Should we fi how to decode words, or should we first focus on teaching chil stand the meaning of what they are reading? Should our approa phonics, whole language, or critical literacy?

One thing we have learned from the many arguments about lea that no one way works best for all children. Some children just words and letter sounds from being read to; other children nee struction in how to sound out words; still others need specific te shaping their mouths and making certain sounds. This is true of regular and special education. As a teacher, you must figure out combination of techniques to use for the students in your class

The programs and devices described below address many facet you read the descriptions, keep in mind any specific needs of y make your selections carefully. As with all other sections of this not complete, but rather describes various popular technologica you a sense of what is available.

Ace Detective (*MindPlay*)	Enhances reading comprehension skills by breaking down text into "cl solve a mystery. Contains some difficult vocabulary at even the easiest built-in dictionary assistance.
Arthur's Birthday: A Living Book (*The Learning Company*)	Arthur and Muffy have planned birthday parties on the same day! The go to Arthur's party, and the girls want to go to Muffy's party. Arthur ar work together to find a creative solution to their dilemma. Even thoug tivities are classified as reading skill builders, many also include comp

WRITING

Writing includes everything from learning to hold a pencil or use a word processor to writing different types of sentences, composing essays, research papers, and short stories—the list could go on. Handwriting and spelling are important skills for writers, and classroom teachers and physical and speech develop techniques to improve both. Spelling in and of itself is a s the field of special education technology, because we all have stor who can use the spell checker to produce a perfectly spelled sente makes absolutely no sense. The following programs can all help w process of teaching students to communicate effectively using the (For programs that teach typing, see the later section on keyboard

MATHEMATICS

Many math programs share the goal of enhancing mathematical skills within a game format. The graphics, characters, and pace closely approximate one of children's favorite pastimes—cartoons. A student can tackle the game requirements at his or her own pace. In addition, most such programs allow a player to store a partially completed game in order to continue during another session. Another positive feature of many math games is the variety of levels they offer. Of course, the child will eventually move on to other programs, but while he or she is working on one skill set, a variety of levels will offer new challenges and reduce the possibility of boredom.

ADDITIONAL RESOURCES AND SUPPORT!

- *A Handbook of Resources* at the back of the book offers a wealth of useful reference material—sources for locating online curriculum materials, discussion groups, and the software and hardware tools discussed in the text.

- Visit the textbook website: **www.cengage.com/education**

  This site contains useful activities for learning about technology and special education, links to downloadable demonstrations of software applications, class activities, a discussion board, and much more.

ABOUT THE AUTHOR

Sarah Irvine Belson is Associate Professor at American University in Washington, DC. Dr. Irvine Belson designed American University's MAT in Educational Technology and teaches both technology and special education course. She earned her Ph.D. in Curriculum and Instruction in 1995 with specialization in Instructional Technology and Special Education at Arizona State University. Prior to this, she worked in both public and private institutions as a special education teacher. Dr. Irvine Belson has been awarded numerous professional distinctions, including the American University Award for Innovative Teaching with Technology. Her research includes investigating effective teacher-education and innovation related to technology in the classroom and the use of technology for exceptional populations. She works with several schools in the Washington, DC, area as a consultant to help all teachers integrate technology.